D1153968

Frank Sullivan
Through the Looking Glass

Frank Sullivan
Through the Looking Glass

A Collection of His Letters and Pieces
With an Introduction by Marc Connelly

Edited, With an Afterword, by
George Oppenheimer

Doubleday & Company, Inc.
Garden City, New York
1970

Library of Congress Catalog Card Number 72–111180
Copyright © 1970 by Frank Sullivan
All Rights Reserved
Printed in the United States of America
First Edition

Acknowledgment is made to the following for permission to reprint their material:

LITTLE, BROWN AND COMPANY

"The Cliché Expert Testifies on Love," copyright 1935 under the title "The Cliché Expert on Love" by The New Yorker Magazine, Inc., and "The Culinary Expert Takes the Stand," copyright 1936 under the title "The Culinary Expert" by The New Yorker Magazine, Inc. Both appeared in *A Pearl in Every Oyster* by Frank Sullivan, copyright 1933, 1934, 1935, 1936, 1937, 1938, © 1966 by Frank Sullivan.
"A Garland of Ibids for Van Wyck Brooks," copyright 1941 under the title "Garland of Ibids" by The New Yorker Magazine, Inc. Appeared in *A Rock in Every Snowball* by Frank Sullivan, copyright 1945 by Frank Sullivan.
"Letter to a Neighbor" and "Apostrophe to a Street" originally appeared in *Good Housekeeping;* "Rover the Partridge" originally appeared in *New York American;* "The Night the Old Nostalgia Burned Down," copyright 1946 by The New Yorker Magazine, Inc.; "The Forgotten Bach," copyright 1950 by The New Yorker Magazine, Inc. All appeared in *The Night the Old Nostalgia Burned Down* by Frank Sullivan, copyright 1946, 1948, 1949, 1950, 1951, 1952, 1953 by Frank Sullivan.
"The Cliché Expert Testifies as a Literary Critic," copyright 1937 under the title "The Culinary Expert: On Literary Critics" by The New Yorker Magazine, Inc.; "A Visit to London" originally appeared in *Harper's Bazaar;* "Proust and the Life Sentence" originally appeared in *New York American*. All appeared in *Sullivan at Bay* by Frank Sullivan, published by J. M. Dent & Sons, Ltd., and Little, Brown and Company.

HARPER & ROW, PUBLISHERS, INC.

"Thoughts Before the Undertaker Came" from *The End of the World*, edited by James W. Barrett. Copyright 1931 by Harper & Brothers, renewed © 1959 by James W. Barrett.

LIVERIGHT PUBLISHING CORPORATION

The Life and Times of Martha Hepplethwaite by Frank Sullivan, copyright R 1954 by Frank Sullivan.

To
Anna Crouse
and to the memory of Russel

TABLE OF CONTENTS

INTRODUCTION

Several theories have been propounded to explain why Frank Sullivan is among the world's most prolific letter writers. One is based on the simple truth that he knows his friends like to hear from him. Getting a letter from Sullivan makes any morning a sunny one. This is because Sullivan is one of this century's most engaging humorists and it's impossible for him to write a letter that doesn't have his talent and affection in it. While this explains why there is always a great demand for Sullivan letters it doesn't make clear why the demand is met. Sullivan has thousands of friends and if statistics were available, I'd bet they would show that during an average day Sullivan writes a letter every eighteen minutes.

People who know and understand writers have come up with another reason for Sullivan's heavy outgoing mail. They say that a law of nature makes writers, especially humorists, do anything rather than produce copy a frantic editor is waiting for. There were occasions when Robert Benchley drove editors crazy. When they telephoned him and begged for an article he had promised to deliver the previous week, his gentle "My goodness, hasn't that boy got there yet?" used to make them walk up walls. I don't mean Benchley was habitually late with copy, but to him conversing with a friend was always more appealing than an editor's tantrums. On the other hand, I can't believe Sullivan was ever late with a commitment. So *that* theory is out.

I think I can throw some light on the multiplicity of Sullivan's letters. Writing one palliates Sullivan's frustrated hunger for travel. All his life he has wanted to go places. There have been moments when he would have sold his soul in order to scale an Alp, pat a llama in Peru, board a liner for a world cruise or dawdle over an *haute cuisine* dinner in London or Hong Kong. Unhappily, none of these dreams has ever been realized. This is because Sullivan suffers from dromophobia. Whenever the opportunity to travel has presented itself Sullivan has panicked and crawled under a rug.

Believe it or not, Sullivan has a psychological inability to go anywhere. I first noticed it in 1927, when the publishers of a book called *Cradle of the Deep* decided to launch it by giving a party on a transatlantic liner berthed at its pier in New York. Sullivan was then doing humorous reporting for the New York *World* and conscientiously forced himself to attend the party and interview the author and guest of honor, Miss Joan Lowell. Even when he ascended the gangplank, Sullivan felt dizzy. He managed to meet Miss Lowell but in a few minutes had to leave the ship because of incipient seasickness. (Incidentally, it may be recalled that Miss Lowell's book, purportedly an account of her childhood on her skipper father's sailing ship, was a fake. Her life at sea had not been much more extensive than Sullivan's.)

Another time, it was in the summer, when most of Sullivan's chums had departed or were about to depart on vacations, Sullivan sought a doctor's help, hoping to overcome his travel block. The doctor prescribed a journey under conditions Sullivan forced himself to accept. Accompanied by a trained nurse—and I assure you I'm not making this up—he got on a train and went as far as St. Louis. When he returned he was visibly unbenefited by the experience.

Once, when his wanderlust wasn't gnawing too cruelly, he was talking about it with a friend. "I doubt that I'll ever be cured," he confided, "but I'm still hoping eventually to go abroad. Every day I'm stepping over larger puddles."

Writing letters, dropping them in mailboxes, knowing they will travel far and wide, have to a degree alleviated Sullivan's frustration in not being able to deliver them personally. This chained world traveler has often shown his interest in unreachable places by writing funny pieces about them (there are examples herein), and making the reader laugh at what Sullivan's basic good sense doesn't let him be sorrowful about.

When George Oppenheimer began assembling this book, many of Sullivan's epistolary debtors reproached themselves for having mislaid letters whose bright warmth was still with them despite their vanished texts. As I don't put things away as neatly as I should, my clutter of important letters, valuable papers, and other memorabilia has been referred to as Collier Brothers Downtown. After it was too late to contribute letters from Sullivan (which I should have kept in a safe-deposit box) I came across one. It obliquely reveals Sullivan's philosophic acceptance of his lot as a reluctant stay-at-home.

As every subscriber to the *National Geographic Magazine* knows, in return for your payment you receive a certificate attesting your membership in the society which publishes it. Many years ago, on receiving my certificate, I sent it to Sullivan, facetiously thanking him for helping me acquire it. Sullivan was impressed by my assurance that I would conduct myself so worthily as a member of the National Geographic Society that on my gravestone could be written: "New York, 22½ miles."

This is what Sullivan wrote in reply:

Dear Con:

Why, you old potato [FDR was then President], I'm tickled pink that you decided to go National Geographic. The rest of the fellows are, too. I saw Brother Admiral Byrd up at the dorm today and I told him, and he was tickled pink. So was Brother Hubert Wilkins. And I know Brother Walter Traprock will be, too, when he hears. I guess you'll have the whole Society as pink as the British Empire on the maps before you're through.

Well, to drop the kidding and be serious, Con old man, I'm tickled pink. I knew those other crowds were rushing you—the National Association of Audubon Societies and the Church Peace Union and World Alliance for International Friendship

Through the Churches—and I'm glad you passed them up and decided to go N.G.S. I think you're the right stuff for us; fact is, I told the fraters so the night we had the meeting to decide on the fellows we wanted to rush. You always were swell at exploring and things like that. Do you remember when we were kids and used to go hunting birds' eggs? You used to shinny up those trees like all get-out. And do you remember the old swimmin' hole and how you used to be able to stay underwater for two minutes at a time? One of the first things I want to do is have you meet Brother Will Beebe.

Of course, while we're darn glad to have you with us, I do think you've got every reason to be proud of being a brother in N.G.S., because it's a pretty swell aggregation. A lot of fellows would give their right eye to be a member of N.G.S., but we don't take in every Tom, Dick and Harry, and that's one of the reasons why fellows who want to amount to something place so much importance on being tapped by us.

When they initiate you and tattoo that old "Member of the National Geographic Society, Sixteenth and M Streets, Washington, District of Columbia" on your left shoulder blade, you want to realize you'll no longer be just plain Marc Connelly. You'll be Marc Connelly, the NGSeke. And as you travel through life, no matter where you go you'll find a brother in N.G.S., ready to lend a helping hand in a pinch. When I was with the Fuller Brush Company some years ago, I was stranded in the Gobi Desert one night without a sou to my name, wondering what the heck I was going to do, when a fellow comes along with the old tattoo mark on his shoulder. I gave him the old high sign and he turned out to be one of the fraters, named Roy Chapman Andrews. And did he have that old Gobi Desert sewed up! Why, I could have had the whole place if I wanted it. Another time when I was with the Hoover Vacuum people, I was stranded on the ocean floor about forty fathoms down, just off the Galapagos Islands, pretty broke and discouraged, and I ran into Brother Will Beebe. He was swell. Put me up for the night

and treated me like a prince. I just mention these incidents to
show you how N.G.S. men stick together.

As for putting you wise to the politics and customs of N.G.S.,
I'll be only too glad to. I suppose you know about leaving the
room if anybody mentions the name of the National Geographic
Society. Sometimes "barbs" from the American Laryngological,
Rhinological and Otological Society, Inc., or crowds like that,
mention N.G.S. irreverently, just to get our goat, but if a fellow
has the right N.G.S. spirit, he pays no attention but just walks
out in a dignified manner.

Another thing, when you're initiated you'll get your copy of
the National Geographic Magazine every month and you always
want to keep that by you, even when you bathe. And above all,
don't give away your copy of the Magazine to every frail you
take a fancy to. A fellow is supposed to give his copy only to the
girl he's engaged to. I don't mean that just because a fellow is an
N.G.S. he can't go around and have fun with skirts, but he
always ought to remember that in the last analysis the most
sacred thing in his life is old Mother N.G.S. herself. She is his
real sweetheart.

You'll have to go out for something, of course. Every frater has
to do something that will reflect credit on the organization. It's
the spirit of N.G.S. and we don't like to see fellows lying idle
around the house, playing ukes or necking dames. Hell's bells, if
we all did that, the other crowds would put it over on us in a jiffy.
You'll have to go out for something, Con. Either dig up some old
ruins, or take a trip across the Atlantic in a twenty-foot yawl, or
race Alan Villiers around the Horn in a ketch.

I asked for the privilege of tapping you. It's simple. When I
hit you on the back and say "Go to British Guiana," you don't
do anything but go to British Guiana. Of course sometimes a
fellow is pooch-head enough to pass up a bid for N.G.S., and
in that case, when the N.G.S. frater taps him and says "Go to
British Guiana," he replies, "Go climb Mount Everest."

Well, congrats, Con old man. I can't wait to see you and give you the grip.

Yours in N.G.S.

Frank Sullivan

But to get back to why all the other letters in this book were written. As I failed to say specifically in the beginning, the fundamental reason is that Sullivan happened to like the people he wrote them to and in doing so sent each one of them a gift. A little piece of his heart.

MARC CONNELLY

THE PIECES

Most of the pieces selected for this volume have been taken from Sullivan's published books which, in turn, were compiled from various newspapers and magazines. Sources are given at the head of each piece.

It is with great regret that, for reasons of space, I am forced to omit such sagas as "Otto Kahn, or, the New Opera Season" (in which the ladies of the Diamond Horseshoe at the old Metropolitan Opera House were required to dim their tiaras so as to avoid collisions); "A Man Never Drops a Hat" (the travails attendant upon parting with an old hat and breaking in a new one); "A Week-end at Lady Astor's" (our hero crashes Cliveden and encounters the Set); "We Have Some Nice, Fresh Crowns Today, Queen" (the late Queen Mary tricks the late King George into letting her buy several bejeweled crowns); "Gloria Swanson Defends Her Title" (the famous movie star outdoes the Manhattan élite by sporting a chapeau that spouts smoke); or "The Moose in the Hoose," a Christmas story that Sullivan wrote for his godson, Timothy, and his sister, Lindsay Ann, the children of playwright Russel and Anna Crouse (later published by Random House).

However, the pieces included will, I hope, make up for those that were reluctantly discarded. So let us start with a Sullivan preface to end prefaces.

—EDITOR'S NOTE

FOREWORD

(*Innocent Bystanding*. Liveright, 1928)

This was to have been a pretty monumental work. At one point or another I planned to brush lightly against almost every topic imaginable, so that anyone reading the book and absorbing its contents could go to dinner parties afterward and talk so well on such a multiplicity of subjects that all the other guests would be driven crazy.

The book was shaping itself nicely along those lines when one day not long ago, as the manuscript lay on a table near an open window, a storm came up and a wind whisked the sheets from under my very nose and scattered them to the four winds. Oh, there were *more* than four winds that day. I counted seven. There must have been nine or ten in all.

It was impossible to retrieve all the sheets. Many of them had been buried in remote, inaccessible sections of the subway excavation in the street outside. Others were filched by the spies who had been stationed outside the house by rival authors immediately after the rumor spread that the book would be monumental.

As a result of this untimely simoom the book may appear jumpy in spots, due to the crevasses caused by the absence of sections of the manuscript. I should like to assure the reader that I am constantly on the lookout for these missing sheets and as fast as I recover them I shall see that each reader is supplied with a new copy of the work, containing the recovered data. With patience I am sure that we shall yet be able to drive most dinner guests crazy.

A word concerning the paper and typography of the book might not be amiss. It is printed on paper the pulp for which was specially chewed by the author from special spruce trees grown in the Canadian forests. This "labor of love" occupied three full years, or two years, eleven months and twenty-odd days longer than the day in which Rome was not built by Romulus and Remus, 752 B.C.

The paper is white. The ink used is a special new color which we are tentatively calling "black," until a better name can be found. "Black" is a little harsh to the ear.

But enough of statistics, which are, at best, apt to be dry!

The author would indeed feel remiss if he were to fail to acknowledge certain debts of gratitude. To *The World, The New Yorker* and *College Humor* for permission to reprint certain pieces. To Mr. Frederick Desmond of Brooklyn Technical High School and the staff of *The World,* who typed the manuscript and, I suspect, quietly wrote in several of the more astounding portions of it. To the Acme Comma Company of Bayonne, N.J., for the commas used in the book. To the authorities of the British Museum for their kindness in furnishing the data on which the chapter on Queen Mary's hats is based. To Sir John Weether Brakemore, professor of philatotemy and don of Ephraim College, Ufton University, England, who was kind enough to read the chapter on "Gladstone, Man or Myth?" and suggest a few changes, one of which was that the chapter be omitted. Finally, to Miss Fifi Kelshy, librarian of Widdle College, Widdle, Iowa, who prepared the index.

F.S.

Manhattan Transfer,
July, 1928.

WELL, THERE'S NO HARM IN LAUGHING

(Front page of the *New York Times Book Review*. December 16, 1951)

Over the course of the past thirty years there has been a dwindling in the number of active practitioners of humor in the United States and the result is a shortage somewhat like that of nurses. I anticipate there will be some to argue that a humorist is not as essential these days as a nurse.

What's amiss? Do budding humorists fear to take the plunge because this is no time for comedy, because they fear their humor might be deemed in bad taste now? Or could it be what we may call the Moola factor, by which promising young humorists, along with other kinds of promising young writers, are lured into writing for radio, television or Hollywood by the promise of vast sums of moola, bigger messes of pottage, more imposing gastric ulcers and anxiety neuroses designed to astound psychoanalysts at a distance of thirty couches?

No doubt many writers of humor do feel edgy about seeming frivolous these days. No man wants to be accused of laughing, or of being *particeps criminis* to laughter in others, during a wake. Yet people have laughed during wakes before this; in fact, that is one reason why wakes were invented. At this point, if I am not careful, I may find myself using the word Escapism.

In another time that tried men's souls Abraham Lincoln was fond of opening Cabinet meetings by reading Artemus Ward's latest. Politicians like Stanton and Chase were shocked at this because they did not think Ward was as important as a battle. Lincoln suspected Ward *was* as important as a battle.

The lot of the humorist is more difficult today than it was thirty years ago but it has never been too easy. Humor has always been regarded with condescension, except by people like

Lincoln, as one of the cadet branches of beautiful letters, and sobersides look at humorists as a duchess looks at bugs; simile borrowed from humorist Booth Tarkington. What are the jesters up to, the Podsnaps wonder. Making fun of Podsnappery, perhaps? This attitude of wary suspicion may stem from a tendency of humorists, especially good ones like Ring Lardner and Mark Twain, to tell the truth, which, though it shall make you free, may also make you uneasy.

It is not difficult to understand any reluctance a young writer might feel toward undertaking the writing of carefree humor today. In the Nineteen Twenties the atom was known intimately to only a few scientists, among whom, unfortunately, was a budding physicist and traitor named Klaus Fuchs. In those days humorists about to be humorous were not in danger of being stopped dead in their tracks by coming across a photograph of Gromyko or Senator [Joseph] McCarthy.

There was plenty wrong with the Nineteen Twenties but from here they seem halcyon. The present mood, to alter a well-known definition of poetry, is one of tranquility recollected in emotion, the emotion being nostalgia. The climate is not propitious for humor. Nevertheless, if the gods have planted humor in a writer's soul he probably will try to write humor, no matter what Gromyko and McCarthy are up to; either he will do that or the angry gods may, as punishment, change him into a weeping willow, or an N.B.C. vice-president.

The feeling exists that there is a suspicion of reproach, a kind of fiddling-while-Rome-burns implication, in writing humor now, and some humorists have tried to alibi themselves against this by putting a Message of Social Significance into their humor. This is a worthy ambition but risky to try unless the humorist is in a class with Vanessa's friend, or James Thurber, or Finley Peter Dunne, or E. B. White. Other humorists just give up and join an advertising agency, or play the piano somewhere else. A well-known former humorist explained to me some years ago why he had quit writing humor to do another kind of writing. He said he felt that his humor was trivial and unimportant. I disagreed. He was a good humorist and I refused to believe it was a trivial thing to bring to harassed humankind as many laughs as he had brought.

Another apostate humorist told me he was giving up writing humor because he had examined his conscience and decided he was not good enough at it. That's the trouble with humorists, they have too much humility. I told this introvert, this traitor to his class, that he was taking a morbid and subversive attitude and begged him not to tell other humorists about it. In fact, I was sorry he had told me. If all the jesters decided they were not competent to write humor, where would we be? Kindly do not answer. But suppose all the politicians and scientists decided *they* were not competent enough, where would we be then? In clover, if you ask me.

It takes ingenuity and courage to write humor at any time but the humorist is more harassed today than ever, and more limited in range. He has seldom, for instance, tackled the subject of Love, or the Love Interest, because experience has shown that when he does, he laughs at love, or takes it lightly, as in the works of Master Wodehouse; or at any rate does not venerate it sufficiently. It pays to take love seriously, as Dr. Freud and Holly-wood long since proved, yet the unabashed Mr. Thurber con-tinues to boot it around as though there had never been a close-up of Garbo kissing John Gilbert.

Today the young novelists of the Latest Lost Generation not only retain the novelist's traditional monopoly on love but they have taken to discussing new kinds of love hitherto confined to Havelock Ellis and medical textbooks. As for the asterisk, it has been put out of business, like the whalebone corset. It is a drug on the punctuation market, for when use of a four-letter word is indicated in a novel redemonstrating that war is hell and that warriors use purple language, the novelist *uses* that word, and to h**l with asterisks. If a humorist were to put such bald words in his attempts to increase the world's store of mirth, or if he were to rewrite Krafft-Ebing for a laugh, he would be run off

Boston Common on a rail as a vulgar and depraved fellow. Is this justice?

Not only that but the Latest Lost Generation has filched despair from the humorists. All the philosophers who have discussed the cause and cure of humor agree that the soul of a humorist is apt to be filled with melancholy, for which his humor is compensation. If melancholy, disillusion, frustration and *Weltschmerz* do act as nitrates to cause humor to burgeon, then it ought to be flourishing today as never before, especially among the novelists of the Decayed-South School. For what has happened is that the novelists of the Latest Lost Generation have taken over despair, and the humorists no longer have enough of it to supply even their modest needs.

Of course I place no credence in the rumor that Gore Vidal, Norman Mailer and Truman Capote each have several cases of prime despair cached in the deep freezer, in case of a sunny day. I am not blaming Gore or Truman. I feel sure that Kafka started this, with an assist from T. S. Eliot.

All in all, no wonder young writers trembling on the verge of being humorists think twice and then take a job at $500 a week writing gags for Uncle Milty or Bob Hope. You cannot blame them for trying to collect the maximum dividends on their talents. In the world we live in, they owe it to themselves to earn enough to provide their wives and kiddies with the very best bomb shelters money can buy. Yet the young humorist who has sold his birthright for a mess of radio gags would do well to remember that nowadays you not only can't take it with you but you can't even have it while you're here.

Of humorists who were with us in 1920, these have departed: George Ade, Robert Benchley, Will Cuppy, Clarence Day, Finley Peter Dunne, Will Rogers, Oliver Herford, Ring Lardner, Don Marquis, Booth Tarkington, Thorne Smith, Ellis Parker Butler, Bert Leston Taylor, Harry Leon Wilson, Irvin S. Cobb, Kin Hubbard, Stephen Leacock, Carolyn Wells, George S. Chappell (Dr. Traprock), Roark Bradford and, latest of the old guard to leave, Gelett Burgess.

Quite a galaxy, you will agree, and their loss is one to make a lamentable dent in the gaiety of the nation.

Holding the fort currently are James Thurber, E. B. White, Arthur Kober, S. J. Perelman, Ogden Nash, Wolcott Gibbs, John McNulty, James Reid Parker, John Lardner, Phyllis McGinley, Peter De Vries—Editor Ross of *The New Yorker* seems to attract humorists as the firecracker attracts the moth. There is Fred Allen, a fourteen-carat humorist who dabbles in radio. I claim P. G. Wodehouse for the United States because his audience is as large here as in his native England, if not larger. Don Quinn's scripts for the Fibber McGee program have proved that a radio comedy can be comic. And we have Corey Ford, Edward Streeter, Al Capp, Red Smith, H. Allen Smith, Robert Ruark, Dr. Seuss and Charles W. Morton.

With these stalwarts in the ring it can hardly be said that American humor is on the ropes. Yet the time will come when at the end of the long day's chores they will want to retire to the peace and the well-earned repose of the Petroleum V. Nasby Home for Aged and Infirm Humorists. And that will be the hour for the younger generation of humorists to take up the torch from the gnarled old hands.

Where are these younger humorists? Come out, come out, wherever you are.

THOUGHTS BEFORE THE UNDERTAKER CAME
(*The End of the World,* edited by James Barrett. Harper, 1931)

On a day at the end of last February I finished my farewell piece for the *World* and then began the task of clearing out the desk I had occupied for eight and a half years.

It took a major crisis such as had occurred to get that desk tidied up. Many times during my first four years on the staff, when I was younger and had more energy, I had been impelled by attacks of orderliness (vestigial remnants, I suppose, of my old Puritan ancestry) to tackle that desk. But the desk always won. Four and a half years ago I gave up and decided to let well enough alone. Thereafter I stuck all my mail into the top drawer and thought no more of it. The early Pleistocene layers of letters probably sank to the bottom of the desk and became carbonized, like little bugs and flowers that become imbedded in a bog and stay there a million years too long.

How did I get such a desk cleaned out before the undertaker's men took charge of the city room? I cut the Gordian knot by throwing away most of the contents of the desk, probably including my soldier bonus certificate, which I can't find and which I may need one of these days. Some of the contents I saved, haphazard. The aspirin, for instance. Many a day following a rough night, when I approached the desk with one eye shut (the better to see you with, little typewriter), that aspirin was a boon.

Pasted about the desk, behind and beside the typewriter, were the December leaves of eight calendars from 1923 on. They were adorned in varying degrees, according to their years, with the grime and dust of time. Also there was a practically new calendar for the year 1931, only one leaf gone. Annually, at New Year's time, I had pasted a calendar in my desk for ready reference, for, true to the time-honored tradition of all newspaper offices, the calendars in the *World* were hung behind files or in spots where to consult them one had to stand on one's head and sprain one's neck. If the day comes when I work in a city room where there are plenty of great big calendars, all visible to the naked eye of the reporter, and where the dictionary is not more than forty paces from your desk, and where the page of the telephone book containing the number you want, is not torn out, I may be greatly disappointed. Half the spice of the game would be gone were these little tribulations absent.

The housecleaning finished, I detached the key of the desk from my ring and left it in the desk. I disliked that key; it was always getting lost. At least I won't have to deal with that any more. And there won't be that window behind my desk which Jack Leary, my neighbor at the next desk, always wanted shut and everybody else wanted open. And there won't be the sun which along about May reached the point in the heavens where it began to stream in on my desk, getting in my eyes and retarding or stimulating the hatching of matchless prose, according to my mood of the moment. There won't be the telephone calls when I'm in the middle of a piece. And there won't be the visitors, seating themselves on my desk as I brooded over an idea (just found, after much travail) to tell me jokes that would make a 156-year-old Turk look like a tot.

There won't be any of the minor crosses that used to make me growl. And I'm just beginning to realize how I shall miss them.

I regret now that I left the typewriter (property of the *World*) in the desk. Certainly I should have borne off some souvenir of those eight and a half years, and we had grown fond of each other, that machine and I. Its predecessor was a doddering mass of clattering incompetence that served me during my first six years on the *World* and wrecked what had been a superb nervous system. Periodically I would demand a new typewriter, and not get one. Then one day I said to Jim Barrett, the city editor, through force of habit: "Jim, how about a new typewriter? This piece of junk is falling apart."

The next day a shining new typewriter was in my desk. I went home with a high fever, suffering from shock, and took to my bed for three days.

I recall the evening in mid-October of 1922 when I walked across the cool dusk of City Hall Park from the *Evening Sun* office to the *World* and was hired by Swope—Herbert Bayard Swope to you. I had in mind a gracious address to deliver to Mr. Swope. I would indicate deftly that he was to congratulate himself on securing the services of such a promising journalist. There was, I believe, to have been a careless reference to an advance in salary.

Swope was dictating to Helen Millar, firing instructions at Bill Beazell and Earl Clauson and talking over the Albany telephone line with Governor Al Smith—all at one and the same time. My speech was not delivered as planned. It was not delivered at all. H.B.S., however, gave me a trenchant address on the ethics of journalism in general, the place of the *World* in particular, my own good fortune in being tapped for that paper, the influence of Stanton in Lincoln's Cabinet, the best method for making raised biscuits, the Tacna-Arica dispute, and the Schick test for scarlet fever.

I went to work and immediately lapsed into obscurity. For a month I did something like paste up bankruptcy reports. I suffered the most awful pangs of homesickness for the old *Evening Sun* office.

Then, quite involuntarily, I leaped into what it would be gross understatement to call prominence. A highly respected lady had died. She bore a surname identical with the surname of a prominent young matron, daughter of a famous financier and inheritor from him of a large fortune. Through some diabolical slip of the mind (to charitably paraphrase what really was sheer incompetence on my part) I got the idea fixed in my head that it was the daughter of the financier who had died. She therefore had the rare experience, the next day, of seeing the news of her passing blazoned on the first page of our first edition (it was yanked out of later editions, after a bewildered butler had telephoned our office for details). I paid glowing tribute to her worth. I was highly complimentary to her. There was nothing she could have taken exception to in that obit—except the statement that she was dead. I was told later that after the first shock she was inclined to regard the incident humorously, but it was no joke to me, nor to the editors of the *World*. The fact that they didn't fire me immediately is testimony of the kind of place the *World* was.

Once afterward I met that matron. We chatted for a moment and then went our ways. She never knew that the obviously nervous young man who had blushed furiously on being introduced to her was he who had tried to shove her prematurely across the Styx.

After that incident Jim Barrett confined my activities largely to such trivia as attending demonstrations of kiss-proof lipsticks and so on. It was all right with me and a period of easygoing assignments followed, out of which I was rudely jolted in May, 1925 by the following note from Mr. Swope:

Adams is going away for more than a month and the brilliant idea has occurred to me to turn his column over to you to play with. You can write long pieces, short pieces, grave or gay . . . We will hit upon a happy head.
Talk to me about this—H.B.S.

The only funny part of that clarion call was the last line.

This ended the glamorous period of ease, with nights of innocent merriment at the now defunct Roymont Club on William Street, back of the *World*. Thereafter, I was a "feature" on the paper, God help me. I had a by-line. A by-line, I can state from experience, is a device which enables your friends to rush up to you the day after a piece has appeared and tell you how terrible it was.

On a sizzling day in that summer of 1925 I was steaming morosely in F.P.A.'s cubby hole (while he was traipsing about Europe on his honeymoon), trying to think of something to feed to the vast maw of that broad-measure column the next day. Suddenly I found myself writing a piece about an imaginary new secretary, Miss Martha Hepplethwaite, who would do no work but insisted on swinging from the chandelier, jeering at me. I was surprised when people seemed to like her. I don't want to seem ungracious, but I never thought Martha was much of a character.

My love goes out to her, however, at this time; and to her colleagues, Aunt Sarah Gallup, the grand old lady of the Adirondacks, and Joseph Twiggle, dean of New York street-cleaners. They were a willing trio and helped me out on many a dull day.

Mr. Twiggle came into being as a result of the flood of ticker tape attending the Lindbergh homecoming. Aunt Sarah Gallup had a more hectic start. I was doing "sidelights" on the Democratic convention in Madison Square Garden in 1924 and had to fill one column a day. One night I found myself a paragraph short. Being in my historic hurry to get good-night from Joe Canavan, night city editor, I simply added a paragraph about a fictitious old lady named Aunt Sarah Gallup, from Holcomb Landing near Ticonderoga, N.Y., who had saved her butter and egg money to come to the convention and root for Al Smith. To give the item piquancy I added that she was 104 years old.

I then walked innocently out of the office and buried my fevered countenance in a tall scotch highball. Next afternoon at the Waldorf I met Fred Edwards of the *Tribune*. He and I were working together in the accumulation of the sidelights. Fred was bitter.

"What do you mean holding out on me?" he demanded.

"What do you mean, 'holding out'?" I asked. I had forgotten about Aunt Sarah.

"My office asked me why I didn't get that human-interest story about the old lady from the Adirondacks."

I explained.

On reaching my own office I found that poor Alex Schlosser, assistant to Barrett, had devoted some minutes of a hot and busy day to locating our correspondent at Ticonderoga, to instruct him to be sure and get a picture of the old lady of 104. The correspondent at Ticonderoga (which is a bona fide place, of course) must have had a baffling time trying to locate Holcomb Landing. There is no such place.

I also learned that the venerable Associated Press had been trying to locate Sarah. It was an outrageous hoax, but it was done without malice. I just wanted to get that column filled.

Aunt Sarah stayed. I increased her age to 287 years. That broadened her scope, I thought.

I can't kick. I had eight and a half pleasant years on the *World*. I realize now what an Eden it was. Nobody, from Ralph Pulitzer, the publisher, to Joe Wilcinski, the head copy boy, ever was anything but friendly and helpful. Nobody bothered me. Nobody told me what to write or what not to write. When Swope hired me he told me the *World* had no "sacred cows." I found that to be true. The editors were glad when I did a good piece, and patiently uncomplaining during the lengthy stretches of the dull ones.

When I die I want to go wherever the *World* has gone, and work on it again.

THE FORGOTTEN BACH

(The New Yorker. The Night the Old
Nostalgia Burned Down. Little, Brown, 1953)

The year 1950, the two-hundredth anniversary of the death of
Johann Sebastian Bach, 1685–1750, was justly made an occasion
to do honor not only to him but to his illustrious relatives, Johann
Christian Bach, Johann Michael Bach, Wilhelm Friedemann
Bach, Karl Philipp Emanuel Bach, Johann Gottfried Bernhard
Bach, Johann Christian Friedrich Bach, Wilhelm Friedrich
Ernst Bach, and the many other scions of that great dynasty
without which the world today would be just about toccata-less.

Yet how much does the average music-lover really know about
the Bachs? Is there a hint of lip service in our current tributes to
them? Does anyone, for instance, know about Johann Wolfgang
Hermann Bach, the Bach the Bachs would like to forget, and,
indeed, have forgotten? I shall not be thanked in some quarters
for bringing his name up, yet he deserves mention; he was unique
in the annals of the family. First, however, a word about that
family.

Johann Sebastian, the principal in the present celebration,
was, of course, the composer of "The Well-Tempered Clavier."
Johann Sebastian was the brother of Johann Christoph, 1671–
1721. Johann Christoph is not to be confused with Johann
Christoph Friedrich Bach, 1732–1795, or with Johann Christian
Bach, 1735–1782. Johann Christoph was the Ohrdruf Bach, and
composed many motets, sarabands, and preludes for the clavier.
This Johann Christoph was the grandson of Christoph the
Weimar Bach, 1613–1661, and the grandnephew of Johann the
Erfurt Bach, 1604–1673. There was also a Johann Christoph
Bach, 1642–1703, who was the brother of Johann Michael Bach,

1648–1694. Johann Michael was known as the Eisenach Bach. No, that's not right. It was Johann Christoph who was the Eisenach Bach. Johann Michael was the Gehren Bach. He was the father-in-law of Johann Sebastian Bach and a nephew of Christoph the Weimar Bach, who was the grandfather of Johann Sebastian and the great-grandfather of Wilhelm Friedemann Bach, Karl Philipp Emanuel Bach, Johann Charles Thomas Bach, Johann Friedrich Christian Bach—I mean Johann Christian Friedrich Bach—no, I mean Johann *Christoph* Friedrich Bach. Johann Christoph Bach, the son of Heinrich the Arnstadt Bach, 1615–1692, was the father of Johann Nikolaus Bach, of Jena, 1669–1753. Johann Nikolaus was the nephew of the Johann Michael Bach, of Gehren, who was father-in-law to Johann Sebastian Bach. Thus, Johann Sebastian was a cousin to his own wife. That is, his first wife. He was no kin to his second wife.

So much for the family background. Though it has never been mentioned until now, I have reason to believe that Johann Wolfgang Hermann Bach, the Forgotten Bach, was one of the many sons of Johann Sebastian Bach, and therefore a great-great-great-grandson of Veit Bach, born circa 1555, who is generally recognized as the founder of the family. Veit Bach played the zither. He had a son named Hans, who was the first Bach to become a professional musician. It seems a far cry from a zither to the Bach oratorio as we know it, and it seems even a farther cry from the Doric simplicity of names like Veit and Hans to the somewhat rococo mazes of Johann Christoph Friedrich and Karl Philipp Emanuel. Yet in accumulating all this nomenclature the Bachs were really only trying to help. As they multiplied, it became increasingly difficult for non-Bach Germans—what there were of them—to tell one Bach from another. (Johann Sebastian alone had twenty children. Well, not quite alone—seven with the help of his first wife and thirteen by courtesy of his second.) The Bachs thought to reduce the confusion by adding more names to each oncoming Bach, but since the names they added were usually Johann or Christoph or Christian or, if they were really in the groove, Friedrich, the result was confusion worse confounded.

At last, the music-loving but baffled Germans gave up trying to identify them by their names and tried associating each with the town where he was court organist.

This plan sounded fine on paper, for there were Bachs at Ohrdruf, Erfurt, Arnstadt, Potsdam, Jena, Bückeburg; in fact, there was scarcely a whistle stop, or organ stop, in Germany that did not have its own Bach. So what happened? When the Germans called Wilhelm Friedemann the Dresden Bach, because he was organist at Dresden, he moved to Halle. When they called Karl Philipp Emanuel the Berlin Bach, because he was court organist at Berlin, he moved to Hamburg. When they called Johann Christoph the Milan Bach, he went to London to teach Queen Charlotte music, if possible. Did they do this to tease? We cannot know. But it was Johann Sebastian Bach who most effectively upset the plan to tell the Bachs apart by tying them up with cities, for he played at one time or another in Arnstadt, Mühlhausen, Weimar, Köthen, Lüneburg, Leipzig, Weissenfels, and Potsdam. Had I been an eighteenth-century German, I should have been tempted to call him just plain Jack Bach.

So much for the family background. But first a word as to why the Bachs all lived in different cities. Well, they *had* to. They couldn't all play the organ in the same place at the same time. It was too dangerous to life and limb. They tried it once at a family reunion in Dresden, and the vibrations were so powerful that Dresden china was shattered for blocks around, and the Bachs themselves proved as subject to the laws of physics as the bric-à-brac. A member of the family named Philipp Philipp Philipp Bach, known as the Philipp Bach, was found unconscious in the buttery after the joint family recital. A powerful arpeggio from a toccata had caught him above the left ear, charred his wig, traveled down his waistcoat, ripping it open, melted the gold watch and seals in his smallclothes, ripped the buckles off his shoes, and knocked him out before jumping the length of the chamber to shatter a two-gallon crock filled with buttermilk, which it instantly turned into several pounds of a highly palatable cheese. After that incident, the Bachs gave each other a fairly wide berth.

So much for the family background. Now for a few revelations about Johann Wolfgang Hermann Bach, the Forgotten Bach. By the time a young Bach was two, he had usually toddled instinctively to the well-tempered clavier (a self-respecting Bach wouldn't give an ill-tempered clavier houseroom) and started work on his first motet. When Johann Wolfgang Hermann Bach got to be two and a half without even an *aria da capo* to his credit, his father grew concerned. One day, he inveigled Johann to the w.-t. clavier, played a saraband, and asked Johann what it was. The boy did not know. Not only did not know but seemed bored. Not only couldn't tell a saraband but was just as ignorant about fugues, fantasias, preludes, capriccios, and Masses in any key, *a cappella* or otherwise. In some alarm, his father had the boy's hearing tested. It was perfect. He was just tone-deaf—the first male Bach in the history of the clan to be so, unless you consider old Veit, who played the zither, automatically suspect. (I specify male Bachs because the Bachs did not require their women to be musical; *"Kinder, Kuchen, und Keine Kantaten"* was the good old German motto for the Bach *Hausfrauen.*)

Naturally, after the scandalous discovery Johann Wolfgang Hermann Bach's position in the family left a good deal to be desired. In fact, he became a kind of male Cinderella, and would soon have become hopelessly mired in inferiority feelings had not his Aunt Sophie taken pity on him and adopted him when he was five. Like most German women of the time, Aunt Sophie, who was one of the famous Froelich triplets of Lübeck, had married a Bach. At the time of her marriage, she had been fond of music, but after the marriage her husband composed fifty-two oratorios. Aunt Sophie used to say it was at about the thirty-ninth that her interest in music began to flag. Her heart went out to poor little Johann, who couldn't tell one note from another.

Tone-deaf or not, Johann Wolfgang Hermann Bach has left

his mark on music. Aunt Sophie kept a diary and engaged in a voluminous correspondence. Her children and grandchildren did likewise. All these documents were carefully preserved, and were found in 1945 in an abandoned salt mine near Munich by a nephew of mine, Lieutenant Sacheverell O'Sullivan, of the Army of Occupation. He has entrusted these papers to my care, as a scholar of some repute. It is possible that this priceless literary and musical find should not be mentioned in the same breath with the Boswell Papers unearthed by Colonel Ralph Isham, but it certainly deserves to be mentioned in, let us say, the next breath but one.

From the Salt Mine Papers, I have already established some data that may make musical history. I find that, like all Bachs, Johann Wolfgang Hermann Bach had twenty children. These children and their children scattered, in time, to many lands. One letter establishes that a grandson of Johann Wolfgang Hermann Bach, named John Herman bbach-ffranchott, of Twickenham, England, was the first person to cry "Bravo!" at the end of a musical performance, a happy custom that has been popular ever since, not only among bona-fide music-lovers but with concertgoers who are not quite sure what the concert was about and wish to chuck a bluff. Another grandson, Giovanni Federico de Bacco, lived in Rome and was arrested there in 1831 for applauding at the wrong place during a performance of *Le Nozze di Figaro*. A great-grandson was publicly snubbed by Wagner at Bayreuth in 1876 for asking the composer when he was planning to write the second act of *Das Rheingold*.

One of Johann Wolfgang Hermann Bach's daughters, Ertrud, married a man from Mecklenburg-Strelitz, who was also tone-deaf, and among their descendants no fewer than twenty-two off-key Wagnerian tenors have been counted. More will undoubtedly come to light as my examination of the Salt Mine Papers proceeds.

Gretchen, another daughter, came to America at the end of the nineteenth century and married later into a prominent American family named Jukes, and many of her descendants,

all, like herself, tone-deaf, have distinguished themselves musi-
cally in this country. A great-grandson, Hans Christoph Jukes,
invented the box of that name and composed a series of preludes
for it, called "The Well-Tempered Juke Box," on a theme suggested by Dinah Shore. Several of Gretchen's descendants are
successful music commentators on the radio, and a round dozen
of the more popular disc jockeys owe their success to the talent
inherited from the tone-deaf matriarch. Others of that branch
have had an important hand in the spread of modern music—I
mean the really *modern* modern music—and it is claimed that
one of Gretchen's daughters was the first person in the United
States to rustle a program throughout an entire concert. I find
no verification of this in the Salt Mine Papers, however,
and until I do that title must remain with Miss Thoughtful
Pumpelly, who rustled the first program on record through a
concert in Boston in 1851. Emerson has described the incident
in an indignant letter to Carlyle.

The foregoing is only the merest outline of what this remarkable, though unrecognized, branch of the Bachs has accomplished
in music. I shall tell the whole story in detail and without pulling
any punches in my forthcoming biography, *The Forgotten Bach*,
to be published either 8vo or 4to in 1954, all of it based on the
Salt Mine Papers my nephew unearthed.

I know my name will be anathema to all except the most advanced music circles for this attempt to do belated justice to the
memory of Johann Wolfgang Hermann Bach, but I like to think
that old Johann Sebastian himself would be proud to know that
his tone-deaf son had turned out rather like the ugly duckling.

LETTER TO A NEIGHBOR

(*Good Housekeeping. The Night the Old
Nostalgia Burned Down.* Little, Brown, 1953)

Dear Butch—

After you went home this afternoon, I fell into a pensive mood
and found myself taking stock of our friendship and what it has
meant to me since that memorable day when we first met. Truly, it
has been a tonic to know you. You have been a stimulating, even a
galvanizing, influence. You have made it necessary for me to ponder
a new set of values—a chore that can be unsettling at my age.

Do you recall the circumstances of our first meeting? Well, I do. It
was a year ago. You had just moved to our block, and you were sitting on your front-porch steps, reconnoitering the neighborhood. I
came along with an armful of groceries. You pulled a gun on me and
cried, "Stick 'em up! I gotcha covered. What's your name?" I told
you. Then you asked if I knew *your* name, and without waiting for
my answer, you told me, and added that you were four years old,
going on five. Then you escorted me the remaining fifty yards to my
home. I did not know until you informed me later that there were
bears and tigers in the block and that they might have hijacked my
groceries and menaced my person. It was mighty friendly of you,
pardner, to escort me home under armed guard that day. It marked
the beginning of a friendship during which I have been held up at
the point of a gun several times a day, answered about a hundred
thousand questions, and learned quite a lot.

Yours is the most scientific mind I have ever encountered. If I
had your curiosity, energy and perseverance, Butch, with my experience, I'd have long since discovered a way to put the atom back together again, minding its own business and doing nobody harm.

You weigh each statement on its merits. You let nothing go un-
challenged. I soon realized the hazard of making rash remarks in
your presence. There was that day in our kitchen when I was host

at our customary midafternoon snack. I had just turned out what I thought was a pretty good job of a peanut butter sandwich, and I handed it to you, saying gaily, "Try that on your zither, squirt."

You said, "What's a zither, Frank?"

I sensed I had made a strategic error and pretended not to hear your question, so you said again, "What's a zither?"

It was useless to dodge the issue. My back was to the wall. I tried to explain to you what a zither was, and under your cross-examination, I realized how little I really knew about zithers. Yet I had thought I knew all I needed to know about them, for mine has been, on the whole, a zitherless life.

There was the morning I went downstairs to breakfast and found you waiting to keep me company, a neighborly act that has frequently enlivened my morning meal and has done much to give the day a cheerful start. I coughed, and explained that I had a frog in my throat.

You demanded to see the frog. You asked how it got in my throat. And why. And when. Thinks I, An up-to-date psychiatrist would answer this tot's questions honestly and not try to duck the issue or fill him with evasions that might confuse his thinking in later life. He should be told that a frog in the throat is only a figure of speech. But if I had told you any such thing, you would have wanted to know what a figure of speech was, and that way, I knew, madness lay. For weeks after that morning, you made daily demands that I produce the frog from my throat. Truly, it has been said—or, rather, is being said by me right now—that elephants and little boys never forget.

You have transformed gardening from the sedative chore of a middle-aged gaffer into an adventure fraught with the unpredictable. Every blossom in the garden, every blade on the sward, trembles when you gallop into view, joyfully crying that you have come to help me weed. And every weed rejoices. There is some consolation in the fact that your range of interests is so wide and you are so busy a man that you cannot spare any one matter your attention for more than two minutes. But in those two minutes, you can help a petunia into a state of advanced debility.

No gardener ever had a more willing apprentice than you. A spirit of scientific inquiry prevades all your activities, though I must admit that the afternoon you sat on the sprinkler to find out how it feels to sit on a sprinkler did neither the sprinkler nor your clean suit any good. Your project to catch squirrels and place them in a large paper bag was original, and it was no fault of yours that the squirrels wouldn't cooperate. That day you decided to tame a bee in a bottle, how were you to know that bees prefer to live in hives and have a very effective means of argument against being placed in bottles? And someday I hope to convince you that the birdbath really does not need to be refilled every five minutes. Birds are not that particular, even though you like to squirt a hose.

On the more constructive side, I think you have really thrown a scare into what you refer to as the Japaneetles. I can believe that word has gone out among them that a young Attila is helping Old Man Sullivan these days, and that the area is not healthy for Japaneetles.

I once read that one must never say "Don't!" to a child, because of the frustrating effects of that word. Something gentler, more persuasive, and less staccato, like "Oh, I wouldn't do that if I were you" was recommended. Well, Butch, as you know, I have tried telling you that I wouldn't do that if I were you on occasions when you were fiddling with the knobs on the gas stove and toying with the Aged Relative's collection of fragile glass knickknacks. I found this warning about as effective as saying, "Tut, tut! I wouldn't if I were you!" to a descending bolt of lightning.

Begging the pardon of the child-guidance experts, I have come to the conclusion that there are occasions in dealing with healthy small boys when "Don't!" or even *"Don't!"* is the only practical command. And I doubt if the moderate amount of "Don'ting" you get on your visits to Sullivan Grange is going to damage as healthy an ego as yours, for I recall the Sunday when you showed up in shining new raiment, and I said, "Why, Butch, you're just about the handsomest fellow I ever saw." And you said, "I know it." Ah, Narcissus, admire yourself while you may. You won't be able to go through life very long as candidly as that. Like the rest of us, you'll learn to dissemble.

It must be great fun to be your age and discover something new almost every day. Words, for instance. Jawbreakers appear quite casually in your budding vocabulary; they're taken from the-Lord-knows-what conversations among your elders and calculated to astonish the unwary. I recall the snowy day when I cautioned you to stay clear of the eaves because of possible avalanches from the roof, and you reassured me, saying, "That's all right, Frank. I'm not allergic to snow." By the way, I'm glad you call me "Frank." It elevates me to comradeship with you on a basis of equality, just as though I, too, were four, going on five.

Why shouldn't I treasure you? You regard me as an oracle and a paragon—well, almost a paragon—and you are the only one who does. You are flatteringly and overwhelmingly interested in everything I do or plan to do. I make no move without hearing, "What are you going to do now, Frank?" . . . "Why?" . . . "What are you doing that for, Frank?" . . . "Why?" . . . "Where are you going, Frank? Can I go, too?" . . . "Why can't I?"

I have learned a lot from you, too. I have become, to my considerable surprise, well versed in the small, personal duties of valet and nursemaid, heretofore entirely out of my line. When you are taking your leave on a winter afternoon, I can button you into your Things with a fair degree of skill, if the Aged R. isn't on hand to do it more skillfully. Your shoelaces come untied every ten minutes, on a timetable as dependable as Old Faithful's. I have learned to tie them. And I remember the small panic that seized me the first time you clambered into my lap (a lap that up to that moment had been undented by any form as small as yours) and demanded that I tell you a story.

This afternoon you were Into Everything. You tried to turn up the thermostat as high as it would go, to see what would happen. The glass *objets d'art* were in mortal peril several times. You were "Don'ted" generously, and finally, when you asked if you might listen to Hoppy, I was only too glad to turn on the television, to keep you quiet. But when ten minutes had gone by, the silence in the living room, save for Hoppy's gunfire, was so marked as to be ominous. I went to the door and peered in the room, to see what was cooking.

You were fast asleep in the big armchair. The recent dynamo was just a tired little boy, worn out by the arduous duties of running the neighborhood and seeing to it that no dull moments crept therein. You looked so small and so innocent, curled up in the armchair, that an odd emotion came over me.

Can it be that you have made me discontented with my status in life? Before I met you, I was a contented bachelor.

PROUST AND THE LIFE SENTENCE

(New York *American. Sullivan at Bay.*
J. M. Dent, London, 1939)

Whenever any one starts bragging about having read *Gone with the Wind,* I quietly mention the fact that I have read all of Marcel Proust. Marcel wrote that vignette of life among the Paris aristocrats called *Remembrance of Things Past.* I refer to it affectionately as *Verbs in the Haystack.* In the English translation Proust, or *Remembrance of Things Past,* runs into seven good-sized volumes.

Everybody ought to read Proust. He is the inventor of the perfected Life Sentence. When the average writer starts to produce a sentence he just throws a subject and a predicate into a bag, gets aboard, and is at his destination in no time. But when Proust started out on a sentence, all the verbs kissed their families good-by and took along their heavy underwear. Proust, embarking on a simple, declarative sentence—or what he would think was a simple, declarative sentence—took along more parts of speech than a movie star does trunks when she sails for Europe.

Proust died in his early fifties. He had been a semi-invalid and a recluse for several years. He rarely left his home, and then only late at night. This was supposed to be on account of his chronic asthma, but I have always had a suspicion that the real reason he shunned society was because he lived in constant dread that he might meet someone who would demand that he parse one of his own sentences.

You can see Proust's characters age visibly during the course of one of his rousing, three-page sentences. Characters, who at the start of the sentence would be vigorous striplings standing on the threshold of life, would be bald, married, and settled down by the time Proust reached the first of the sentence's concluding phalanx of clauses. I have watched Proust characters with sympathy through some of his heftier sentences; have seen the roses fade in their cheeks; have seen them mature, age, and sink, slippered pantaloons, into the grave, before Proust had reached the period or question mark that brought the sentence to an end.

Reading Proust is an adventure not to be missed. In one of his sentences you get everything that Margaret Mitchell had crammed into *Gone with the Wind*. Proust makes all other novels, even Miss Mitchell's, seem like exclamation marks. And you can imagine how magnificent an exercise reading Proust is for sweeping cobwebs out of the brain. Only one must be vigilant, lest Proust sweep out the brain, too.

When I started reading him, I was completely out of condition, with a cerebellum flabby from disuse. I recall how stiff my brain was the day after I read those first few pages of *Swann's Way*. I couldn't even read a simple little exercise like a newspaper editorial. Before I finished Proust, however, I had taken three inches off my head, and was fit as a fiddle. Every ounce of fat gone. I must reread Proust.

One thing I find it difficult to understand about Proust. That is to say, in addition to *Remembrance of Things Past*. He was rich, and yet he wrote. Why the hell should anybody who is rich want to write?

A VISIT TO LONDON

BY ONE WHO HAS NEVER BEEN THERE
(*Harper's Bazaar*. *Sullivan at Bay*.
J. M. Dent, London, 1939)

We arrived in London in a fog. The great sprawling metropolis was completely enveloped in a pea-soup mist which, we were told, had descended a month and a half previously. We didn't mind, because somehow it seemed right that we should have our first sight of the great sprawling metropolis in a fog. Nell's only regret was that on account of the fog we could only get a dim view of the famous old Waterloo Station, which we heard had been built on the cricket fields of Eton.

Nell wanted to put up at one of the fashionable caravansaries in Tooting Bec, but I vetoed that. I told her as long as we were in London we ought to try to get the flavor of the great sprawling metropolis (which I shall refer to from now on as London) by stopping at one of those cosy old inns replete with historical interest and devoid of modern plumbing. Nell then suggested we go to the Cheshire Cheese, but I demurred again. I wanted to stop at the famous old inn frequented by Dr. Johnson and those other noted Regency bucks, but for the life of me I couldn't think of the name of the place, so to the Cheshire Cheese we went.

It proved utterly charming, exactly as we had pictured an old English inn—mullioned windows, mullioned waiters, ceilings with broad beams, barmaids with broader beams, et cetera. There was a room where Queen Elizabeth hid from Essex and his army, and another room where she hid with Essex and his army, and a third room where Essex and his army later hid from her.

There was a room where Shakespeare had been arrested for poaching and a room where Charles I hid from the Parliament while the Parliament was hiding from him in the room next door, which was the same room where Titus Oates hatched his plot. It was called the Plot Hatching Room on account of the fact that Guy Fawkes had also hatched his plot there.

Off the kitchen was a room where King Alfred let the cakes burn. And the tapster looked exactly like Sam Weller. Nell and I were delighted at our good fortune in finding such a really mellow old place.

We hired the Plot Hatching Room and proceeded to make ourselves comfortable. Both Nell and I had been looking forward with considerable interest to tasting British food, and we were not disappointed, for we dined excellently: a typical English meal of clotted Devonshire cream, roast beef, port wine and plum pudding. Afterward we took a tram (short for terambulator) to His Majesty's Theatre in Ludgate Circus and there saw a play by Noel Coward.

Next morning we were awakened bright and early by the cries of the hawksters, tipsters, drapers, mercers, et cetera, vending their wares in the streets below. (London newsboys are not permitted to shout their headlines. They come up and whisper the news in your ear. This often tickles your ear, particularly if the whispered headline contains a lot of sibilants, such as "Lady Susan Sursingham Shoots Sire, Sir Seth Sursingham.")

There was a dense fog out. It was much denser than the pea-soup fog that had greeted our arrival. It was more the consistency of creamed cauliflower soup. You could scarcely see Windsor Castle.

A rosy-cheeked serving wench who reminded Nell of Sam Weller came in and laid a fire of sea coals and we breakfasted cosily by it. Typical English breakfast of clotted Devonshire cream, kedgeree, roast beef, Yorkshire pudding, mulled ale, crumpets, sack and port. The girl was curious about America and wanted to know if the Indians still used bows and arrows in attacking Manhattan. Then she asked if we would give her an Indian yell, so Nell and I obliged with the old Ojibway war cry:

"Cornell I yell yell yell Cornell!"

"Team Team Team!!!"

She was quite impressed, even a bit terrified.

We spent that day sightseeing and went in the evening to Their Majesties' Theatre to see a play. It was by Noel Coward.

What a fog next morning! I thought it was like *potage à la reine,* but Nell said it reminded her more of *borsch.* And those fascinating London noises, coming at you out of the mysterious fog. Nell and I are greatly interested in the noises characteristic of the various cities we visit. In Paris her favorite sound was the scrunch of the French burying the family sock, full of gold, in the backyard. Mine was the low hum of models posing for artists in the nude. Her favorite London noise was the click of pearl buttons dropping from costers' weskits, but I preferred the throaty drawl of duchesses snubbing persons in trade.

Nothing daunted by the fog, we sallied forth on our sightseeing, first taking the precaution of donning our raincoats, or waterproofs, as the English call them.

The English have the most peculiar words for things. Our subway, for instance, is their tube. I believe they have no word for our tube. They call baggage luggage; a cracker a lift, and an elevator a biscuit. Their meat is our poison and our drink is theirs. They call a spade a spade. In telephoning they say, "Are you there?" where we say, "Hello. Hello. Hello. Operator. Operator. Yes, they do answer. There's always somebody there. Ring them again."

The English are a great people for clipping their words, for making one syllable do the work of two or three. For instance, if an American were dining with a British lady of quality and he wanted the Worcestershire sauce, he would say, "Lady Ursula, could I trouble you for the Worcestershire sauce?" but an Englishman would say, "Lady Ursula, pass the Woosh."

On the other hand, they sometimes go to the other extreme. When they wish to express skepticism or incredulity they say, "Oh, I say now, not really, you know, what?" when we achieve the same effect by saying, "Nuts!" A London society woman says, "too perfectly divayne," where a New York society woman says, "too poifectly divine." And when the British want to express disapproval of conduct they consider unsportsmanlike or unethical they say, "That's not cricket," where we say, "That's probably wrestling."

One soon gets used to these little strangenesses. By the time we had been in London a week, nobody would have dreamed we were Americans had it not been for our tortoise-shell glasses, Nell's habit of chewing tobacco and saying, "Waal now, I reckon," and of course the large American flags she and I always carried.

The following day was Thursday and there was a really superb fog, like lobster bisque with toast Melba, I thought, but Nell said she saw it as cream of asparagus. She read in "The Old Lady of Threadneedle Street," as the British call the London *Times,* that a debate on the Boston Tea Party was the order of the day in the House of Lords, so we gulped a typical English breakfast of fish and chips, jugged hare, and gin and bitters, and hurried over to the Houses of Parliament. But the debate was not very exciting and there was such a dense fog in the House of Lords that we couldn't see anything anyhow, so we went over to the Commons in the hope of hearing Lady Astor, the American-born peeress, in action.

They were debating the oakum situation in Woking (or it may have been the woking situation in Oakum) and the Prime Minister was being interrogated by the Opposition, Mr. Winston Churchill.

Next morning there was a glorious fog, just like oyster gumbo. I wanted to go over to Rotten Row to see the regatta, but Nell had her heart set on going down to Trafalgar Square to see the famous statue of Lord Nelson. This is the statue which according to the old story (see any high-school textbook in English history) tips its hat every time a virgin passes. We no sooner reached the Square than Lord Nelson tipped his hat to Nell. Not only tipped his hat to her but told her in a low but quite audible whisper that she reminded him of Sam Weller. Nell was furious, on both counts, and strode off muttering, "It's a fake. It's a fake."

Nell went shopping the next day but flopped badly. The shopkeepers wouldn't sell her anything because she had never been formally introduced to them. British shopkeepers are very strict about this. Nell came home angry and desperate.

"I need a new toothbrush," she wailed, "and I don't know a single druggist in London socially. What am I going to do?"

"Well, for one thing, don't say druggist," I warned her. In England a druggist is a chemist. A public school is a private school. The left side of the road is the right side, and gasoline is petrol. And "My Country 'tis of Thee" is "God Save the King."

That night we thought we'd go to Soho, the Italian or Bohemian quarter of London, as we had heard there were some very good Italian restaurants there. We found a very good one and dined magnificently for two and thruppence hapenny on clotted Devonshire cream, roast beef, bubble and squeak, ale and ravioli.

Passing through Upper Tooting on the way home, I was interested in seeing the offices of the famous humorous weekly *Punch,* or "The Thunderer," as the English affectionately call it. Once a week the staff of *Punch* lunch together and then, over the port, decide on the cover for the next week.

Nell and I liked the London cops, or bobbies, very much. They are a highly efficient body of men who wear chin straps and never allow a murderer to escape. Murder is rare in England and an unsolved murder is rarer. The low rate of homicide is due to the fact that the British never get well enough acquainted to kill each other. Once in a while a foreigner kills an Englishman for being too reticent, but if you see an Englishman murdering another Englishman you can be pretty sure the victim is either a blood relative or a friend of long standing.

The suicides in London are mainly foreigners driven to despair by attempts to understand the difference between the city with a small c and the City with a capital C. It seems that the City is part of the city, but the City is not all of the city. You can be in the city and not be in the City, but you cannot be in the City without being in the city. Nell spent two days trying to figure this out and then I had to take her to a nursing home, where she spent a week in a dense fog.

Our stay in London ended rather unexpectedly. After she returned from the nursing home Nell did not seem her usual self. Irritable and upset. One morning when I passed her the clotted Devonshire cream she glared at me and hissed, "I don't want any clotted Devonshire cream. See?"

And a moment later she added:

"Nor any clotted Yorkshire pudding either. See?"

I thought this rather odd. Nell generally has a good appetite and cleans her plate.

I looked out of the window after we finished breakfast.

"My, there's a magnificent fog out, Nell," I said, to make conversation. "Just like mulligatawny soup."

"It's not like mulligatawny soup at all," she snapped. "It's like clam chowder."

For some time past she had been growing more and more unreasonable on the subject of the fogs. It seemed to me she had an uncanny faculty for picking the wrong soup to fit a fog, and while much of the happiness of our life together has been based on mutual respect for each other's opinions, I considered this a plain question of fact on which it was my duty to set Nell right. The fog was certainly mulligatawny, not clam chowder. I told her so.

"The other day," I added, "when it really was clam chowder, you said it was like Philadelphia pepper pot."

She flew into a rage, told me that it was I who had been quoting the wrong soups all along; that she was sick of it, sick of the fogs and sick of me. With that she packed her bag and left for Cannes.

I dined alone at a pub that night and later went to a play. But somehow I could not enjoy it. Something was missing. Suddenly I realized what it was. The play was not by Noel Coward. I went home, restless and uneasy.

Another day went by and then, feeling very blue indeed, I was on the point of sending Nell a wire telling her she could name her own fogs if she would only come back, when a message arrived from her. It read as follows:

"Sorry I dusted off in such a huff. Lovely cream of tomato soup down here. Do come on down before it's all gone. Love. Nell."

I took the next train for Cannes.

THE NIGHT THE OLD NOSTALGIA
BURNED DOWN

MY OWN NEW YORK CHILDHOOD
*(The New Yorker. The Night the Old Nostalgia
Burned Down. Little, Brown, 1953)*

When I was a boy, Fourteenth Street was where Twenty-third
Street is now, and Samuel J. Tilden and I used to play marbles
on the lot where the Grand Opera House still stood. Governor
Lovelace brought the first marble from England to this country
on August 17, 1668, and gave it to my Great-Aunt Amelia van
Santvoort, of whom he was enamored. She had several copies
made, and Sam Tilden and I used to amuse ourselves with them.

I remember the Sunday afternoons when Governor Lovelace
would come to tea at our house, although I could not have been
much more than a tad at the time. I can hear the rich clanking
of the silver harness as his magnificent equipage, with its twelve
ebony outriders in cerise bombazine, rolled up to our house at
No. 239 East 174th Street. I was the envy of all the kids on the
block because I was allowed to sit in the carriage while the governor went in to take tea with Great-Aunt Amelia. I always chose
Ada Rehan to sit beside me. She was a little golden-haired
thing at the time and none of us dreamed she would one day go
out from East 174th Street and shoot President Garfield.

Great-Aunt Amelia was a dowager of the old school. You don't
see many of her kind around New York today, probably because
the old school was torn down a good many years ago; its site is
now occupied by Central Park. People used to say that the Queen,
as they called Great-Aunt Amelia, looked more like my Aunt
Theodosia than my Aunt Theodosia did.

But Aunt Caroline was really the great lady of our family. I can still see her descending the staircase, dressed for the opera in silk hat, satin-lined cape, immaculate shirt, white tie, and that magnificent, purple-black beard.

"Well, boy!" she would boom at me. "Well!"

"Well, Aunt Caroline!" I would say, doing my best to boom back at her.

She would chuckle and say, "Boy, I like your spirit! Tell Grimson I said to add an extra tot of brandy to your bedtime milk."

Oh, those lollipops at Preem's, just around the corner from the corner! Mm-m-m, I can still taste them! After school, we kids would rush home and shout, "Ma, gimme a penny for a lollipop at Preem's, willya, Ma? Hey, Ma, willya?" Then we would go tease Jake Astor, the secondhand-fur dealer around the corner. I shall never forget the day Minnie Maddern Fiske swiped the mink pelt from Jake's cart and stuffed it under Bishop Potter's cope.

Miss Hattie Pumplebutt was our teacher at P.S. 67. She was a demure wisp of a woman, with white hair parted in the middle, pince-nez that were forever dropping off her nose, always some lacy collar high around her throat, and paper cuffs. We adored her. Every once in a while she would climb up on her desk, flap her arms, shout "Whee-e-e! I'm a bobolink!," and start crowing. Or she would take off suddenly and go skipping about the tops of our desks with a dexterity and sure-footedness truly marvelous in one of her age. When we grew old enough, we were told about Miss Pumplebutt. She took dope. Well, she made history and geography far more interesting than a lot of non-sniffing teachers I have known.

One day, Jim Fisk and I played hooky from school and went to the old Haymarket on Sixth Avenue, which was then between Fifth and Seventh. We had two beers apiece and thought we were quite men about town. I dared Jim to go over and shoot Stanford White, never dreaming the chump would do it. I didn't know he was loaded. I got Hail Columbia from Father for that escapade.

Father was very strict about the aristocratic old New York ritual of the Saturday-night bath. Every Saturday night at eight sharp we would line up: Father, Mother, Diamond Jim Brady; Mrs. Dalrymple, the housekeeper; Absentweather, the butler; Aggie, the second girl; Aggie, the third girl; Aggie, the fourth girl; and twelve of us youngsters, each one equipped with soap and a towel. At a command from Father, we would leave our mansion on East Thirtieth Street and proceed solemnly up Fifth Avenue in single file to the old reservoir, keeping a sharp eye out for Indians. Then, at a signal from Papa, in we'd go. Everyone who was anyone in New York in those days had his Saturday-night bath in the reservoir, and it was there that I first saw and fell in love with the little girl whom I later made Duchess of Marlborough.

My Grandmamma Satterthwaite was a remarkable old lady. At the age of eighty-seven she could skip rope four hundred and twenty-two consecutive times without stopping, and every boy on the block was madly in love with her. Then her father failed in the crash of '87 and in no time she was out of pigtails, had her hair up and was quite the young lady. I never did hear what became of her.

It rather amuses me to hear the youngsters of today enthusing about the croissants, etc., at Spodetti's and the other fashionable Fifth Avenue patisseries. Why, they aren't a patch on Horan's!

Mike Horan's place was at Minetta Lane and Washington Mews, and I clearly remember my father telling a somewhat startled Walt Whitman that old Mike Horan could bend a banana in two—with his bare hands! But I never saw him do it. We kids used to stand in front of his shop for hours after school waiting for Mike to bend a banana, but he never did. I can still hear the cheerful clang of his hammer on the anvil and the acrid smell of burning hoofs from the Loveland Dance Palace, across the way on Delancey Street, which was then Grand. Then the Civil War came and the property of the Loyalists was confiscated. I still have some old Loyalist property I confiscated on that occasion. I use it for a paperweight. Old Gammer Wilberforce was a Loyalist. We used to chase her down the street, shouting "Tory!" at her. Then she would chase us up the street, shouting:

"Blaine, Blaine, James G. Blaine!
Continental liar from the State of Maine!"

or:

"Ma! Ma! Where's my Pa?"
"Gone to the White House, ha, ha ha!"

Of course, very few white people ever went to Chinatown in those days. It was not until the Honorah Totweiler case that people became aware of Chinatown. I venture to say that few persons today would recall Honorah Totweiler, yet in 1832 the Honorah Totweiler case was the sensation of the country. In one day the circulation of the elder James Gordon Bennett jumped seventy-four thousand as a result of the Totweiler case.

One sunny afternoon in the autumn of September 23, 1832, a lovely and innocent girl, twelfth of eighteen daughters of Isaac Totweiler, a mercer, and Sapphira, his wife, set out from her home in Washington Mews to return a cup of sugar—but let the elder Bennett tell the story:

It is high time [Bennett wrote] that the people of these United States were awakened to the menace in which the old liberties for which our forefathers fought and bled, in buff and blue, by day and night, at Lexington and Concord, in '75 and '76, have been placed as a result of the waste, the orgy of spending, the deliberate falsifications, the betrayal of public trust, and the attempt to set up a bureaucratic and unconstitutional dictatorship, of the current Administration in Washington. Murphy must go, and Tammany with him!

After dinner on Sundays, my Grandpa Bemis would take a nap, with the *Times*, or something, thrown over his face to keep out the glare. If he was in a good humor when he awoke, he would take us youngsters up to Dick Canfield's to play games, but as he was never in a good humor when he awoke, we never went to Dick Canfield's to play games.

Sometimes, when we kids came home from school, Mrs. Rossiter, the housekeeper, would meet us in the hall and place a warning finger on her lips. We knew what that meant. We must be on our good behavior. The wealthy Mrs. Murgatroyd was calling on Mother. We would be ushered into the Presence, Mother would tell us to stop using our sleeves as a handkerchief, and then Mrs. Murgatroyd would laugh and say, "Oh, Annie, let the poor children alone. Sure, you're only young once." Then she would lift up her skirt to the knee, fish out a huge wallet from under her stocking, and give us each $2,000,000. We loved her. Not only did she have a pair of d———d shapely stems for an old lady her age, but she was reputed to be able to carry six schooners of beer in each hand.

I shall never forget the night of the fire. It was about three o'clock in the morning when it started, in an old distaff factory on West Twelfth Street. I was awakened by the crackling. I shivered, for my brother, as usual, had all the bedclothes, and there I was, with fully three inches of snow (one inch powder, two inches crust) on my bare back. The next morning there were seven feet of snow on West Twenty-seventh Street alone. You don't get that sort of winter nowadays. That was the winter the elder John D. Rockefeller was frozen over solid from November to May.

On Saturdays we used to go with Great-Aunt Tib to the Eden Musee to see the wax figure of Lillian Russell. There was a woman! They don't build girls like her nowadays. You can't get the material, and even if you could, the contractors and the plumbers would gyp you and substitute shoddy.

I was six when the riots occurred. No, I was *thirty*-six. I remember because it was the year of the famous Horace Greeley hoax, and I used to hear my parents laughing about it. It was commonly believed that Mark Twain was the perpetrator of the hoax, although Charles A. Dana insisted to his dying day that it was Lawrence Godkin. At any rate, the hoax, or "sell," originated one night at the Union League Club when Horace chanced to remark to Boss Tweed that his (Horace's) wife was entertaining that night. The town was agog for days, no one having the faintest notion that the story was not on the level. Greeley even threatened Berry Wall with a libel suit.

Well, that was New York, the old New York, the New York of gaslit streets, and sparrows (and, of course, horses), and cobblestones. The newsboy rolled the *Youth's Companion* into a missile and threw it on your front stoop and the postmen wore uniforms of pink velvet and made a point of bringing everybody a letter every day.

Eheu, fugaces!—

YVONNE

(The New Yorker. In One Ear.
Viking Press, 1933)

Every afternoon at three o'clock a little girl with a deep bass voice appears at the corner of Beekman Place and Fifty-first Street and shouts "Yvonne!" for an hour and a half. On Saturdays she starts in the morning.

Apparently she wants to get in touch with another little girl, named Yvonne, although I admit this is only one man's opinion. Up to now, Yvonne has not, to the best of my knowledge and belief, given any sign of responsiveness, and, frankly, I am worried.

At first I didn't care whether Yvonne answered or not. Then I hoped she wouldn't, just to spite the little girl. But now I want her to answer. More than anything else in the world I want Yvonne to answer that little girl, so that I can pick up the threads of my disordered life and try to make a new start.

I do not know how long the little girl with the bass voice has been on that corner shouting "Yvonne!" This is my third winter in this neighborhood and I do not think she was shouting it the winter of 1930–1931, although I wouldn't want to say for sure, because that was the winter the little boy was shouting "Glurk!" and I was working on the glurk case to the exclusion of all other interests. She might have been shouting "Yvonne!" and it just might not have registered with me. Your ear does acquire a certain selectivity about noises after you have lived in New York since January 6, 1919, and particularly after you have worked in newspaper city rooms from January 7, 1919, to February 27, 1931.

My guess would be that she has been at it a considerable

length of time, judging from the obvious condition of her vocal chords. Because even the fact that she is out on that corner in all kinds of weather shouting "Yvonne!" could not account for her present voice. Even if her mother had been frightened by a fire siren, it wouldn't account for it. A little girl certainly not more than ten or eleven does not develop a voice like Bert Lahr's unless she has been shouting "Yvonne!" or something for a long time.

Furthermore, it is plain she is no novice at shouting. She has a technique that would do credit to a Wagnerian soprano. When she shouts "Yvonne!" she accents the first syllable and holds it, crescendo, for as long as thirty seconds. (I've clocked her on this.) Then she gives you the "vonne," in pear-shaped tones audible for about two of our city blocks.

The little boy who glurked had no particular technique. He just traveled up and down Beekman Place shouting "Glurk! Glurk! Glurk!" in a voice which, although of a treble appropriate to his years (he was about seven), had a curiously carrying quality. Now, I defy anybody with a spark of curiosity in his make-up to sit by idly without wondering why even a *little* boy should want to spend the better part of his waking hours shouting "Glurk!" I dropped everything and went out gunning for the little codger. After several unsuccessful forays, I found him one day, lurking in the wake of a vasty beldame who came sailing down East Fifty-first Street laden to the gunwales with groceries.

He had a stick, whittled into something approaching a resemblance to a rifle. He would aim the stick at her, cock an eye, make a trigger motion with his finger, and say "Glurk!"

"Playing, little boy?" I asked, pleasantly.

He regarded me suspiciously.

"Is that a gun?" I pursued, ingratiatingly.

"Yes," he conceded. He was pretty short with me, too.

"My goodness, don't tell me you're shooting that lady with it!"

"Aw, she's my mother."

"But don't you know you must never shoot your mother in the back? You should fight fair, and give Mummy a chance to defend herself. Why do you say 'Glurk'?"

"Aw, that's the noise when the gun shoots," he explained, with impatience.

"Did you ever hear of a Maxim silencer?" I asked.

He hadn't. I explained that it was a gadget that eliminated the glurk in guns. Then I asked him if he thought it would be worth while to accept a retainer of fifty cents a week to put a Maxim silencer on his gun. He accepted.

"But there's one condition," I warned him. "When I'm up there in that apartment, trying to work to keep body and soul together, every time I hear a glurk out of you, off comes three cents from the fifty. Remember, now."

The first week he owed me sixteen cents. The second week he wiped that out and made two cents. The third week he made twenty-three cents. The next week he collected the full half-dollar, and the week after that he demanded a raise of ten cents.

Thus, at a trifling cost, I had not only abolished glurking on our block, but I had also taught that little shaver a lesson in self-control and thrift, and at a formative age when it was apt to do him the most good. Not to mention the fact that when he grows up, if he should decide to take up a career of crime, he will, thanks to me, know how to use a Maxim silencer.

I would like to be of some similar service to the little girl who shouts "Yvonne!" but, damn it all, I can't *catch* her.

Every afternoon when school is out, I make ready to dart down to the corner at the first shout of "Yvonne!" but no matter how fast I get down those twelve flights, she's gone when I reach the street. As soon as I get back to the apartment, she's at it again.

She's a fool to elude me, because, if she only knew it, I'd be an eager and valuable lieutenant. She's got me completely sold on the idea of locating Yvonne. I never was so bent on anything in my life. I'll bet you Carnegie would snap me up if he were alive and on the corner of Beekman Place and Fifty-first Street

shouting "Yvonne!" Carnegie was a canny old party. The secret of
his success was his ability to pick the right lieutenants.

I could help the little girl in lots of ways. I could help her
shout "Yvonne!" and I could shout it at hours when she does not
have access to the corner, such as three o'clock in the morning.
How does she knew that three o'clock in the morning isn't the
very time to reach Yvonne? I tried it at half past two the other
morning, but when I stood on the corner and called for Yvonne,
two taxicab drivers, a doorman and a cop responded and none
of them would admit he was Yvonne.

Maybe it would help if we organized Beekman Place to help
in the search for Yvonne. I could do that and it would not be
difficult, because, thank God, the old husking-bee spirit has not
disappeared from our little community. No Beekmanite in distress is suffered to go for long unaided. Outsiders may call it
parochialism, but we have another name for it. We call it
Loyalty. We of Beekman Place are a simple, rugged people without any frills. Life is no bed of roses for us. The soil is rocky, the
climate none too salubrious, and the East River, which is our
outlet to the sea (and the secret of our greatness), is full of float-
ing tomato cans. But we eke out an existence on our little rock
over here. It was good enough for our grandfathers, and at least
we can look any man in the face, which is more than most of
our critics from the effete tribes of western Manhattan can do.
And we have given three Presidents to the country: Millard
Fillmore, Guthrie McClintic, and Katharine Cornell.

But enough of braggadocio.

I thought that if everybody on Beekman Place would gather
en masse on the Fifty-first Street corner on a day to be known as
Find Yvonne for the Little Girl Day and then, at a given signal,
set up a community roar for Yvonne, the resulting hullabaloo
might fetch her, because I'm sure that with all our talent over
here, we must have some mighty good Yvonne-shouters among
us. If that uproar didn't fetch Yvonne, then I think we could
fairly assume that nothing ever will; that she is a myth. We can
then take her little friend aside and explain gently that there is

no use shouting "Yvonne!" any more; that, in fact, it is henceforth taboo on Beekman Place.

After that, if she shouts for Yvonne again, we can throw her into the East River for breaking the taboo. This may seem harsh, but it is the law of the tribe and it will be for the common good.

A GARLAND OF IBIDS FOR VAN WYCK BROOKS

(The New Yorker. A Rock in Every Snowball.
Little, Brown, 1946)

I have just finished reading a book[1] which struck me as being one of the finest books I have read since I read *The Flowering of New England,* by the same author.[2] But there is a fly in the ointment. I have been rendered cockeyed by the footnotes. There seem to be too many of them, even for a book largely about Boston.[3] I do not know why the author had to have so many footnotes. Maybe he had a reason for each one, but I suspect the footnote habit has crept up on him, for I got out his book on Emerson,[4] published in 1932, and he used practically no footnotes in it.

You read along in *New England: Indian Summer,* interested to the hilt in what Van Wyck Brooks is telling you about Long-

---

[1] *New England: Indian Summer.*

[2] Van Wyck Brooks, author of *New England: Indian Summer, The Flowering of New England, The Life of Emerson, The Ordeal of Mark Twain,* and other books.

[3] Sometimes referred to as The Hub. Capital and chief city of Massachusetts. Scene of the Boston Tea Party and the arrest of Henry L. Mencken. Bostonians are traditionally noted for their civic pride, or, as an envious New York critic once termed it, their parochial outlook. It is related that on an occasion when Saltonstall Boylston learned that his friend L. Cabot Lowell was leaving for a trip around the world, he inquired of Lowell, "Which route shall you take, L.C.?" "Oh, I shall go by way of Dedham, of course," replied Mr. Lowell. On another occasion, the old Back Bay aristocrat Ralph Waldo Mulcahy said to Oliver Wendell Rooney, "By the way, Rooney, did your ancestors come over on the *Mayflower*?" "Oh, no," replied Mr. Rooney. "They arrived on the next boat. They sent the servants over on the *Mayflower.*"

[4] Ralph Waldo Emerson, Sage of Concord and famous transcendentalist philosopher, not to be confused with Ralph McAllister Ingersoll, editor of *PM.*

fellow,[5] Thoreau,[6] Phillips,[7] James,[8] Alcott,[9] Lowell,[10] Adams,[11] and other great figures of the Periclean Age of The Hub,[12] when suddenly there is a footnote.

[5] Henry Wadsworth Longfellow, Good Gray Poet. Longfellow was no footnote addict. He preferred foot*prints*. Cf. his "Psalm of Life":

> And, departing, leave behind us
> Footprints on the sands of time.

[6] Henry David Thoreau, philosopher who lived at Walden Pond for two years on carrots, twigs, nuts, minnows, creek water, and, as Margaret Fuller suspected (booming it out at Brook Farm in that full, rich voice of hers, to the dismay of William Ellery Channing, Henry Wadsworth Longfellow, Edward Everett Hale, John Lothrop Motley, Charles Eliot Norton, and William Lloyd Garrison), sirloin steaks and creamery butter smuggled to him by Emerson. Suffering as he did from a vitamin deficiency, the result of too much moss in his diet, Thoreau became somewhat of a misanthrope and would often creep up behind members of the Saturday Club and shout "Boo!" or, as some authorities maintain, "Pooh!" The matter is not clarified very much, one must admit, by a letter Mrs. Harriet Beecher Stowe wrote to her son, Harriet Beecher Stowe, Jr. (not to be confused with Herbert Bayard Swope), on June 7, 1854, in which she states: "Not much to write home about, as the saying goes. Dave Thoreau here for supper last nite [*sic*]. He got into an argument with John Greenleaf Whittier, the Good Gray Poet, as to whether snow is really ermine too dear for an earl, and Greenleaf called him a Communist. Dave then crept up behind Greenleaf and shouted either 'Boo!' [*sic*] or 'Pooh!' [*sic*], I couldn't make out wich [*sic*]. All well here except F. Marion Crawford, Sarah Orne Jewett, Charles Dudley Warner, Thomas Wentworth Higginson, and William Dean Howells, who complain of feeling sic [*sic*]. Your aff. mother, H. B. STOWE, SR."

[7] Wendell Phillips. He was about the only Bostonian of his time who wore no middle name and he was therefore considered half naked. Even Mark Twain, when he went to visit Howells in Boston, registered as Samuel Langhorne Clemens.

[8] Probably not Jesse James. Probably is either William James, deviser of Pragmatic Sanctions, or his brother Henry, the novelist. It was about this time that Henry James was going through his transition period, and could not make up his mind whether he was in England living in America or in America living in England.

[9] Amos Bronson Alcott, educator and bad provider. The Mr. Micawber of his day. Not to be confused with Novelist Bus Bronson of Yale or Mrs. Chauncey Olcott.

[10] James Russell Lowell, poet, essayist, and kinfolk of late rotund, cigar-smoking Back Bay Poetess Amy Lowell, no rhymester she.

[11] Henry Adams, author of *The Education of Henry Adams*, by Henry Adams. Not to be confused with Henry Adams, Samuel Adams, John Adams, John Quincy Adams, Abigail Adams, Charles Edward Adams (not to be con-

The text is in fine, clear type. The footnotes are in small type. So it is quite a chore to keep focusing up and down the page, especially if you have old eyes or a touch of astigmatism.[13] By and by you say to yourself, "I be damn if I look down at any more footnotes!" but you do, because the book is so interesting you don't want to miss even the footnotes.[14]

When you get to the footnote at the bottom of the page, like as not all you find is *ibid. Ibid* is a great favorite of footnote-mad authors.[15] It was a great favorite with Gibbon.[16] How come

---

fused with Charles Francis Adams, Charles Henry Adams, or Henry Adams), Maude Adams, Franklin Pierce Adams, Samuel Hopkins Adams, Bristow Adams, George Matthew Adams, James Truslow Adams, Adams Express, Adams & Flanagan, Horace Flanagan, or Louis Adamic.

[12] Sometimes referred to as Boston. One is reminded of the famous quatrain:

> Here's to the City of Boston,
> The home of Filene and the Card.,
> Where the Rileys speak only to Cabots
> And the Cabots speak only to God!

[13] In this connection, it is interesting to note that Louisa May Alcott had a touch of astigmatism, if we are to accept the word of Charles Eliot Norton. Edward Everett Hale states in his *Letters*, Vol. XV, Ch. 8, pp. 297 *et seq.*, that William Cullen Bryant told Oliver Wendell Holmes that on one occasion when the fun was running high at Thomas Wentworth Higginson's home and all barriers were down, Thomas Bailey Aldrich had put the question bluntly to Charles Eliot Norton, saying, "Now listen, has Louisa May Alcott got astigmatism or hasn't she?" Charles Eliot Norton answered, perhaps unwisely, "Yes." Cf. the famous dictum of General William Tecumseh Sherman, sometimes erroneously ascribed to General Ulysses Simpson Grant: "Never bring up a lady's name in the mess."

[14] Ah there, Van Wyck!

[15] So is cf.

[16] Edward Gibbon, English historian, not to be confused with Cedric Gibbons, Hollywood art director. Edward Gibbon was a great hand for footnotes, especially if they gave him a chance to show off his Latin. He would come sniffing up to a nice, spicy morsel of scandal about the Romans and then, just as the reader expected him to dish the dirt, he'd go into his Latin routine, somewhat as follows: "In those days vice reached depths not plumbed since the reign of Caligula and it was an open secret that the notorious Empress Theodora *in tres partes divisa erat* and that she was also addicted to the *argumentum ad hominem!*" Gibbon, prissy little fat man that he was, did that just to tease readers who had flunked Caesar.

writers of fiction do not need footnotes? Take Edna Ferber.[17] She doesn't use footnotes. Suppose Edna Herford[18] took to writing her novels in this manner: "Cicely Ticklepaw* sat at her dressing table in a brown study. She had 'a very strange feeling she'd ne'er felt before, a kind of a grind of depression.'† Could it be love?‡ If so, why had she sent him§ away? She sighed, and a soft cry of 'Aye me!'¶ escaped her. Seizing a nail file desperately, she commenced hacking away at her fingernails, when a voice behind her said, 'O! that I were a glove upon that hand, that I might touch that check!'** Cicely reddened, turned. It was Cleon Bel Murphy! Softly, she told him, 'What man art thou, that, thus bescreen'd in night, so stumblest on my counsel!'"††

What would Van Wyck Brooks say if Edna Ferber wrote like that?[19] Yes. Exactly. Now, where were we?[20] No, I was not. I know what I was saying. You keep out of this. You're a footnote.[21] Yeah? Well, just for that, no more footnotes. Out you go![22] I am, that's who.[23] See what I mean, Van Wyck? Give a

---

[17] Edna Cabot Ferber, contemporary New England novelist. It is related of Edna Ferber that she once met Oliver Herford in Gramercy Park and recoiled at the sight of an extremely loud necktie he was wearing. "Heavens above, Oliver Herford!" exclaimed Miss Ferber, never one not to speak her mind. "That is a terrible cravat. Why do you wear it?" "Because it is my wife's whim that I wear it," explained Oliver Herford. "Well, land sakes alive, before I'd wear a tie like that just on account of a wife's whim!" jeered Miss Ferber. "You don't know my wife," said Oliver Herford. "She's got a whim of iron." Miss Ferber later made this incident the basis for the dramatic battle between the husband and wife in her novel *The Cravat*.

[18] No, no, no, not Edna Herford! Edna *Ferber!* Edna Herford is the fellow who had the wife with the iron whim.

* Blond, lovely, and twenty-one.

† See "I'm Falling in Love with Someone"—Victor Herbert.

‡ Sure.

§ Cleon Bel Murphy, the man she loves.

¶ *Romeo and Juliet*, Act II, Scene 2.

** *Ibid.*

†† *Ibid.*

[19] And what would Edna Ferber say if Edna Ferber wrote like that?

[20] You were saying Louisa May Alcott had astigmatism.

[21] Yeah? And how far would you have got in this article without footnotes?

[22] Who's gonna put me out?

[23] Yeah? You and who else?

footnote an inch and it'll take a foot.[24] I give up. They got me.
And they'll get you too in the end, Van Wyck. You may think
you're strong enough to keep 'em under control; you may think
you can take a footnote or leave it. All I say is, remember Dr.
Jekyll! Lay off 'em, Van. I'm telling you for your own good.

—UNEASY BROOKS FAN[25]

[24] Yoo-hoo! Footnote!
[25] Frank Saltonstall Sullivan.

DEAR OLD PARIS
MEMORIES BY ONE WHO HAS NEVER
BEEN THERE BUT HAS HEARD
AND READ PLENTY ABOUT IT
(*The New Yorker. In One Ear.* Viking Press, 1933)

Several days ago I went up to the attic to get some moths for my new blue serge suit, and in going through an old trunk came across a faded velvet beret and a small reddish beard.

The beret and the beard I had worn in my student days in Paris! . . . I sat there for what seemed an hour—and, in fact, was an hour—lost in dreams of those dear, dead days.

Father had not wanted me to become an artist. He wanted me to join the business and learn it from the bottoms up. He was a brewer. I tried, but I couldn't do it. Milwaukee stifled me. I felt that there was something in me that was very precious that Milwaukee would kill unless I escaped. I knew I had to get away, or perish. I had to be free; free to live my own life in my own way, free to express myself. Father could not understand. There was a scene.

I left, and went to Paris. But Mother sent me plenty of money.

It seems ages ago that I dropped into the little *pension* in the Rue de la Paix, behind the Gare du Nord, off the Boulevard des Capucines, and bought that red beard. It cost but a franc. (Imagine getting a beard these days for a franc.) I remember Liane, the little *cocotte* who sold me the beard. She was my first love in Paris, a gay wisp of a girl, as affectionate as a puppy. We used to wander hand in hand, back and forth, over the Pont Neuf on spring nights when the air was soft with that wonderful softness the air has in spring in Paris.

I bought the beret at a quaint little shop in the Faubourg St.-

Germain, just off the Rue St.-Honoré. A dear old Frenchman in a smock and wooden *sabots* kept the shop, but his daughter, Marie, a ravishing blonde, did most of the work. She was the fourth sweetheart of my student days in Paris. On a summer night when the air was soft with that marvelous softness the air has in Paris in summer, I would finish my painting, hurry over to the Rue St.-Honoré, and help Marie put up the shutters. Then we would leave *Maman* (as the French call their father) sitting in front of the shop, smoking his pipe contentedly, and we two would wander off, hand in hand. The old gentleman would smile and wave at us with that tender understanding of young love which the French display so well whenever there is a sufficient *dot*.

Marie and I would go to Foyot's, in the Place Pigalle just off the "Boul' Mich'," for *escargots*. Gad, when I think of those *escargots* at Foyot's in the old days, prepared as only Pierre could pierre them, with that heavenly sauce that only he could conjure. Pierre could do things with a leek, some white wine, a bit of parsley, an onion, and a piece of old shoe leather, that you wouldn't believe possible. The sauce prepared, he would place it near the snails. Entranced by the magic concoction, they would troop out of their shells and pop one by one into the sauce, willing martyrs in the cause of good cuisine. *Et voilà!* There were your *escargots à la Pierre.*

Pierre's daughter, Diane, used to help him. I wonder what happened to that dainty, delightful minx who was the seventh love of my student days in Paris. On autumn evenings, when the air was soft with that divine softness of air in Paris in autumn, I would call at Foyot's for Diane.

"*Mais,* aren't you going to help me *avec les escargots ce soir, ma petite fille de joie?*" her father would inquire.

"*Enfer avec les escargots,*" Diane would retort gayly, and off we'd go to a little *bistro* called the Chat Rouge. No, it wasn't the Chat that was Rouge; it was the Moulin that was Rouge. The Chat was Noir, and it was on the Place de la Concorde, just behind the Madeleine (an *église*).

In those days only a few of us knew about the Chat Noir. George Moore used to come there, for one. He was a struggling young *concierge* at the time, or struggling *with* a young *concierge;* he told me which, but I have forgotten. Marcel Proust used to come there, too. A strange sort of chap, Proust. He was a neurotic, and an asthmatic to boot, and he would never leave his room. I shall never forget what an odd sight it was to see Proust come walking down the Boulevard des Italiens, in his room.

Of course, when I was studying in Paris, French cooking had not yet been invented by George Jean Nathan, but one could get perfectly good food at Napoleon's Tomb, which was run by a magnificent old rip named Margot. I can see her now— grizzled, bearded like a pard, fierce of eyebrow, keys jingling at her apron—taking her seat at the cash register and shouting *"Alors!"* at the harassed waiters.

Dear old Margot. She was like a father to me.

Matisse used to go to Margot's, also Matosse and Matasse and Matoose. I often saw Monet and Manet there, and Manit and Manot and Manou, and sometimes W.

And the singing we students used to perpetrate! *Mon Dieu,* it's a wonder our singing didn't bring on a second Terror. Our favorite was an old Provençal ballad called *"Samedi soir le bain,"* and if I remember correctly, it went like this:

> Tais toi, mon bijou,
> Tu sais que je t'aime,
> Allons, dis donc, au Sorbonne!
> Zut! Alors!

It used to make us cry, especially if we were homesick. Then there was another, called *"Peut-être,"* if I remember rightly:

> Mon Petit choux,
> J'adore vous;
> Il n'y a pas des papillons?
> Hein! Alors!

We sang that one when we were happy.

And such arguments as we students used to have, while the

saucers piled higher and higher. We knew it all, or thought we did. How innocent, how naïve we really were, yet how furious we should have been if anyone had told us at the time that we were naïve or furious. The *vin rouge* wasn't potent enough for us Americans. We had to improve on it, greatly to the disgust of the French. We used to mix the *vin rouge* with *vin bleu* and drink the result, which was *vin pourpre*. But the French wouldn't drink the mixture. They used it for their fountain pens.

Fountain pens remind me of those Sundays at Versailles, watching the Fountains play. There were five of them, all accomplished musicians. There were the mother and father (piano and harp, respectively); a son who played the violoncello; another son, "Poodles," who supplied the comedy relief; and Louise Fountain, the daughter—dark, beautiful Louise, with such eyes! She played the B-flat cornet. Naturally, I was not long in making the acquaintance of Louise and that acquaintance quickly ripened into—ah, but one does not kiss and tell.

I shall never forget my first Quat'z' Arts ball. It was there I met Lucienne, the twenty-seventh sweetheart of my student days in Paris. A group of riotous, fun-loving students had stripped poor Lucienne of every last vestige of her costume. She didn't seem to mind awfully. I, *moi-même*, was no better off, a crowd of souvenir-hunting midinettes from Les Invalides having swept gayly over me, leaving me as bare as a tree after a visit from a swarm of locusts.

"Aren't you a mannequin in Worth's on the Rue Lamarck?" I asked Lucienne.

"Yes," she replied.

"I thought I recognized your face," I said. "It makes dawn. Will you drive out the Bois to Les Halles with me for some of that onion soup for which it is famous?"

"Oh, Monsieur is kind, but I am not dressed for onion soup."

"Nonsense, little goose," I told her. "Come just as you are." So off we went to Les Halles to watch the farmers and their oxen trudging in at the dawn laden with onion soup from the Hautes-Pyrénées, Normandy, and the Côte d'Azur. It was in December, and the air was soft with that entrancing softness of air in Paris in winter.

I recall the picnics at St.-Cloud—the funny, middle-class French families having their Sunday outing; husband, wife, children, mistress, all very gay. And Prunier's. I wonder if the chicken à la King à la Prunier's is still as good as it was. And the dear old Paris sewers—ah, but I ramble on until I grow tiresome.

They unveiled a bust of me at the Hall of Fame the other day. I looked about me at the eminent men who had gathered to honor the "greatest painter of the ages," as they were kind enough to term me. There were Dr. Nicholas Butler, Professor Irving Babbitt, Dr. John H. Finley, President Lowell, Edwin Arlington Robinson and a host of others. And as I looked about me, I became sad. The years had passed. Father was wrong and I was right. I had fame, wealth, honor; but, as I said to myself that day, what does it mean to me? Now that I've got it, what does it *mean* to me? Has it brought me happiness? I wondered.

And suddenly I thought that, with all due respect to Dr. Butler and all those eminent gentlemen, I would gladly give them all up for one hour of youth and happiness with Liane, or Marie, or Louise, or Diane, or any one of the two hundred and seventy-four sweethearts of that first rapturous year as a student in Paris!

APOSTROPHE TO A STREET

(*Good Housekeeping. The Night the Old
Nostalgia Burned Down.* Little, Brown, 1953)

Technically it is an avenue, but that title is a bit of swank the
village elders thought up after the War between the States when
they renamed The Street for Mr. Lincoln and in his honor raised
it to the dignity of a boulevard. Before that it had been plain
South Street.

A stranger seeing it for the first time would not note anything
special about it except perhaps that it is richly blessed with elms
that make a cool green arcade of it in summer. Yet it has somewhat more charm for me than Peachtree Street in Atlanta, or
Euclid Avenue in Cleveland, or Beacon Street in Boston or the
Champs Élysées.

This may be because I never took off my shoes and stockings
and sailed boats in the gutters of the Champs Élysées after a
heavy rain, and it was not from a home on Beacon Street that I
once went forth to be confirmed, wearing glittering new patent
leather shoes that pinched. Nor was it from Euclid Avenue that
I stepped one June evening, garbed in a borrowed tuxedo, to
orate at the high-school graduating exercises on the topic, The
Political Morals of the United States. (I denounced corruption
in high places.)

It was The Street I left on one crisp morning in September
1917, to march to the depot behind flying banners and the rem-
nant of Post Luther M. Wheeler, G.A.R., on my way to help
make the world safe for democracy. I have left it many times
since and come back many times, on occasions glad and sad.

Our clan first moved to The Street before my time, about the
year my father was voting for whatever Democrat opposed

Chester A. Arthur. They moved away twice and twice moved back. The last trip we've stayed fifty years and have about decided we like it; at least the two of us who survive have so decided.

Michigan Avenue in Chicago is a splendid boulevard, no argument at all about that, yet I prefer Lincoln Avenue on a fair Sunday morning in summer. Neighbor Rydberg is hoeing his garden. Neighbor Alice Norton is washing her car. Neighbor Rose Dunn reads the Sunday paper in her hammock under the spruces. The younger set pass by on their way to Sunday school, shining in their best duds and Sunday faces. Our special Lincoln Avenue sun toasts us pleasantly from our special Lincoln Avenue sky, two shades bluer than any other sky. A sweet Sabbath calm prevails, picked out, you might say, by the hum of bees, the warble of orioles and an occasional holler from me at pups choosing my flower beds for their frolics.

It boosts my morale to play lord of the manor on the 250 × 150 chunk of The Street to which I hold title; to walk about, surveying *my* elms, *my* maples, *my* spruces—and *my* crabgrass—to a choral accompaniment from *my* orioles and *my* robins, and occasional jeers from catbirds and jays whom I ignore. I cannot make one tulip or a single spruce paw show up a day earlier in the spring any more than I can delay the fall of one maple leaf in October. All I can do, being human, is destroy, but I do not want to destroy anything on my demesne except the crabgrass and the ants. This illusion of possession does me good and does the trees and birds no harm. Maybe they feel possessive about me. I'd take it as a compliment if they did.

"Ah," says the senior elm to the oriole, "I see *our* mammal is back from the city. Hmm, his foliage is getting a bit thin on top."

"It is," the oriole agrees. "Perhaps a little judicious pruning . . ."

"I wonder," the willow muses, "if *they* die at the top, like us."

The Street is at its best at twilight in winter when the snow takes on that bluish tinge. I like the moment at dusk when the street lights come on, but I liked that moment even better about forty-five years ago, when it was not a man at a distant switch who turned on the lights but a boy who came up the street and lit the gas lamps with a long pole.

For two decades I lived during a large part of the year in apartments in New York City and never once knew who my next-door neighbors were, but when I walk down The Street of a morning to get my newspapers at Rod Sutton's store, nearly everyone I meet calls me by my first name and I call them by theirs. I have known some of them since I was a boy, and that, friends, is no putt. I take it as an even greater compliment that the neighborhood youngsters call me by my first name.

One odd thing about The Street is that when you come back to it after an absence it always seems to have grown younger. We who live on it grow older, but The Street is far more chipper today than it was fifty years ago. Then it was little more than a country road, but it was a gay country road. In the summertime trolley cars loaded with merrymakers creaked and swayed along it, bound for the dancing and vaudeville and swimming at the Lake, or for the races at the track. In the dog days it was magnificently dusty or muddy, depending on the weather. When it was dusty sprinkling carts traveled its length, sending out gushing fans of water to lay the dust. It was a favored sport of my generation to see how close to the spray we could frisk without getting soaked.

At Christmas time you could usually count on The Street being handsomely banked with snow and if a thaw came later it was slushy beyond the dreams of the golosh trust. In January we hitched our sleds to the big sleighs that drew ice from the Yaddo ponds to the icehouses out Jefferson Street. Separated by layers of straw the ice cakes were piled high in the houses, against the summer's needs, and what a playground those barns made for small boys on hot summer days! The memory of their dark coolness is a part of the patina of The Street, though the ice houses were a quarter of a mile away.

Homes line both sides of The Street today, but in 1900 only its north side was inhabited. Fields stretched off to the south, reaching for all we knew to Albany, a fabulous forty miles away. In May the fields were golden with dandelions, and boys were handed a dishpan and a knife and commissioned to gather a mess of greens for the family dinner. And there were the chokecherry trees, into which, in August, boys could climb and gorge themselves until they were purple, quite literally, in the face, and also all over the shirtwaist. The only surviving chokecherry tree, as far as I know, stands now in our yard, enjoying a lusty and respected old age and honored each spring with a healing spray of DDT.

The Street has long since been paved and macadamized and marcelled and modernized. The trolley cars gave place years ago to a bus line. Ice cubes have supplanted the ice houses. The drainage is so efficient that after a thunder shower the water doesn't linger in the gutters long enough to make it worthwhile to sail boats there. Anyhow, boys don't sail boats now. They fly airplanes.

The Street gives a sense of permanency, of continuity, that is good for the soul in These Troubled Times. For instance, I often see my neighbor Jack taking an evening stroll with his two-year-old heir. I have known Jack for a long time. He is a fine fellow. He belongs to The Street, too, and was glad to get back to it after his four years in the South Pacific. He is now the husband of a pretty girl, father of two remarkable babies and proprietor of a thriving business. Yet I recall the spring, and it doesn't seem too long ago, when I came back to The Street and was greeted by Jack, not in his familiar boyish treble, but in a new and melancholy croak, which seemed to startle him as much as it did me. Nature, I saw, had just deprived Bethesda Episcopal Church of one of its most lyric boy sopranos.

There was also the lively evening when Jack and several other Peck's Bad Boys got to fooling with a steam roller the street department had parked on our block for the night. One of the kids pulled the wrong, or right, lever and the steam roller started careening down the road like a bull elephant on a rampage. The boys jumped. The housewives on the front porches dropped their evening papers and screamed. A neighbor dropped his rake, hotfooted it after the juggernaut, hopped aboard and stopped it just as it was about to climb the curb and chew up the Widow Peets' front porch.

In a few years history will repeat. Jack's heir will assume the mantle of Peck's Bad Boy. It will be Jack who will be stopping berserk steam rollers and young Jack in his turn will be despoiling the grape arbors in September, or sending baseballs crashing through parlor windows. Rather comforting to know that this will be so.

It cannot be claimed that The Street has made any outstanding contribution to the nation's life. It has produced no famous poets, musicians, atomic physicists or tycoons. It has given the country no President, though named for one of the greatest. Nelson Avenue, the thoroughfare just to our east, really boasts more distinction, claiming a summer resident worth a couple hundred millions and—certainly to the youngsters—an even more glamorous citizen, who is a retired snake charmer. Yet the United Nations statesmen might learn something from a visit to The Street. We are Americans of—let's see—Austrian, English, Jewish, Irish (both Eire and Ulster), Canadian, Italian, Scotch, German, Swedish and Norwegian descent, and until his death in his nineties a few years ago the patriarch of the neighborhood, respected and liked by all, was a mighty fine American who was a Negro. We get along great. Always have, and that goes for Eire and Ulster. No blood is shed, unless you count an occasional nose incarnadined in a row among the junior set. We know each each other's virtues and appreciate them; we know each other's foibles and wink at them. None of us cares how the others vote or worship and we respect each other's privacy, yet we aren't so dull as to have no neighborly curiosity at all about one another. We're only human. We put our neighbors on the pan occasionally, provided they are absent at the time, and give them a neighborly broiling. But let illness or trouble of any kind strike, and watch The Street go into action to help its own.

Well, you must have recognized The Street by this time. Of course you have. With a change here and there it's your Street, too.

QUIGLEY 873

(*The New Yorker. The Night the Old Nostalgia Burned Down.*
Little, Brown, 1953)

Perhaps no class of scientist is more apt to encounter the un-expected in the course of his work than the student of folklore. My wife and I appreciated this last summer when we discovered the refreshingly unique Lovers' Leap at Wassamattawichez Notch, New Hampshire, which for research purposes we have catalogued as Quigley 873.

My wife, Dr. Johanna Bracegirdle Quigley, and myself (Professor W. Hungerford Quigley) may possibly be recognized as co-authors of "The Role of the Lovers' Leap in American Folk-lore," the rather monumental study that, we flatter ourselves, has effected a sweeping change in thought on the subject since its publication, a decade ago. We narrowed our field of research to the Lovers' Leap because it seemed to us not only a fascinating but a neglected aspect of folklore, and we have never regretted our decision. Dr. Johanna, a mite more thorough as a scientist than am I, has several times actually made the jump from a Lovers' Leap, just to get the feel of the thing, but on each occasion she used a parachute; I have been adamant on that point.

I might say a word or two here about Lovers' Leaps, for the benefit of readers unfamiliar with the colorful tradition. In North America, which is rich in precipices of all heights, the Lovers' Leap has reached its fullest flower, and in American folklore it is almost always a beautiful Indian maiden and a hand-some young brave who, thwarted in their love by parental or tribal opposition, solved their problem tragically by leaping from a ledge at the top of the precipice to the rocks below. The scene later becomes known in legend as a Lovers' Leap. The investigations of Dr. Johanna and myself, up to our discovery of Quigley 873, had revealed eight hundred and seventy-two authentic Lovers' Leaps in the United States and Canada, and we thought we had exhausted the field. The jumps ranged from fifty to three thousand feet and the leaping lovers represented every tribe in the country except the Seminoles, of Florida. Florida, being very flat, affords no facilities for lovers desirous of leaping, and how the star-crossed Seminoles solve their difficulties is a nice problem that Dr. Johanna and I hope one day to probe.

It was during a motor trip in the White Mountains that we discovered Quigley 873. We were bowling along a road near Lake Wassamattawichez on an idyllic June afternoon when, rounding a bend, we saw before us, on the opposite side of the valley, a crag that we both realized instantly might be a Lovers' Leap, and one of the most perfect we had ever encountered— sheer drop, magnificent view, parking space. It had everything!

"It *must* be a Lovers' Leap, but I don't seem to recognize it," I said to Dr. Johanna. Was it possible that we had stumbled on a new Leap? We hardly dared hope.

Well, the thing was to find out, and to do this it was necessary, of course, to locate the oldest inhabitant of North Wassamattawichez, the village nestling in the valley below. My wife and I once differed, though not seriously, on the best method of verifying oldest inhabitants. If a birth certificate was not available, she favored a thorough physical examination by a competent physician, but oldest inhabitants, she found, often displayed a nettling resistance to such a test, and she finally gave up her method and adopted mine, which I do think works as well in the long run. My system is simply this: if a native sufficiently advanced in years uses "mebbe" for "maybe," "allus" for "always," and "sezee" for "says he," and if he recalls that his father carried him to the railroad station to watch Lincoln's funeral train pass by, in 1865, then I ask him his age, deduct fifteen years from his answer, and accept him as a bona-fide oldest inhabitant.

Dr. Johanna and I soon found our man, a venerable patriarch named Jonas Atkinson, one hundred and four-minus-fifteen years old, and we engaged him in conversation over a mug of foaming ale at the quaint tavern in the village. By way of breaking the conversational ice, I asked him the traditional question demanded by protocol. "To what do you attribute your great age, Mr. Atkinson?"

"I allus sweat good," he replied, and, gazing into his already empty mug, added slyly, "An' I allus enjoy my ale."

I smiled, and commanded the landlord to fetch more ale.

Dr. Johanna then took up the ball. "My husband and I were attracted by that odd-looking cliff yonder side of the valley," she said with assumed nonchalance. "Has it by any chance got a name?"

"Yep," said Mr. Atkinson. "It's called Lovers' Leap."

The astronomer who has found a new comet or the botanist who has uncovered a hitherto unknown trillium will recognize the excitement that filled us at this confirmation of our hope.

"Lovers' Leap, eh?" said Dr. Johanna, still with pretended indifference. "What ever for?"

"Two Injuns leapt there a long time ago," said Mr. Atkinson.

"Dashed themselves to death on the rocks below, clasped in a last fond embrace?" asked Dr. Johanna, now scarcely able to control her excitement.

"Shucks, no, Sis," said Mr. Atkinson. "Nothin' like that."

Dr. Johanna and I exchanged perplexed glances. "You mean they jumped off that cliff and *lived?*" I asked.

"Didn't say they jumped offen it, Bub," said Mr. Atkinson. "I said they leapt."

"Well, what's the difference?"

"Well, sir, I'll tell ye—Consarn it, I can't. M'throat's gone scratchy on me agin."

"Landlord, more ale!" said I.

"Thankee. Drat this foam. Most of it gits in a feller's beard. Sheer waste o' good ale. Well, sir, it was like this. This maiden an' this here brave from the Wassamattawichez tribe fell in love. Made a fine-lookin' pair, too. He was an all-around athlete and could jump better'n any brave in the tribe, an' they called him Standin' High. She was almost as good as he was at track, so they called her Leapin' Trout. Well, things would o' gone all right, but her father promised her hand to an old buck that happened to have a lot o' wampum. So the kids decided to elope. One day they slipped away an' met down yander in the ravine, all set to light out fer the West. Well, they git jest underneath the cliff thar when who comes rushin' at 'em from one end o' the ravine but a mob o' her folks in hot pursuit. So Leapin' Trout and Standin' High started for th'other end o' the ravine, but who shows up thar but Got Wampum, th'old buck she was supposed to marry, with a mob o' *his* folks. Escape was cut off.

"Leapin' Trout pulled a pizened arrow out o' her quiver an' cried, 'At least we can die together!' but her lover stayed her hand. 'Don't puncture yerself,' sezee. 'There is yet a way out.'

" 'Whar?' s'she.

" 'The cliff up thar,' sezee.

" 'Jump fifty feet straight up?' s'she. 'Are you crazy, Standin' High?'

" 'You can do it, with a little help,' sezee. 'I got an idea.'

"There was a log restin' a-teeter across a boulder. He told her to stand on the end that touched the ground.

" 'Now,' sezee, 'when I jump on th'other end, you'll shoot up into the air, and when you do, just hunch and scrunch yerself along all you can an' you'll make the top o' that cliff, understand? It's our on'y chance.'

" 'But you, Standin' High,' s'she, 'what'll become o' you?'

" 'Don't worry about me,' sezee. 'I'll take off right after ye. Come along. We got no time fer argufication.'

"They didn't, nuther, because by now mobs o' kinfolk was comin' down at 'em from both ends o' the gulch, whoopin' and yellin' like savages, and makin' a reg'lar garboil.

"So Leapin' Trout crouched on the grounded end o' the log. Standin' High sprang up onto a big boulder that was nigh. 'Git ready!' sezee. 'Git set! Go!' An' with that he jumps offen the boulder onto th'other end o' the log with all his might, an' up shoots the beautiful Indian maiden like a bat out o' hell. You know, the way the acrobats do it in the circus. An', by gum and by golly, she lands on the edge o' the cliff fifty foot above, teeters there a second, then grabs a bush and hauls herself to safety."

"And what became of Stanley High?" asked Dr. Johanna eagerly.

"*Standin'* High!" corrected Mr. Atkinson. "Well, he can't use the log. He ain't got no friend down thar to catapult *him* up. He has to rely on the stren'th the Lord gave him. So he grabs a fifty-foot pine trunk layin' nearby, gits a good runnin' start, takes off, an' sails into the air in as purty a pole vault as this nation ever see."

"Did he make it?" asked Dr. Johanna.

Mr. Atkinson turned purple and gave out gasping, choking noises. "Landlord, more ale!" I cried. "Hurry!"

Mr. Atkinson quaffed and the spasm passed.

"That ale didn't come a minute too soon, Bub," he said. "Thirsty work, spinnin' these legends."

"Yes, yes, Mr. Atkinson, but tell us—did Standing High make it?"

"Missed it by ten foot."

"A-a-h, what a pity!" Dr. Johanna mourned. "He fell back on the tomahawks of his enemies?"

"I never said that, Sis. He got away all right. But he'd o' bin a gone goose if it hadn't bin fer J. Fenimore Cooper."

"J. Fenimore Cooper?"

"Yep. Standin' High was a great reader, fer an Injun. Allus claimed he learnt everything he knew about Injun lore from J. Fenimore, an' when he left home that mornin' he'd slipped his well-thumbed copy o' *The Deerslayer* into his pants pocket. That saved his life."

"How?" I asked.

"Well, when old Got Wampum reached the spot, jest after Standin' High took off fer the top o' the cliff, he gave a yell o' baffled rage an' let fly an arrow at his rival's retreatin' form. Old Got Wampum was a good shot."

"He hit Standing High?"

"Right where it done the most good, as things turned out. The arrow passed clean through Cooper's book an' penetrated Standin' High to a depth of mebbe half an inch. Not so deep as a well but deep enough to encourage, as the Bard would say. Standin' High gave a sharp cry an' sprang three more feet into the air."

"And that got him to the top of the cliff?" I asked.

"Nope. He was still shy seven foot."

"So he fell back on the arrows of his foes after all?"

"Not by a durn sight. He grabbed Leapin' Trout by the hair."

"By the hair?"

"Sure. Leapin' Trout had hair seven foot long, like that gal in the fairy tale."

"Rapunzel?" suggested Dr. Johanna.

"Don't mind if I do," said Mr. Atkinson quickly.

I said, "Landlord, more ale!"

"Thankee," said Mr. Atkinson. "Yarnin' suttinly makes a feller spit cotton. Yep, Leapin' Trout got a good hold onto a tree, let her hair down over the cliff, Standin' High grabbed the hair, an' she hauled him up."

"To safety?"

"Yes, ma'am," said Mr. Atkinson.

"What an utterly charming legend!" said Dr. Johanna, brushing what I fear was a not quite scientific tear from her cheek.

"They didn't leap *offen* that cliff," said Mr. Atkinson. "They leapt *onto* it. I reckon this here's the on'y Lovers' Leap in reverse in this country, and the on'y one with a happy endin'."

"I can just see old Got Wampum, the disgruntled lover," I chuckled. "I'll bet *his* face was red."

"Why not? He was an Injun," said Mr. Atkinson.

"Did Stanley High and Running Broad live happily ever after?" asked Dr. Johanna.

"Her name was Leapin' Trout," corrected Mr. Atkinson. "Yep,

they done all right. Toured fer years with the Pawnee Bill show and retired with a small fortune. I heard tell they had a grandson went to Yale, class of 1922, and he was the best one in all the colleges at vaultin' with the pole."

Sullivan invented two deathless but far from lifeless female characters (see page 13)—Aunt Sarah Gallup, the Grand Old Lady of the Adirondacks, who thought she had lived forever, known everybody and done everything, and Martha Hepplethwaite, his mythical secretary, who was even more apocryphal than her employer. A trio of their didoes appears on the following pages.

ROVER THE PARTRIDGE
(New York *American. The Night the Old Nostalgia Burned Down.* Little, Brown, 1953)

Aunt Sarah Gallup brought her blunderbuss to her shoulder, took careful aim, let go, and brought down a pheasant, a partridge, a quail, a woodcock, a deer and a sizable portion of an elm tree.

"Good shot, Aunt Sarah."

"I've done better," said the Grand Old Lady of the Adirondacks modestly, as she rose from the sitting posture to which the kickback from the blunderbuss had thrown her. "Hunting ain't what it used to be."

"You seem to be doing all right."

"No use talking, hunting ain't what it used to be, young man. There's too much coddling of partridges. And it's made 'em lose their spunk. When I was a gal there warn't no open seasons and shut seasons and all that claptrap you have nowadays. We allus knew when the partridge season was open, all right, and no mistake about it."

"How, Aunt Sarah?"

"When the partridges flew up to the log cabin and dared us to come out and fight, that's how. Partridges was partridges in those days. They could give you a tussle for your money. Here you, Rover, put that down."

Rover, our retriever, deposited the elm limb which Aunt Sarah had potted, at her feet, and wagged his tail.

"That's a good dog. I hope he never turns partridge on you."

"Turn partridge on me. What do you mean, Aunt Sarah?"

"Like a dog I had once. His name was Rover, too. He turned partridge. Leastwise, I'm not sure whether he turned partridge, or whether he'd been a partridge secretly all along and had just turned dog for a while."

"What on earth are you talking about, Aunt Sarah?"

"You don't have to believe me, sonny. I'm not asking you to. I'm just tellin' you I had a dog once name of Rover that went over to the partridges."

"Why did he do it?"

"I think mebbe it warn't all his fault. He got off to a bad start. He never had a chance to find out what kind of dog he was, and I think he got to brooding about that. When he was a pup we all thought he was a pointer, and I think he thought so, too, and mebbe he might have got to be a first-class pointer if it hadn't been for my grandma."

"What did she have to do with it?"

"Well, you see, she was a great stickler for manners and one day when she caught Rover pointing, she told him it wasn't good manners to point, and to stop it right away. So he did. He stopped pointing and started out to be a setter. But it was too late, and he got sort of confused, and the upshot of the whole thing was that poor Rover never did get to be what you might call any definite kind of dog at all. I felt sorry for him. He wasn't overbright to begin with, and the strain was too much. I think he did the best he could, under the circumstances. How would you like to get well started in life as a pointer and then have to try to make yourself over into a setter?"

"I wouldn't like that at all, Aunt Sarah."

"Well, neither did Rover, and he was never the same after he started trying. His mind seemed unbalanced, sort of. And fust thing we know, he was back to pointing. Next thing, he'd gone over to the partridges, hook, line and sinker."

"But how do you mean he went over to the partridges?"

"Well, Simple, he just went over, like I say. He just went out into the woods and instead of pointing partridges for us, he pointed us for partridges."

"He helped the partridges hunt you settlers?"

"He suttinly did, and it was quite a blow to us settlers. In fact, it was the last straw, to have Rover leave us like that. After that we didn't have a chance against the partridges. Didn't dare go out of doors during the partridge season for fear one might grab us and carry us off to his nest."

"Then you didn't shoot any partridges in those days, after all, Aunt Sarah?"

"Yes, I did. I was able for 'em. I killed many a one, but it was always in self-defense."

MISS GALLUP AND NIAGARA

(New York *American*. *The Night the Old Nostalgia
Burned Down*. Little, Brown, 1953)

Aunt Sarah Gallup, the Grand Old Lady of the Adirondacks, laid down her newspaper with a snort.

"I knew no good would come of it," she declared.

"Of what, Aunt Sarah?"

"Of letting all those people go over Niagara Falls in steel barrels. No falls can stand that. I knew it would happen and it did. They chipped a big piece off'n the falls."

"But if people go over Niagara Falls, Aunt Sarah, they've got to protect themselves some way. Personally, I fail to see why anybody should want to go over Niagara Falls at all."

"You don't? Well, let me tell you, young man, there's no rarer sport in the world than going over Niagara Falls."

"Aunt Sarah, you don't mean to tell me you've been over the falls in a barrel?"

"Not in any barrel, certainly not. In my day people would have laughed at anybody used a barrel in going over Niagara."

"How did you go over?"

"Just stepped in and went over, that's all."

"And nothing happened to you?"

"Got a good wettin'. Oh, it was fine. Your cold showers aren't a patch on it, to cool off on a hot day. We used to do it all the time. Put on some dry clothes afterward and feel like a million dollars. And in those days, remember, a million dollars was equal to about five million today. And the falls were bigger."

"I didn't know you knew Niagara Falls so well, Aunt Sarah."

"Suttinly. In the 1750's we used to go there for the summer. Either there or to the Two Thousand Islands."

"You mean the Thousand Islands, Aunt Sarah."

"There were two thousand then."

"What happened to the other thousand?"

"Indians stole 'em. I can taste that good old Two Thousand Island dressing still. M-m-m."

"It's called Thousand Island dressing now, Aunt Sarah."

"Twice as weak as it was, I suppose. We used to go to Niagara to bathe and shoot the falls. Afterward we'd try and bag a salmon for supper."

"Why, come, Aunt Sarah. A salmon wouldn't stand a chance in the Niagara whirlpool. What are you trying to give me?"

"The kind of salmon you get wouldn't, of course, no more'n you could go over Niagara without a barrel. These salmon I'm speaking of were eighteenth-century American salmon. Real salmon. They used to think nothing of jumping the falls to get up the river to spawn. I landed one once weighed two and a half tons."

"How did you get it home?"

"Didn't get it home. Didn't want to. I just wanted it for the roe. We used to dry the roe and then use them for croquet balls. During the Revolution we used to use the salmon roe for ammunition. They made swell cannon balls. Properly dried, they was much more effective than iron cannon balls, as well the redcoats knew. Heaven alone knows how many British were mowed down by salmon roe from our ten pounders. For a long time the British were frantic trying to find out what mysterious stuff we was a-makin' our cannon balls of, and finally, when they did find out, they sent a regiment to Niagara right away to catch enough salmon to supply roe for the British cannon."

"So that equaled things up, I suppose."

"Not at all. Not a man came back from Niagara."

"What happened to them?"

"The salmon ate them. Guess they were fascinated by the red color of the British uniforms. For years after the Revolution, when I'd go to Niagara to catch me a salmon, like as not I'd find a button or two from a British uniform inside him. Sometimes you'd find a whole British soldier, still alive. . . ."

"Oh come, Aunt Sarah!"

"You don't believe me, eh? I suppose you think Benedict Arnold escaped to England?"

"He died there, in disgrace."

"So you think. Well, sir, so did I, until one day when I opened a peculiarly large salmon I had bagged just this side of the falls, who walked out but Benedict . . ."

"Goodbye, Aunt Sarah."

JULY 3.

(New York *World*. *The Life and Times of Martha Hepplethwaite*.
Boni and Liveright, 1926)

Looks like rain, Miss Hepplethwaite. . . . See that little
cloud over there? . . . Well, that's what is called an ominous little cloud. . . . All severe electric storms start with ominous little
clouds. . . . It's getting bigger. . . . You are pale, Miss Hepplethwaite. . . . Are you afraid of lightning? . . . You're not
afraid of it but you are afraid of being hit by it. . . . Well, I'd
call that quibbling, and there's only one thing worse than
quibbling, Miss Hepplethwaite, and that is quoits. . . . No,
I like quilts. . . . Crazy or not, I like quilts. . . . You are afraid,
my dear. . . . You can't conceal it, because your teeth just
dropped out and they are still chattering down there behind the
incoming letter basket, or, as you like to call it, the wastebasket.
. . . Don't be afraid, my dear. . . . Ah, that was a crash. . . .
It will be a magnificent storm. . . . I wish Ben Franklin were
here. . . . Child, you're positively shimmying with fear. . . .
Is it as bad as all that? . . . Put your typewriter down and come
over here by Mr. Sullivan. . . . There, there, poor child. . . .
Nothing can harm you while Mr. Sullivan has you in his keeping. . . . Nestle close. . . . Put your arms around Mr. Sullivan's
neck. . . . Ah, ah, don't touch that watch and chain now. . . .
Watches and chains are conductors of lightning. . . . You know
you're quite an armful, Miss Hepplethwaite. . . . You ought to
avoid butter, sweets and eggs. . . . I know it's awfully hard to
avoid eggs. . . . No matter where you go you meet them. . . .
Oh, THAT was a clap of thunder, wasn't it! . . . I never heard
such baritone thunder. . . . Don't hug Mr. Sullivan so tight,
my dear. . . . You'll choke him. . . . After all, I'd prefer death

by lightning to death by slow strangulation. . . . They say your whole life passes before you when you die by strangulation and I'd have to see mine over again. . . . Yes, indeedy, a bum show. . . . It's getting darker.

How magnificent an electric storm is if you're not out in it. . . . The rain comes slashing by in white sheets. . . . Drops as big as your solitaire are splashing on the ledge outside. . . . The black clouds are scurrying across the sky like pickaninnies late for school. . . . The trees in City Hall Park are bent under the weight of the storm. . . . Hark to that thunder, how it cracks and roars. . . . See the men down on the plaza. . . . How small they look from up here. . . . See how they scud for shelter before the gale, like ants rushing to escape from some giant's heel. . . . Poor little fools. . . . Don't be nervous. . . . Cuddle close to me. . . . Lightning cannot strike this office, my dear, because everything in here has been charged. . . . That one looks as if it struck the boss's office. . . . Yes, it did, see it falling down all crumpled and torn and baffled. . . . I wish it would stop. . . . I am not trembling. . . . Anybody is entitled to a tremble or two a week, and if I choose to take mine now, who shall say me nay? . . . Mm, it's coming louder and louder. . . . I ought to clean out beneath that desk, do you know it? . . . No, I'm not afraid. . . . I've been going to clean out beneath that desk for years. . . . And I've been promising myself to spend an afternoon under that desk for months. . . . Bang, there goes another one! . . . Let go, Miss Hepplethwaite, I'm going underneath the desk. . . . I am NOT afraid, let go my neck. . . . What you trying to do, beat me under that desk? . . . No, you don't. . . . "Women and children last" is the motto around this office. . . . You get under your own desk. . . . There goes another one. . . . Good-by. . . . Let me know when it's stopped raining.

THE LETTERS

With the possible exceptions of Horace Walpole, James Boswell, Lord Chesterfield and Lady Mary Wortley Montagu, few men or women of letters have written as many of them as Frank Sullivan.

I have limited these letters to those that *he* wrote, since this is his book. Also I have not arranged them in chronological order, but have put them under the names of the recipients. One reason for this procedure is that this latter-day Walpole sometimes omits month, day, year or all three.

As with the pieces, so with the letters. There is not sufficient space in this Space Age to include many that are eminently worthy of inclusion. In fact, many that are included have been edited with Sullivan's approval. Almost without exception, his legion of friends has co-operated wholeheartedly in helping me to prepare this missive program. My gratitude to all of them is boundless.

A word of warning. Sullivan has many aliases. If you come upon a letter signed Augustine Whitpenny or Havelock Frothingham, do not be misled. It is merely his expression of a passion for strange names. He and Nunnally Johnson, the director, producer and writer of stage and screen, and Stanley Walker, the newspaper editor, formed the Nomenclature Club, the purpose of which was to collect such names of actual people as Totton P. Heffelfinger, Ulric Wiesendanger, Judge Kug Fake, Mrs. Marshall Parshall, Wambly Bald, Chief Mark Raspberry, Sir Crisp English, Giok Pooey, Lycurgus Spinks, Byrd Mock, Kim Ng and Woodenasse Keith. He has also the diconcerting habit of signing himself with the cognomens of John Roach Straton, Dr. Krafft-Ebing, Secretary Stanton, Porfirio Rubirosa and other notables.

According to Lord Byron, "One of the pleasures of reading old letters is the knowledge that they need no answer," while William James insisted that, "As long as there are postmen, life will have zest." So, without any obligation on your part but with Sullivan's infinite zest and jest, there follow epistles to practically everybody but the Romans.

One last word—Sullivan's spelling, punctuation and lower-case letters, in the style of Don Marquis' archy the cockroach, have been left as is. Some things are sacred, even to an editor.

—EDITOR'S NOTE

TO VARIOUS LADIES

Patricia Collinge[1]

Sullivan wrote a piece (see page 40) about a little girl who raged through Beekman Place (where he lived at that time) yelling her lungs out for a playmate named Yvonne. Miss Collinge then wrote an open letter to Frank via *The New Yorker* about how the name Yvonne kept her awake. How it kept running through her head and getting itself mixed into things like "Yvonnetually, why not now? Yvonne Yvonneovitch," and so on.

New York City [no date]

Dear Pat,

Your piece moved me to the core of my being and I think as a result you have a right to know that Yvonne did me the honour of paying me a formal call several days ago. She was accompanied by Charlotte, the Yvonne shouter, and by a male escort, Charlotte's four-year old brother, Harold (in case of emergency and for the sake of propriety). Yvonne and Charlotte are about eight and go to school on the corner. Harold said *he* wanted to go to school, too, but Yvonne and Charlotte corrected him sharply, telling him he didn't. He said he did. I asked Harold if he would like an orange, but Yvonne and Charlotte said he wouldn't. Harold will grow up with some kind of a neurosis or sister fixation, I think.

Now, I don't wish to hurt you, Miss C., but I must be frank and relate the next incident. I said to Yvonne, "There'll be another piece about you in the New Yorker this week, Yvonne."

"By you?" she asked rather suspiciously. I told her no, by a Miss Patricia Collinge. "She's a well known actress," I explained. "Oh, you mean Lillian Gish," said Yvonne. (You know that Lillian lives next door, I suppose.)

Then I produced some home made candy I happened to have on hand and Yvonne and Charlotte decided that Harold could have some of that, the real reason being, I suspect, that they wanted some too, and couldn't see a way to shut him out. So Yvonne and Charlotte and Harold had not some but all of the candy, and were probably sick all night. I left them in the hallway, scrapping to see who would push the button to summon the elevator, so they all pushed it, madly.

File this in the Yvonne archives.

Sincerely,

F. Sullivan

Anna Erskine Crouse[2]

Saratoga, May 27 [no year]

Dear Anna,

If it would be convenient for you to have me I'd very much enjoy coming to Annisquam from about July 25 to Labor Day. Please don't hesitate to say so if this doesn't fit in with your plans but after all you have asked me repeatedly and now that you have made your bed you must lie in it. I thought I'd let you know early so that you and Crouse and T. and Lindsay A.[3] would have plenty of time to find other quarters. You see, when I go visiting I don't like to have anybody else in the house with me, including the host and hostess and any relatives they may have. It disturbs my privacy. I have grown so used to living alone I do not really think I could adjust to having my host and hostess around, but I would greatly enjoy seeing you all from time to time.

The reason I have got to get out of Saratoga is the approaching celebration of the centennial of racing here. I may have to leave town even earlier than I thought, for there is a possibility I will be run out of town after being tarred and feathered by a mob of angry parents, as soon as the results of the Essay Contest are published. It is a long story and if I bore you please let me know by return mail. Last winter a professional director of centennials (name of Demetrios Sazani) arrived here to start preparations for this big wingding. He is a pleasant fellow, and able, and I met him duly at the Colonial bar. I could tell from the lecherous look in his eye and a few remarks he dropped that he had singled me out as a sucker on whom he could wish ten or twenty centennial chores. But I quickly disabused him of any illusions and told him I had no intention of doing a damn thing about the centennial as I was too close to my own centennial for comfort. Later, not wishing to make myself more of a curmudgeon than I am (no small feat in itself) I relented to the extent of writing a piece for the centennial program and then I allowed myself to be persuaded to be a judge in the Essay Contest—essays on Saratoga by 500 kids from the public and parochial schools. The teachers winnowed out fifty essays they considered the best and I went through those fifty right careful, and after much prayer I picked the two I thought best and handed the result to Demetrios. About half the essays were done by students whose parents or grandparents I know. What was my consternation then to find that I am the ONLY judge of the essays. Not a goddamn other judge to share the rap inevitable in such situations. Picture to yourself the carnage that will follow when the names of the two winners I picked are announced and the 498 mothers and 498 fathers of the kids who didn't win a prize start out after me. A cross will be burned on my lawn. Four-letter words will be chalked on my front stoop. Poisoned chocolate drops will arrive in the mail. Pails of water will be placed above my front door to spill on me when I go out. Ground glass will be slipped into my milk bottles. Abusive anonymous letters will arrive accusing me of being a Communist, a sex deviate and a stealer of pennies from widows, orphans and blind men.

On top of all that what else do you think happened? After I read the essays for him, risking my life, Demetrios asked me if I would be judge of the BABY CONTEST. I struck him. I know it was hasty and wrong but I saw red. He will be out of the hospital, they say, in time to collect a large fee for directing the centennial.

That is why I am going to leave here and live with you this summer, unless of course you are having a centennial at Annisquam. I will send you a list later on of what provisions I'd like to have you leave in the deep freeze. You can get excellent caviar at S. S. Pierces.

Your true friend,

F.

LINDSAY ANN CROUSE

Saratoga, Feb 20, 1960

Dear L.A.,

How are you coming on with that bird feeder? This is only a question meant to give me a chance to tell you how I'm coming on with my bird feeding this winter. I have gone into this thing this winter on a much greater scale than ever before and have had more success than even John Kieran,[4] the famous naturalist, could hope to have. But I am broke from buying sunflower seeds for the grosbeaks and I would appreciate it if you would send me ten thousand dollars by return post so I can buy some sunflower seeds or the equivalent for myself. If you haven't got ten thousand dollars your mother has, and you can get it from her.

In the first place I made some extensive changes in my feeding system. I have a feeder exactly like the one I sent you. It hangs outside my bedroom window and I can lie abed in comfort and watch the birds feeding. This gives me an excuse not to work, so you see I feed two birds with one stone. There was only one drawback this winter. It gets mighty cold up here. Saratoga is not like New York where you never have snow and the palm trees bloom all winter. Many mornings it is zero up here and sometimes it lasts during the day. So the suet cake I had put in the feeder was of course frozen pretty hard and I noticed that the little nuthatches who thronged there to get a bite to eat had a hard time digging a piece of frozen suet out for themselves. I wouldn't like to have to eat frozen suet myself, so I thought the matter over and hit on a new plan. I found an old wooden cocktail tray in the pantry and I nailed it outside the bedroom window and on it I placed a supply of peanut butter and English walnuts. English walnuts were the only kind I happened to have in stock at the moment. I fixed them up for the birds in the following manner: I shelled a half dozen or so and put them on a newspaper. Then I took a wooden rolling pin, of the kind your dear mother throws at your father when he enrages her, and I rolled out the English walnuts into fine pieces that the birds could pick up and eat with ease. If they tried to swallow a whole English walnut they would choke, and that would mean that the Society for the Prevention of Cruelty to Birds would arrest me. Well, the new feeding station was a smash hit right from the start. I am taking reservations up to next May. The fighting that goes on among my feathered friends to get onto the cocktail tray is something horrendous. Apparently nobody ever thought to feed English walnuts to nuthatches and other birds and a good reason why, too. They are expensive. But now that I have started them on English walnuts, they demand them every day. When I cracked up some ordinary peanuts one day, thinking to economize on bird feed, you should have heard the cries of protest and rage. The birds beat their fists against the bedroom window and called me names you'd think no respectable bird would call a nice fellow who has been as kind to them as I have. So I had to get them the English walnuts. It seems I spent half my time crushing up walnuts for the nuthatches, chickadees, sparrows, bluejays, etc. (The bluejays are especially loose in their talk and they all ought to be arrested). Of course, I also have to provide sunflower seeds, too. Then one day I had a great triumph that makes all my trouble worth while. THE EVENING GROSBEAKS CONDESCENDED TO VISIT MY COCKTAIL BAR. Do not tell John Kieran this, or he will gnash his teeth in envy. The grosbeaks are a quite rare bird. They stay in the far north but have been coming this far south recently. They are big as a robin, have stubby short bills, and are yellow, with black and white wings, and they go for sunflower seeds. They can eat a pound of them a day, without any trouble at all.

None of my feathered friends go for the old hanging feeder, the kind you have. They like the tray better. More room for them to fight on it. There was a storm here night before last and yesterday morning when I arose, the cocktail tray feeder was six inches deep in snow and all my friends were lined up on the roof, wondering where I was with the snow shovel. I scraped the snow off and filled the tray with a generous allowance of sunflower seeds, wild bird seed, peanut butter and English walnuts, and did they have a spree. For this good deed I will be rewarded in Heaven, if not here below. The only thing I fear is that they will get tired of English walnuts and demand caviar. Caviar I simply cannot afford. I thought you, as a bird lover, would be interested in hearing all this, and might get some pointers if you decide to go in for feeding wild birds.

I understand Timmy has invented a new substance called oxygen. Please tell him to get to work on some useful invention, and invent a Scotch that will cost only 25 cts. a highball. I have to have three Scotches every evening, my doctor says, and they cost me an aggregate of $2.40. What with all this and English walnuts too, whither are we drifting?

A charming couple of my acquaintance named Mr. and Mrs. Russel Crouse live in New York and oddly enough right at the

same apartment house where you live. If you see them, please
introduce yourself, tell them you are a friend of mine and ask
them What HO!

Love,

Uncle Frank

JEAN DIXON ELY[5]

Saratoga, February 9 [no year]

Dear Jean,

It is a fitting comment on the slapdash way I arrange my life
that I have to wait for Geri Souvaine, Milton Cross and Edward
Downes[6] to bring me back to the arms of an old pal like you.
When Edw was on the opera quiz this afternoon and said, "The
next question is from Jean Dixon of Annisquam, Mass," I raised
up in bed and hollered, "Hey, I know her, she's a friend of mine."
But there was no answer as there was nobody in the house but
me.

Anyhow I'm glad you made it and got that book and I predict
that you will go on to greater triumphs on other quizzes.

I hope you and Ted are sitting out the winter comfortably.
It has been a terrible one here, eighteen below and nonsense
like that all the time. I am whiling away the time writing the
libretto for an opera, "Der Fliegende Humperdinck." It's about
this King that has a daughter, and he announces that any Prince
that succeeds in scaling a glass mountain or Zauberberge, outside
the Palace, will be given the hand of the Princess in marriage.
If not, if he doesn't scale the mountain, the candidate's head
will be cut off. Several princes try and they all slide down before
reaching the summit and lose their heads until one comes along,
Prince Florizel, and he gets right to the top of the glass moun-

tain (Zauberberge). The Princess is up there waiting but when Prince Florizel gets a look at her he says, "Good God!" (Lieber Gott) and chooses death rather than marry her, as she turns out to be a terrible old bag. The King, sly minx, hadn't said anything about *that*. So just as the King is about to cut off Prince Florizel's head, his fairy godmother comes along just in the nick of time and changes the King into a past participle. The glass mountain disappears, the Princess turns into a frog, and Prince Florizel says, "Well, that's more like it," and he marries her.

Do you think it's got a chance?

Love,

Frank

EDNA FERBER[7]
[*This letter was written after the death of Russel Crouse.*]

Saratoga, April 19, 1966

Dearest Ferb,

I was about to write you when your letter came, because I have been thinking about you as you have about me. I knew all about your visit to the Crouses and I wish all visits of that kind could be modelled on your visit. I talked with Anna and the two youngsters shortly after and they told me about how you had come in and how you all had found yourselves glowing and laughing and telling fond stories about him. Both Anna and Lindsay Ann said that lovely thoughtful and genuine thing you and Dick[8] did was the kindest thing that happened during those rough days. God will reward you. If He doesn't, I will . . . Now I will confess that the right thing you did, I didn't do. Poor Anna had the thoughtfulness to telephone me Sunday night so that I would not hear it cold over the radio and I rewarded her thoughtfulness by blowing my top and busting into tears. I was ashamed of myself. It didn't make her sad errand easier. I apologized later and it is all right. I talked with Anna last night. She seemed somewhat harassed, the excitement and exigencies following immediately after his death are over and she is now facing all the talks with lawyers, etc. And poor Howard is not able to be much of a tower of help. I talked with Dorothy[9] and him the day after Russel died and he sounded so ill and, of course, broken by what had happened—and had a really rough cough which I didn't like.

It is remarkable and consoling the way you and so many other friends have included me in the sympathy. Last week, the day after it happened, the phone rang constantly, from friends of mine up here who never knew Crouse but knew he and I were close friends. They were offering me their sympathy. It touched me. And of course I was on the telephone with some of the old friends—the merry widows, Mady Sherwood[10] and Alice Guinzburg,[11] George Oppenheimer, Jean Dixon and then Howard and Dorothy. And poor Ford[12] called early Monday morning from Hanover because he had heard about it over the radio! I had taken an extra amytal tablet and was groggy when he woke me in the middle of the night (9 a.m.) and had to call him later on to explain.

The last time I saw Crouse was here, last August, when Anna and he came for an overnight stay and we went to the races. I treasure that memory because it could not have been more pleasant. I introduced them to two old Saratoga High School chums of mine, John and Linda Heslin. John is a doctor in Albany, and they have a summer home here, and they are the salt of the earth. The Heslins and the Crouses liked each other at first sight. At the track, even the weather was perfect. To my surprise I found it was the first time Anna had ever been at a racetrack and won herself a bet that put her in the seventh heaven. Crouse, a veteran horseplayer (he had been here many times in August) also won several good bets. I lost, as is my wont. Even better, he met quite a few old friends he hadn't seen in a

long time, like Mike Casale, a racing writer he worked with on
the Mail years ago. And Gene Markey,[13] and others; and then
who loomed up but Max Gordon,[14] in a gay and festive mood.
He delighted us by telling about his system of beating the races,
which was roughly to bet on every horse in the race. That of
course ensured that he would win and it also made sure he would
lose. It was Broun's* system, too, I recalled. Everything was
funny and nice that time, even to the moment when Anna
needed an electric iron to press a dress and I found an old one of
Kate's[15] in a kitchen closet; it hadn't been used since her time
and I felt sure it was useless and would blow up. But Anna took
it back to the hotel and by gum it worked! Then she raised gentle
hell when she came into my kitchen and found I had left the
butter on the table on that August night. She popped it back in
the icebox and I heeded her advice and kept it there, until she
left.

I suppose it is sententious to say that Crouse had a good life
but he surely did, didn't he? He saw to it in part (The Lord helps
those who help themselves) but some of it was just bestowed on
him because he deserved it. He had a fine if riotous time with
dear old Alison[16] and was loyal to her to her last moment. I remember the tears in his eyes when, along toward the end he told
me she no longer wanted a taste of champagne. All she could
take in those days. I think about two years passed before he
married Anna, and Ferb, take it from me, he was the most lonely
man in the world in those two years. He was just not cut out to
be a bachelor. Then he had scruples about asking Anna to marry
him because of the difference in their ages, and I was so glad
when he got rid of those scruples. And how grand his life with
Anna has been, how good she has been for him, and he for her;
and those two splendid children coming along after he had passed
fifty. He had a score of years of their companionship and I wish
he had had ten or more years of it. And with all else a most
satisfying and successful career, full of the inevitable aches and
pains of playwrighting but full of rewards, too, and with a per-

---

* Heywood Broun. See note 16, page 263.

fect collaborator to work with for thirty-two years. And above all that born capacity for friendship that brought him the love of everybody who really knew him. . . . . . Good God, what a long letter! Yes, Ferb, I do know there's nothing like work and it fills me with guilt to know that I haven't worked. I'd feel absolutely useless and unjustified if I hadn't, along the way, made friends like Crouse and you. *That's* an achievement.

Love,

Frank

RUTH HAMMOND AND DONALD MACDONALD[17]

New York, Dec. 13, 1927

Dear Macdonalds,

Now about this business of eating tomorrow (Friday) night, let us get the thing systematized and not go about it in any haphazard fashion. We Americans are too much on the go; we are becoming a race of neurotics, and I for one propose to take my time from now on and plan everything in a leisurely manner.

You are eating on me, that is to say, I am paying. "On" is a slang expression. Now, I'll meet you in the north end of the peacock alley in the Astor at seven o'clock sharp. I'll be dressed as a peacock and will have my tail with me. She's really a rather good sort, you know.

The reason I am meeting you at the Astor is because this restaurant I am taking you to is near there, but I have to blindfold you before I take you to the speakeasy, as they don't want people to find out about it. They charge $2.50 a dinner. The liquor is free.

Now also, by meeting you at the Astor I save a trip away over to Beekman Place, and then you have to pay for a taxi from

Boikman Place to the Astor. I figure that at about sixty cents and I can apply that to the check. It is just such little coups like this that have made me known as the Wolf of Wall Street. I always say that if you take care of the pennies the caretaker's daughters will take care of themselves.

Now there'll be people there who matter socially, so let's have no shenanigans. No cutting throats with knives. No indiscriminate throwing of peas by Hammond. No wiggling of fingers in the soup. No puttering about in the mashed potatoes, and don't, for Christ's sake, blow on the coffee from above to cool it. If you want to cool the coffee, ring for the waiter, and tell him to send the blow-boy. Then the blow-boy will come and you stand up and hold your coffee cup aloft. Then he bends to the proper degree until his face is below the bottom of the coffee cup and he blows on it from below. It cools the coffee more rapidly, and the picture of the quaint little fellow there in the subdued lights going pooh, pooh, pooh at the cup of amber-colored fluid is really one of the sights that the average stranger in New York never sees.

I wash at home because if you wash at this place you have to tip the attendant. And in the second place there is no place to wash, and no attendant. In time there will be a place to wash and there will be attendants. Fifty years ago people scoffed at the idea of airplanes, and yet look at today!

Informal dress. Clean clothes, if possible.

Love,

Sullivan

Saratoga, April 30, 1968

Dear Ruth,

Your letter about our dear Edna said it. After I heard she was desperately ill I wanted to write her but I was stumped—I simply did not know what to say. I was afraid it would sound like a fare-well letter and I had no way of knowing whether she knew she was hopelessly ill. Of course she must have. She was too forth-right and courageous not to face death and stare it down. And she wouldn't be fooled by any doctors trying to make things easier for her. She knew.

I'll never forget the night here in Saratoga when Ferb, George Kaufman[18] and I had dinner at the Gideon Putnam Hotel. She had brought George here on a mean sleety winter day to interest him in doing a play about old Saratoga with her. After she had conducted him on a tour through the cold, damp United States Hotel, George had enough. He was taking the first train to New York in the morning. We were having a cordial in the bar when news came over the radio that some big shot had taken his own life, so the conversation veered to suicide. After a few minutes of that George decided to get us off that gloomy subject and he said, "Well, I've decided to kill myself when I reach 60." Edna was the perfect straightman; she said, "What with, George?" And he said, "Kindness." I reminded him of that years later and he had forgotten it. (Ferb, of course, thwarted about doing the play, turned it into a novel, Saratoga Trunk, which made her a half million or so.)

I will now bid you good day, and settle back and look at the flowering crabapple tree outside my bedroom window. It is a mass of pink beauty and I am going to look at it eight hours a day, because its blossoms fade after a few days. I wish it would stay in bloom nine months of the year.

Yours ever,

Frank

HELEN HAYES[19]

March 28, 1936

Dear Helen,

I suppose you get so many mash notes from fellows "out front" that they must be quite a nuisance, but I would indeed be derelict in my duty as an American citizen, a true patriot and a lover of the arts were I not to tell you that thanks to you and Housman[20] I had on Thursday one of the most gratifying afternoons I ever spent in a theatre. That goes also for evenings. I would have liked to have gone backstage to tell you this but did not want to bother you as I knew you had an evening performance coming.

In addition to my veneration for Hayes the Artiste, I have an affection for Hayes the Gal that amounts practically to a typhoon.

Love,

Frank Sullivan

Give my love also to that Zephyr, MacArthur.[21]

BEATRICE KAUFMAN[22]

Saratoga, July 13, 1944

Fairest Daughter of the Finger Lakes Region:

I have Aleck's[23] Letters,[24] with your and Joe's inscription, and I wouldn't exchange this gift for the Hope Diamond. I read the two volumes the day they came and will re-read them many times in the future. You and Joe have done a perfectly fine job of editing. All will concur in this, except possibly Tallulah who may soar to new and even more vivid heights of language on reading the letter in which Aleck set forth his opinion of her as a comedienne. I told Joe I had only one criticism. Too damn *few* of the letters. I told Joe also how pleased and flattered I am that he and you included me in this memorial to Aleck. I wanted very much to have a small part in it, so thanks. I was proud that Aleck chose to accept me as a friend.

That talent for friendship he had, that insatiable interest in people, simply fills me with envy and admiration. God, I wish I had some of it. You have had experience with that curiosity of his, of course. He wanted to know everything about everybody, and he never forgot a detail about anyone. Everything interested him, and that is a hell of a good trait to have. That is why I think Aleck had a good time, as good times go, during his life, and that is why I feel sorry that anyone with that talent for living and for giving his friends an exciting if not always a strictly happy time should only have had fifty-five years for life. It is nonsense to say that he lived more in the 55 years than an ordinary man would have lived in 70. Aleck should have had as many years allotted to him as Justice Holmes. What a time he would have had for himself.

I have heard Aleck criticised during his life as being interested in cultivating only Names, or what you might call Famous People. We who knew him know how silly that is. He was one of the greatest non-respecters of Names I ever saw. It was what a person was that took his eye, not any name the guy bore. Sure he took a childish delight in being in the White House as a guest. Why not? Who wouldn't? The point is I'll bet my last dollar Aleck never would have set foot in the White House while Hoover was there, or if he had to do so, he wouldn't have said much about it.

I see you are nodding now, Trixie, so I'll lower the shade and steal quietly from the room. Get well fast, dear; good girls are scarce and I need you around for my morale. God knows your benign influence on me is wielded mostly by remote control these years but the important point is that it is wielded.

God bless you.

Love,

Frank

ADELE BROWN LOVETT[25]

Saratoga, December 20, 1937

Dear Adele,

I arrived in Saratoga intact, and with your fragile Christmas gift intact, although I had to battle every porter on the New York Central. They have a sixth sense that tells them whenever a body has a bag he wants to carry himself and that's the bag they always want to carry. They paid no attention to the suitcase full of soiled, unbreakable linen; they wanted to get their clutches on the one containing the Jingle Bells cocktail glasses so they could smash them.

I wrote O'Hara[26] yesterday and tried to do justice to the floral display in your room but I must admit that the job boggled me somewhat, and I do not boggle easily. I told him that the room was filled with floral tokens and that you looked not unlike the Queen of the Santa Barbara Rose Festival sitting on her Float; also a little like Our Lady of Lourdes, but I neglected to say to O'Hara that parakeets and flamingoes ambled in and out of the tropical jungle that surrounded your bed of pain and that it took me a safari of several minutes before I wound my way through the dense foliage, arrived at your bedside and said, "Dr. Lovett, I presume." I did not tell O'Hara those details because I did not think that he would believe them. I did however mention that you looked blooming as I thought he might relish a little mot or two of that calibre; my more subtle cracks being over his head. And I said that I left rather nervously before I expected to, having a premonition that at any minute the nurse would come in with a giant sequoia from some consoling Lovett fan.

Put out the lights respectably at midnight last night, intending to get up early today and do some work and just as I was dropping off, the fire siren sounded. I looked out and there was a red glow off to the west. I stood it for a while but when the crackling sounds began to come through I gave up, threw a shawl over my head and chased out and stayed out until five this morning watching a honey of a fire. One of the dormitories at Skidmore; fortunately, no one in the place on account of Xmas vacation. That being one reason why the place was what is called a roaring inferno by the time the firemen got there. If it had been found earlier it might have been squelched but there was no squelching it by the time I arrived and that being the case I stayed to see the fun and believe me there is nothing more exciting or awful than a good bangup fire, particularly at night, to give you the creeps. This was an old Saratoga mansion the college had acquired a couple of years ago and was using as a dormitory for freshmen and it is full or was full of those unexpected cupolas and balconies and whatnots that the architects who designed Saratoga liked so much. One by one they would crash and fall into the raging inferno and then a hell of an eruption of flames and sparks. Oh boy! The place had been the home for fifty years of an old family that had been identified with Saratoga for a long time and which has gradually been dying off, or going to seed, or moving away and this house was the last relic and I could not help thinking of the Magnificent Ambersons. It was a real good fire.

Well, Lady Macbeth (as I call you, now that Birnam Wood has come to Room 1021) I wish you a speedy recovery and a happy Christmas in the—if you will pardon the expression—

bosom of your family, and I wish your family, and their respective bosoms, the happiest of Christmases also, and I hope that if you can't afford turkey on account of the business recession you will at least dine substantially on limb of lamb. Farewell, Miss Santa Barbara of 1937, I adore you with an ardor that would make Dante's for Beatrice seem like one of those pale crushes an amoeba gets on itself just before it divides in two.

At your service,

F.S.

Saratoga, September 38, 1939

Friend Addie,

Or Alkali Addie, as I like to think of you as, since your trek through the cactus and gopher country. I meant to tell you by the way to be sure and bring me back one of those horse's skeletons that always litter the Mojave desert in pictures in which Joan Crawford gives up a life of ease to follow the man she loves to his ranch. I want it for my den.

You doubtless had an adventurous and pleasant summer but although I did not stir from Saratoga hardly, I have not been idle. A woman fell madly in love with me, for one thing. Name of Miss Mary Teresa Burke, age, three and a half. For a month or so she nursed her passion in secret, allowing the canker of her love for me to gnaw at her heart, and every time I showed up she would lapse into complete silence and shyness. I spent a month trying to psychoanalyze her out of her inhibition and now I think maybe it could be argued that I overdid it, as I cured her, and let loose an avalanche of conversation which has been pouring down on me ever since. She is present at my levee every morning and has a piece of toast, bootlegged because her mother would give Kate hell if she found out about it. She wants to know everything I do, and why I do it, and won't take any unsatisfactory account for an answer, and after I wipe the toast and eggs off my jowls and bow my excuses to her and come upstairs, she comes up two or three times to see if I am warm enough or cold enough, before she goes home. What is this power I have over the female sex? I kind of like it.

Will you tell Bob I have two or three little chores I would like him to do. First, have him get Pennsylvania RR up to 40. That's all I ask. That's what I bought it at. Well, of course, if he could shoot it up to 42, that would give me a $200 profit to compensate me for my worry and mental anguish during the two years it has been around 15. And of course if he wishes to shoot it up to, let us say, 70, please tell him to feel perfectly free to do so, and to allow this to serve as a written authorization from me. So this is power of attorney, as the girl said when the lawyer hit her over the head with the croquet mallet.

Don't forget now, you and I are going to splash some soup on each other in about a week, and in the meantime you can take it for granted that my letch for you continues unabated, with

Love

Frank

Margaret Leech Pulitzer[27]

Saratoga, July 17, 1941

Dear Peggy,

The last few sweltering days I was in New York were spent mainly on a bench in the shade in Central Park reading "Reveille in Washington." Congratulations on a magnificent job.

I admit to some bias about any book written by you, but nobody would have to know and cherish you to see how grand a book that is. Everything else aside, it was a tonic for me to read it at this particular time for I was low in my mind about the Lindberghs and the Wheelers and their ilk and what they are trying to do to disunite us, but after reading about what Lincoln had to put up with, I must admit we seem like the Rock of Gibraltar today by comparison. I did not realize I knew so little about the Civil War. My God, how did the Union ever survive? Survive McClellan and that long train of incompetents that followed him. You know the old story about the race track tout whom a Southerner had been giving an argument about how Lee really won the Civil War, and the tout said, "Yeh, Lee may have won, but they paid off on Grant." While I was reading "Reveille" I chanced across a ten volume pictorial history of the Civil War in the Cornell Club library, so that complemented the illustrations in "Reveille." You list the ten volume pictorial history in your bibliography but I can't think of the editor's name.

I am very happy about this book because I never had a first-rate historian for a friend before, and have always wanted one.

Yours,

Frank

A Pleasant Old Custom.

Seasons Greetings to Dear Margaret from Frank.

Saratoga, October 23, 1950

Dear Peg,

The first to cry Huzza at your resolution to write more letters will be the undersigned old party, but it will be an uphill struggle to revive the Art of Correspondence, as Horry Walpole knew it. This dont seem to be the age for correspondence except those starting "In re yours of the 29th inst." I guess maybe Woollcott was the last of the letter writers. I always thought his were in the best tradition. I'm a sucker for them anyhow, in every way. I like to get 'em and I like to read published letters. There is a 20 vol set of Walpole's in the Cornell Club library and I have dipped into it, but 20 volumes is too much for my eyes. I thought during the last war that the revival of letter writing was at hand, and I made a note to do a piece about it, or explore possibilities of same. It was because all the lads who went to Attu and Guadalcanal and Murmansk got homesick and being homesick wrote letters back home by the ream. They were goddam good letters, too, in spite of censors, and I have a drawerful of them here in this room. But after the war was over and they got home, they quit writing letters, of course, and Walpole and Aleck ceased twirling apprehensively in their graves.

Ross[28] writes a unique letter, as you know, and I have saved a lot of his, but he shows signs of degenerating. I once had a 3 page, single space typewritten letter from him about some minor matters, and he explained that he was too busy to write a shorter letter. Now he must be taking it easy, because he is giving out telegraphic, staccato communications, like one I got the other day: "Dear Frank, Here is a list of ideas you are down for. Do six pieces in the next four weeks." Or it may have been four pieces in the next six weeks. I had a hilarious lunch with Ross day after I saw you. I was telling him that Cleveland Amory[29] was up here getting Saratoga background for a book he plans on old resorts like Newport, Bar Harbor, this place, etc. Ross said, "I hope he's gonna do Lenox. That's the goddamdest most colorful resort in the country. Most exclusive. I found out all about it when I was in the bughouse up there." This was boomed thru the Barberry Room in the well known Ross tones, and everybody stopped to listen. The bughouse was of course a sanitarium where Ross had once taken a rest cure. I hadn't heard that term "bughouse" used in years. I was delighted.

Love,

Frank

MADELINE HURLOCK SHERWOOD

Saratoga [no date]

Dear Daughter,

Hope this finds you well. All well here. Crops very good this year in spite of the drought. Just got the fall plowing done and the winter wheat sowed and now if we can only keep them dang crows from eating the tarnation stuff. Remember the old pasture down by the lea across from the wen? Waal, we plowed that this summer and planted corn, but the dang woodchucks et it all up, so the corn crop was a bust. But Aunt Bill did right good with her hens this year and took in a passel of money so we was able to make the payment on the mortgage for the tractor. That dang Buster, Uncle Jed's boy, has gone and got a gal in trouble. Aunt Bill says she knew no good would come of lettin' him go to the camp meeting the Reverend Perkins held down by the grove across from the fen. That's where it happened. Just to punish him for skylarkin around, Ma says he caint have any party on his thirteenth birthday next month. That'll teach him to fool around. Remember Bessie, the old hoss down by the wen across from the lea? Waal, she got spavins and we had to shoot her last August. We had to shoot Grandpa too. He had glanders. Mighty fine turnout at the funeral. Bessie's, that is. Waal, Merry Christmas Daughter. Don't take any wooden nickels.

Pa

February 7, 1932

My ducks,

I had intended to write you before but owing to the Japanese crisis I have not been able to leave the Foreign Office except almost literally to sleep. Then, as if we didn't have enough on our hands, the Right is making trouble for Dizzy, and I think the House will rise and put the question next Tuesday, if Gladstone and the Tories succeed in winning Uxbridge from the Whigs, who are led, of course, by Mr. Heppner. I saw Her Majesty yesterday at Tony's,[30] and she was simply furious with Gladstone; says he addresses her as if she were a public meeting. Dizzy is wonderfully calm in spite of it all. Lord Castlereagh is sitting for Wimbledon, and Lady Castlereagh is sitting for company. Truly we live in an exciting age.

You may be interested in learning that at a meeting of the Academy of Arts and Sciences and Arts at Tony's three nights ago Mrs. Parker,[31] Mr. Oppenheimer, Mr. Lederer[32] and self got to work on that Passengers ode, and completed it. The completed text, if I remember rightly, is as follows:*

> Passengers will please refrain
> From flushing toilets while the train
> Is standing in the station, I love you.
> While the train is in the station
> Concentrate on constipation
> Lovely sunsets make me dream of you.
> Don't tip the porter
> While you're making water
> Oftimes colored folks have souls as white as we.
> Passengers will please refrain
> From flushing toilets while the train
> Is in the station—could you care for me?

* To be sung to the tune of "Humoresque."

I was at a party at the MacArthurs last night but the host was absent until one a.m., when he arrived in a butcher's coat and bearing a side of beef which he had bought as a little trinket for Helen. At three a.m. Charlie Winninger[33] phoned and stated that he wanted to cry over the telephone to Helen and Charlie, which he did. We all listened in, it was a very good cry, especially the sobbing.

How is dear Ferber? Tell her that the secret of her departure from New York so hastily is out, and that Hoover is issuing a statement tomorrow acknowledging the child. I told her to keep away from that White House dinner.

Well, love. Have a good time. But I'll bet you'll be glad to get back to the good old U S A.

Yours always,

Frank

Saratoga, January 19, 1956

Fairest Gloxinia in the Dell:—

A romance is springing up between me and an English lady you know named Lady Juliet Duff. She wrote me a pleasant letter a year ago about something in the NYorker and, by dad, come this past Christmas I put her in that Christmas litany I do, and she seems pleased, judging from a letter I have. Two letters in one year. She mentions you warmly, and also that toast of 2 continents, Alan Campbell.[34] Anybody mentions you and Campbell warmly is a friend of mine, and will never lack a crust of bread or a pallet to sleep, unless I need them for myself.

Damn it all, I have been reproaching myself ever since New Years for not being able to come down to see you and the Gov and Governess. I didn't know what to do. I read a chapter of St Paul to the Ephesians and a chapter from Emily Post every night before I go to bed, yet I always seem to go around pulling boners,

and antagonizing loved ones I would give me eye teeth not to
antagonize and committing gaffes generally. I can smell a gaffe a
mile off and go right to it and commit it. When the Gov of the
Empire State does you the honor to invite you down to the
Executive Mansion twice in one year and you don't show up, it
simply comes under the head of simony, or barratry, or lèse Harriman, and I wouldn't be a bit surprised if he and Marie im-
peached me very soon. I mean well, but it's just that that hole in
my head never closed, after the Bishop dropped me on it at my
christening. I would have loved nothing better than to have come
down that New Year's eve and spent it with you and Marie and
Averell and the Guinzburgs and Backer[35] but I had this here
sentimental date with Dr. John Heslin and Linda, his bride of
some forty years. They are old friends and classmates of mine of
the Saratoga High School Class of 1910—"Roga, Roga—Sara-
TOGA! Sis Boom Bah! Sara-toga HIGH School, Rah! Rah!
Rah!" He is a famed urologist, now of Albany, and in addition
to the ties of affection that bind me to him, a prostate man is a
mighty handy fellow for a fellow my age and decrepitude to
have up his sleeve, just in case. Well, they have a home up here
at Saratoga Lake (the scene of your debacle some years ago, when
you were ordered off the floor at Arrowhead for dancing cheek to
cheek with a young gigolo: I think that fellow that ordered us
off later did time in the clink as a common gambler) and they
were having this party and when Averell talked with me I was
just torn, that's all. I wanted nothing more than to come down,
and yet I didn't want to seem as tho I was walking out on John
and Linda because a better offer came along. And I would have
been all right except that when I got out to Heslin's, the matter
came up and when they heard I'd been invited down to see you
and the lady and gentleman who are our democratic equivalent
of Grace Kelly and Prince Ranier of Monaco, Linda, or Mrs.
Heslin, said, "Oh, why didn't you go? You'd have much more
fun than you would with us." So that fixed me up fine. So what
do you think I'm doing tonight? I'm going out to that Saratoga
Lake place to have dinner with the Heslins.

Remember the pajamas you gave me, with "Voulez vous couchez avec moi" embroidered on the pocket? Did I ever oblige you? My files were destroyed in a small fire several years ago and for the life of me I cannot remember whom I couchezed avec in the 1930s.

If anybody says I don't love you and regard you as the finest flower of American womanhood, he is a cad and if I can catch him, believe me, he'll smart for it.

Your loving grandfather,

Frank

Saratoga, Feb 16, 1959

Little Girl,

I had a delightful experience last night. It was zero and sleeting into the bargain so I stayed at home and, looking about for something to read, I came upon a Wodehouse I had never read, called "If I Were You." It was like finding the pot of gold at the end of the rainbow. And right at the end of chapter one I came upon the following:

"Bah!" said Mr. Waddington.
It was not much of a last word,
but, such as it was, he had it.

I laughed so hard I woke up the lady who was in bed with me. I'm always having experiences like that. One night I picked up an old Stephen Leacock volume and opened it at a piece called "Gertrude the Governess." The first sentence went something like this: "It was a wild and stormy night on the west coast of Ireland but this need not concern us, as our story takes place in the south of England." I laughed so hard I woke that lady up again; she's an old sleepy head anyhow.

It made me think of one of my favorite openings in Mr. Benchley. "While rummaging through my bureau one day I came across some old snow."

Guess who are bowling up the Thruway at this very moment, thinking they are going to have a restful week of crisp, cool winter here. Mr. and Mrs. Crouse are, but do you know what they are going to find when they get to the Gideon Putnam Hotel? Frozen slush, icicles, damp freezing weather and everybody's noses running red with colds. Dirtiest winter in my memory, which is far from what it used to be.

Love and kisses,

Gadge

ALISON SMITH

Saratoga, Nov. 17, 1942

Dear Alice J. Smith,

I trust this finds you feeling well. It ought to, because I ordered these recent events in the Solomons especially as part of your therapeutic treatment. Boy, was that news from the Solomons like a shot of adrenalin for me! I was half prepared for bad news, because I knew we had a smaller force than the Japs and that they were working from that big base of theirs only a few hundred miles away. The news perked me up no end. I hope it keeps up. We are probably in for some fighting in Tunisia. At least Hitler will make some kind of stand there. Bizerte won't fall into our hands as easily as the other African points did but I guess it's in the bag. It's nice to feel that the tide has turned. Nice, hell. That doesn't half express it.

I was absorbed in Mark Twain this winter. Fascinating, fascinating! I read Mark's Autobiography and then started reading his biography, written by Albert Bigelow Paine. What a man! I mean Mark. I started this reading with a strong prejudice against his wife because I had read a lot about her habit of censoring his stuff, but you can't help like her. She was a gentle, good soul, according to her lights, and they loved one another, and he apparently didn't mind her bowdlerizing his stuff in the least; in fact, respected her judgment highly and always thought he was in the wrong. But good God, she didn't even know what he was about; hadn't the slightest comprehension of his genius. Or certainly not a sufficient insight. Why, she thought "The Prince and the Pauper" was far and away a better book than "Huck Finn!" When Mark had Huck say he wouldn't go back to the widow's home because "she'd comb the hell out o' me" old lady Twain made Mark change it to "she'd comb thunder out o' me." She made him take the word "breechclout" out of a scene describing some Fiji islanders! ! ! Poor old Mark. Well my goodness if I rattle on like this you'll think me a veritable bookworm.

Your loving

F.S.

DOROTHY STICKNEY AND HOWARD LINDSAY

(On the publication of Sullivan's book for children, "The Moose in The Hoose," he was given a dinner by his fellow Saratogians.)

Saratoga, December 23, 1959

Dear D. & H.,

Thank you for that lovely wire you sent on the occasion of the big gala for you know who. It was a wonderful occasion and it is wonderful to get the roses while you can still smell them but as a result of the experience I now know just what you thespians go through in the way of butterflies on the stomach before an opening. I had a marvellous collection of butterflies on my stomach for two weeks before the event, and more kept joining every time I heard that too many people were coming to the dinner, and many more were sore because they didn't get invitations. You must have got invitations. The energetic girls at the Library who thought up and managed the tea, invited everybody of prominence in the haut monde since Chaucer.* It started as a little hullabaloo which was to have taken place at the Library and wound up as a dinner for 260, representing the Worden Hotel dining room capacity. First time I was ever SRO and undoubtedly the last. Russel M. Crouse was darling. Gave a short speech insulting me and then, on demands from the audience, did his famous bird calls and as an encore, his imitation of Bea Lillie† imitating Ruth Draper‡ doing a Railroad Station on the Western Plains. He wowed them. John O'Hara sang the Bell Song from Lakme, and was in marvellous voice. He also did a few card tricks and took a rabbit out of my coat pocket. I put the rabbit there myself, to carry for luck, before I left the house, and I damn well made him put it back. I hate a fellow that takes liberties with one's rabbit. I made a speech too but kept it down to 190 words, out of respect for Lincoln's Gettysburg which ran to something like 280, I believe. Neither Crouse nor O'Hara had a drink and neither did I, for that matter, but I had four Miltowns and felt as tho the world was my oyster. It could well have been, too, as there is an R in December and the shindig took place on Dec. 1.

The radio has so mangled and cheapened Christmas this year with unutterably sordid commercialization that I am unable to wish you a Merry Christmas. In fact I think if Scrooge were around now, he never would reform and Tiny Tim would be indicted by this time for being a quiz kid fake. I cannot report

* He couldn't come. Pleaded another engagement.

† Beatrice Lillie, popular British and American comedienne of stage and screen.

‡ Ruth Draper, famous monologuist who for many years toured in her one-woman show.

on what television has done to Christmas this year as, thank God, I have no television. However, I love you both and hope your every slightest wish for 1960 is gratified tenfold.

Frank

DOROTHY STICKNEY

(*This letter was actually written in September, 1952, when Sullivan sent Miss Stickney a copy of an old report card.*)

Sept 11, 1908

Dear Dorothy,

I wanted you to be the first to know. 93 in English! Isn't it wonderful, and all due to the help you gave me in the examination when Miss Gorman wasn't looking. I only got 70 in geometry but who cares about old geometry. You ought to of sat closer to me in that geometry exam, Dotty, and where was you in Ceasar. Divisa in tres partes, I suppose.

We are going to have a spread, or maybe we'll make it a marshmallow toasting, sometime soon, for the benefit of the Trip to Washington Fund of the Class of 1910. We plan to make the trip to the "Nation's Capital" next Easter vake, you know, and do the "sights" and I would like to invite you to be my girl when the roast takes place. Just because Lindsay '09 is on the varsity football twelve is no reason why all you frails should fall for him. Our class will also have some strawrides when the weather gets cooler and I hope you'll be my girl on them, too. Oh, what fun we shall have spooning!

Yours in Delta Omicron,

Francis John S.

TO SUNDRY GENTLEMEN

LORD JEFFERY AMHERST[1]

(Every year since 1932 Sullivan has written a poem of Christmas greetings in The New Yorker. *See page 234.)*

Saratoga, January 10, 1965

Dear Jeff,

Enclosed is a clipping of the New Yorker Christmas greeting. I thought it would be more expeditious to send the clip rather than the entire magazine. It was in the issue dated December 26 but which appeared two days before Christmas. Clemence Dane[2] is about two-thirds down the first column, having a toddy with John Slade and Paul Schrade.[3] Tell her I think she would enjoy a toddy with John and Paul, two congenial gentlemen. John is president of Yaddo, a retreat for impecunious writers established here forty years ago by a wealthy New York banker who had a home here. Paul is an up-and-coming lad who is an aide to Walter Reuther, the late labor leader. And Miss Dane won't feel she's among strangers. Some London neighbors are nearby—Sir Winston, Peregrine Worsthorne (a London columnist whose name fascinated me) and others . . . I was most sorry to hear Miss Dane has been so ill and I hope this finds her vastly improved. Ask her to do a Yank admirer a great favor by galloping along to convalescence, so that she can have that toddy and many companion toddys. I appoint you as my proxy to join her in one of them—or more.

I've been doing that Christmas greeting for the New Yorker annually since 1932, God help me, and for several years before that did a kind of quickie version of it for the World. Lots of comical things happen in connection with it, as, for instance, a letter I had last week from an indignant woman in Philadelphia demanding to know how I dared compose that entire litany without once saluting that "great American, Barry." (That's the only name she gave him.) Well, it happened I did originally have a reference to Goldwater in the Pome but it was so mean and un-Christmassy that the New Yorker suggested it would be kinder to leave him out, so I deleted him. I returned the lady's note and wrote on it, "Barry WHO?" If I am any prophet this will so infuriate her that she will write a screaming letter to the New Yorker demanding my head on a platter. The Goldwater aficionados, especially the ladies, are really quite nuts. Makes me think back to 1940 when the isolationists were doing their obscene dances here, and I wrote some verses for the New Yorker deriding them. In one devoted to Lindbergh I referred to him as a Knight in Shining Pewter. It was about the time he was predicting England's defeat. Ross got about a dozen letters from embattled isolationists cancelling subscriptions and threatening dire things because of this affront to their hero. It delighted Ross; he loved to stir up the animals.

All my best and give my heartiest wishes for a speedy recovery to that valuable lady, Clemence Dane, and may the Lord's grace come down on her and make her whole.

Yours,

Frank

Saratoga, March 5, 1965

[*The ceremonies referred to were for the funeral of Sir Winston Churchill.*]

Dear Jeff,

The Illustrated London News arrived and herewith a thousand thanks for it. Your sending it satisfies me that there is something to telepathy, or extra-sensory perception, or whatever it is. When your note came I had just been pondering ways to get a copy of that issue from New York, for I knew it would have complete pictorial coverage of the ceremonies.

On the day of the funeral I sat before my television from nine in the morning until four in the afternoon, watching it, and I have never been so moved in my life. It was a noble farewell to a noble hero and nowhere but in London could it have taken place; all the dignity and splendor of centuries of tradition. Sir Winston never hesitated to proclaim his fondness for tradition and all it means . . . We got the excellent BBC coverage, relayed to the US and Canada along with some sections from the independent British network and some very clear pictures from that amazing Telstar satellite. It was a fine piece of work; the ceremony was covered every foot of the way from Westminster Hall to St. Paul's, through the service there and finally that moving shot of the funeral train gliding silently out of Waterloo Station. I was 3,000 miles from these scenes but I saw more of the cavalcade than any Londoner watching from one spot in the Strand. But I still have printers ink in my veins and I wanted to see the accounts from the reporters and from the photographers. Life magazine was on the stands here immediately almost, with an excellent issue devoted largely to the funeral but it was nowhere near as complete as the coverage by the Illustrated London News. I'm keeping my copy beside the pictorial record of President Kennedy's funeral. Those two occasions were so different. With John Kennedy one felt the waste, the bitter tragedy of a brilliant young man cut off by murder scarcely before his work had begun. In Winston Churchill's case there was the sadness of parting with one everybody regarded as an old friend; it would have been good to have had the vital, reassuring personality around for years to come. But you had the comfort of knowing that he died full of years and ended his days in peace, with his work gloriously accomplished. He was the greatest man the world has seen in this century and very probably much longer.

I hope you are well. T. S. Eliot was wrong—April is not the

cruelest month. March is. Dirty weather. Dirty, cutting winds blowing. Dirty snow, the dregs of the winter. Dirty sidewalks.

Many thanks again for the ILN, it was grand of you to think to send it.

Yours ever,

Frank

NATHANIEL BENCHLEY[4]

Saratoga, Feb 6 1955

Dear Nat,

I live a secluded life these days and nobody tells me anything. Russel and Anna Crouse were at this Spa for a rest a couple weeks ago and it was from them I first heard you were doing a biography of your father. The news delighted me and a bit of news in your letter delights me, too—that Bob kept a diary. How he found time or patience to do it I don't know. It must be a rare document and with it as a source I don't imagine you have had to worry too much about assembling the biography.

I will put down some incidents about Bob that come to mind, on a chance that you will not have heard all of them. I find that my feeling is really more one general, pleasant diffused memory of a thousand good meetings at Tony's, or 21, or Jim Moriarty's, or other places we frequented in those days. You are not interested in a memorial or eulogy since you know how I feel about him, so I will just repeat that I loved him. The trouble was, so many other people loved him, too, and there were so many claims on his companionship that I always felt reluctant to intrude. But if it happened that I had an hour or an evening with him that was so much velvet, and it was always fun and always rewarding. It was Bob who first took me to the place called the

Puncheon Club that Jack Kriendler and Charlie Berns ran on the south side of 49th Street. That was a kind of milestone, because it marked the first of many visits to one Kriendler establishment or another, very often in Bob's company.

I am glad to remember that not too long before he died I had an entire old-fashioned evening with him. We met at 21, went to Bleecks[5] when 21 closed and went to the Royalton[6] when Bleecks closed, and talked on. It was dawn when I walked home to the Cornell Club and I knew I was nicely oiled because it was only when I was nicely oiled that I insisted on walking, to prove I could walk straight and was therefore not nicely oiled.

I can't claim to have shared too many of Bob's evening adventures, but I know they were robust. I recall a night when he and I and some others were in a speakeasy called Chez Florence, somewhere up a loft in the mid-West 40s, and there was a massive and loud-mouthed oaf at the bar who annoyed Bob a good deal. So Bob started giving a very good imitation of the oaf, who, as it turned out, was a gangster of considerable standing. Instead of resenting the imitation, the gangster was so entranced that he fastened himself on us, or really on Bob, and insisted we tour the hot spots with him. We had a hard time getting rid of him. Now if I or another had baited that fellow we'd have drawn a punch in the jaw, or worse. Bob had a way with him.

One night I did try to keep up with him. I was taking care of him and I must have had delusions of grandeur to think I could handle that job. It started early in the evening when we met at Tony Soma's. Bob was low in his mind about something and what was unusual for him, showed it. He told me he was worried and that if I was his friend I would stick by him that night. That was enough for me. I was concerned about him, so I determined to stick with him, come hell or high water. I did my best. We visited a great many places, including a lot I had never visited before. About four in the morning erosion set in with me, and I found myself being escorted home to Central Park and 105th Street by Bob. I got out, with some kind of fuddled idea that I had not failed him and had taken care of him, told him goodnight, and fell flat on my face. Bob and the taxi driver helped me up to the apartment, and that was the last time I tried to chaperone Mr. Benchley. I believe he finally told me what caused his low spirits that night—a Morris Plan note was due and he had no funds.

He came to Saratoga one August in the 1920s with Jock Whitney, for a weekend, and telephoned me. We made a date to meet in the clubhouse Saturday afternoon, after the first race. There was a mob at the track that day. I was the one who ought to have known better than to make the meeting place vague, at any rate the upshot was that we didn't locate each other until ten minutes or so after the time we set. And Bob had gone to the trouble of dressing himself to look like a tout, or what he considered a tout ought to look like, in order to astonish me. I remember the getup included a very British bowler hat, and a flamboyant vest, and his best toutish expression. Although I was late in locating him, it worked out all right, because while he was standing at the foot of a stairway, I suppose a thousand or two busy racegoers were also astonished and delighted by this exotic figure, and wondered who he could be. Then I came along, and was astonished and delighted in my turn.

Directly, we went into the bar to celebrate his taking possession of Saratoga. The bartender who took care of us happened to be named Sullivan, and he happened also to come from Worcester, so we each had a link with Sully the Bartender. But not only did Sullivan come from Worcester, he had known Bob's brother who I believe died in the Spanish American War, and had served in that war with the brother. That settled it. Sullivan of Worcester more or less quit waiting on the other customers and devoted himself to Bob. We stayed with him quite a while. Someone, I think it was Jock's mother, had given Bob a talisman of some kind, a lucky piece, which he was to hold during a race that one of the Greentree horses was entered in, but when the race was run, we were still visiting the Worcester Sullivan and the talisman lay neglected on the bar. The Whitney horse did not win, and of course this was Bob's fault, because he was supposed to go out and look at the race and hold the talisman, and get the horse home in front by doing that. Necromancy plays a larger part in horse racing than many people think. I never heard how he squared himself with Mrs. Whitney, but I know he had no trouble, for I know what a great affection she had for him.

One time Bob and I talked about our respective fathers and agreed they had a good deal in common, especially considerable charm. Bob talked about his father, Charlie (am I correct there?), and I told him something of my dear old gent, who could have gone on at any performance as Mr. Micawber, and spent a rather happy life betting most of his substance, unsuccessfully, on the horse races. Bob was puzzled by my coming back to Saratoga so much. He said he had no desire to go back to Worcester. He was through with Worcester and said he had no wish to re-visit it voluntarily.

A delightful moment comes to mind, involving Bob and Ross, and you no doubt already know about it. It happened at the wedding festival of Marc Connelly and Madeline (now Mrs. Bob Sherwood) which took place at Jim Moriarty's pleasant place at 109 East 61st Street, on the eve of the nuptials. Marc asked Jim to keep the place open after hours and the party started around midnight and went on from there. In the middle of the festivities there was a moment's lull in the noise, just long enough for Marise Hamilton[7] and I to overhear Ross saying to Bob, at the bar—"Now, Bob, I don't want you to think I'm not incoherent."

Other memories, of Bob and the Dutch Treat Club shows in the days when those shows were good, being written and played by Bob, and Ring Lardner, and Kaufman and Connelly, and such. Bob was a knight in armor and I was the ghost of King Charles I, in a sketch Marc wrote for one of the shows. Buck Crouse and Marc were also in the cast. I had stagefright, took a couple of long shots of brandy to overcome it, and did overcome it, but forgot my lines. It more or less ruined Marc's sketch (about an American who had leased an English castle haunted by us ghosts) and he was sore as hell at me, quite justly.

Well, these are all more or less bacchanalian but nobody is

better aware than I am that this side of Bob was only one side, and not the most important side at all. I was well aware of other sides, of his capacity for indignation, for instance, if he thought someone was getting a raw deal, e.g., the Sacco Vanzetti incident. In fact, I admired his courage in another episode he told me about. On one of his nocturnal journeys, he and some other fellow landed in a kind of clip joint. Mr. B. was highly interested in the place and unworried, but the pal didn't like it and wanted to leave. The managers of the joint, irked at his not appreciating their place, got rid of him by giving him a mickey finn. I don't recall who he was. He went away and left Bob, perforce, I suppose, and when Bob found out about the trick next day, he started right back to the place that night to tell the thugs what he thought of them. I don't think many of us would have had the nerve to do that.

Alison Smith told me about a review Bob wrote and the effect it had on him. The review took some actor over the coals, quite justly, for an execrable performance, but after it was published Bob was tortured by his conscience, lest he had done some harm to the actor's career. I don't think many drama critics have that much conscience. I don't think he was taken in, either, by any of the people who tried to force themselves on him in public, more or less the types who thought themselves privileged to call him Bob on first meeting or no meeting at all.

Well, he was unique. So many of my companions of those years are now on the Other Shore that it makes it a little simpler for me to hope that when my time comes, I will at least know a good many of the Committee on Admissions. . . .

Please give my devotion to your mother, and to your sainted wife. I am awaiting the biography with eagerness. I doubt very much if anything herein will be of use, but here it is, for what it's worth.

[no signature]

JOSEPH BRYAN, III[8]

Sullivan's Bluff, July 9, 1954

Friend Joe:

I know of little to tell you except that I wrote Marc Connelly after reading that a tot had dropped a chair on him from a roof top and was pleased to hear from him immediately, this proving that the concussion had not damaged his brain pan. I have learned by heart the last line of his letter. The letter was written from The Players.[9] The last line proceeds as follows: "Guess who I just had a drink with at the bar. Corey Ford. Give up?"

By this time, with your sources of information, you no doubt know that a man was arrested by indignant neighbors in Syracuse on a charge that he had a pet boa constrictor eleven feet long, named Julius Squeezer. This sort of thing revives my faith that this nation under God will survive and triumph over McCarthy.

Yours,

Arthur Wing Pinero

Saratoga, June 25, 1958

Dear Bryan,

The usually accepted version of the origin of the Saratoga chip is that it was "invented" accidentally, in 1853, at Moon's Lakehouse, Saratoga Lake. Very popular eating place in those days run by a man name of Cary Moon. One of Moon's cooks, Aunt Katie Weeks, did the inventing. The story is that she was getting ready to make crullers or doughnuts and had a kettle of fat on the stove, sufficiently hot. She also happened to be peeling potatoes at the time and she happened to cut off a thin slice of potato which fell into the sizzling fat. By the time Aunt Katie got the slice of potato out, it was done to a turn. She threw it aside on a table and then someone came by, tasted the piece of fried potato, and found it delicious. Moon knew a thing or two and he immediately had Katie make regular batches of chips, which he made a regular item of the menu, to the delight of Commodore Vanderbilt and the other swells who patronized his lakehouse. Soon Moon was selling cornucopias of the chips to diners who wanted to take some home to munch on, and so the Saratoga chip was launched. If Aunt Katie and/or Moon could have patented the Saratoga chip they would have made millions.

What the hell do you think I am? A walking encyclopedia. Be off or I'll kick you downstairs.

FS.

Saratoga, Sunday, July, 1959

Dear Job Ryan,

I just made a discovery and goodness knows why I didn't make it before. I am the only person in this town who walks to church. (Yes, I *go* to church; wanna make something of it?) Everybody rides to church. I suppose if they were commanded to walk to church on the two legs God gave them, you would hear screams of horror and protest. The church is only five blocks from this house and when the day comes when I can't walk the distance for the glory of God and the limbering up of my leg muscles, in the order named, I'll quit going. But my neighbors view me as suspect because I actually prefer to walk. They regard my walking as subversive propaganda. Maybe I'll get somebody else to walk to church, or somewhere, and maybe the fashion will take hold and people will start walking. It is a possibility my devout fellow Catholics cannot bear to contemplate (not that the Protestants walk, either; they're just as auto-ridden as we are). Every Sunday when I walk to Mass I am offered on an average of three rides by friends who cannot understand why I should walk when they have offered me a ride. They put it down to senile dementia. This is because they have, away back in their minds, the uneasy feeling that they ought to be walking too, and that they are paving the way for the complete loss of the functional American leg. That's the way Russia will beat us. They'll be able to walk, and we will be so used to being wheeled around in autos that we won't be able to walk, so they will win. In a walkover. Why, the kids here would be shocked if told they had to walk to school, even if the school is only a few blocks away. I remember when I was about kindergarten age and I damn well walked, in rain and snow and blizzard, three quarters of a mile from where we lived in the racetrack to No. 4 School, and did it four times a day. I offer all this to you as a comment on whither we are drifting. You might call it to the attention of the proper authorities. I can think of no adequate remedy for the situation except to stop making all autos for two years. Oh, what a vision of peace. That would be Glory, Glo-o-o-o-ry indeed (old hymn).

I had a surprise at Mass. The celebrant preached about *you*. I was delighted to see you thus honored. He didn't exactly mention you by name but there was no mistaking whom he meant as he referred to the scurrilous and degenerate minds who sent pornographic matter through the mails to children. I am a child at heart, so I qualified there. I would have risen in my pew and denounced you, too, except that this is some kind of Quaker practice, to let the congregation speak out, and we don't allow it in our church. Just put your dough in the collection plate, and shut your trap is our motto. I would say it in Latin for you except that I have for the moment forgotten Latin. By the way, continuing in this saintly vein, I do wish you had been at the evening Mass at St. Patrick's Cathedral on Ascension Day. I would have given anything to have had you or Ford or somebody like that present. I was in a pew minding my own business when

an usher came up and handed me a basket, and said, You pass
the basket at the offertory. I said, "I never passed a basket in my
life." I was panic-stricken. He said, Nothing to it, you just pass
up to the third pillar there, and that's all. So perforce I did, and
was just getting into my stride, when I noticed I began to get
hard looks from guys in the pews and finally, after several of
these, it dawned on me that I had passed the third pillar and was
trying to collect twice from these guys. Then the usher came up
and relieved me of the basket. Later the Cardinal came out and
thanked me publicly for doing a fine job. The least he could have
done was to have made me a Knight of Malta. But if you had
been there, the sight of me passing the plate might have instilled
in you a respect and reverence for my sterling qualities which
has been all too conspicuously absent from our relations these
many years.

I note your new address. Riding to hounds every day, I suppose, in a pink coat, and drinking stirrup cups made of pink
ladies.

Yours,

Jorrocks

Saratoga, 4th of July . . . 1963

Dear Bryan:

. . . and what has all this vaunted freedom got us? Television commercials, DDT and anti-biotics that make you itch
and break out in a rash. We'd have fared better if we had stayed
subjects of Czar Ivan the Terrible. I was thinking of moving back
to Ireland where my ancestors came from until I read that they
are going to raise social security payments—now I guess I'll stay
here. While you were returning those knives and forks you took
from the Gideon Putnam (as "souvenirs" I suppose) you might
have returned the dozen Queen Anne solid silver teaspoons

bearing my family crest that were missing shortly after the last visit you paid me, a year last summer. You announce your intention of calling here in August when you come to visit my wealthy neighbors and of course under the laws of hospitality of my clan I must receive you, but I will be distant to you and in mixing a Scotch and soda for you I may feel justified in adding just a dash of mickey finn, to remind you that respect for other people's silverware is one of the cardinal precepts of us Yankees, no matter how loosely the First Families of Virginia interpret that virtue. George Washington was the wealthiest American of his time. How do you suppose he made all that money? Yes. *White* slaves.

Our friend Admiral Markey now has a costly swimming pool on his estate, so bring your water wings. I am just putting the finishing touches on an invention of mine and I hope to persuade the Markeys to let me inaugurate it at their new pool while you are here. It is a bottomless bathing suit, to go with the new topless bathing suits which are all the rage now. The admiral's pool is enclosed and heated, in case of chilly weather in August, and champagne will be used to fill it, as there is a severe drought here and water for swimming pools is prohibited.

I must report on Sue, a four-year-old, who was visiting her kinfolk next door. I presented her with a copy of A Moose in the Hoose, a marvellous children's book I wrote but which because of the machinations of the capitalist imperialists never got the kudos nor brought in the cash I had expected. Sue said, "Did you print this book all by yourself?" I said I did. She pondered this for a moment. Then: "I didn't know old men could print." The more I think about that crack the surer I feel that I will not tell it again. Goddam little capitalist imperialist.

Lucius Beebe[10] writes that he has been commissioned by American Heritage to write a "definitive" article on Dan Moriarty's famous speakeasy on East 58th Street. Lu spelled it "Moririty" in his letter and I trust he will grow more definitive than that when he starts writing the piece. This may not be too much of a chore because he asked me to put down everything I could recall about Dan's. I sat down in a glow of nostalgia and tossed off a thousand or two words and if others do this too, all Lucius will have to do will be to copy off our reminiscences— and of course cash the check.

Come to think of it, I have spent a good deal of time the past few years writing reminiscences for other people's books. I guess word gets around, and authors who figure on doing books about the 1920s or thirties or Ross, etc., usually write me, among others, and I always respond. Then people upbraid me for not writing any more. The next one pulls that on me is going to get a poke in the snoot. A chap writing a biography of Faulkner is stopping off here to talk to me about Faulkner and a chap writing about Jim Forrestal* ditto, though I was not an intimate of either of those men and have no detailed information to impart except that I liked them both. (I found a copy recently of The Sound and the Fury, inscribed to me by Bill Faulkner, in 1931, when Ford and I shared the apartment on 51st Street. I remembered the occasion. And the tumult that followed. IT WAS FORD'S COPY of the book that Bill autographed to me. Took me quite some time to calm Ford when he got back from New Hampshire and found what had happened.)

You better make it a point to come see me in August, because I am getting old, and am very tired. That time of year thou mayst in me behold when yellow leaves or none or few do hang upon those choirs where late the sweet birds sang, or words to that effect. When my time comes I plan to die with my boots on. I suppose I ought to get fitted for a pair of boots suitable to the occasion. Could you send me the name of that London shop where they make boots for the dukes and guardsmen. Brooks, isn't it? No, that's the club you joined, isn't it, after they wouldn't let you in White's.

Your true friend

FJ Sullivan

* James Forrestal, Secretary of the Navy under F.D.R.

Saratoga, Queen of Spas, April 4, 1964

Dear Jos,

Yes, that clipping reminded me of Kate. Once when I was laid up here with the grippe she was my nurse and dosed me so valiantly that I got a piece out of the experience for Ross, called A Ministering Angel Thou. It later appeared as a sketch in a movie musical with Mary Boland[11] playing Kate and Chas Ruggles[12] playing me, no doubt to his intense astonishment. Whenever I started to Fix things around this house Kate retired to a safe distance, knowing that within a few moments I would do something traditional, like hitting my thumb with the hammer, or dropping a glass storm window on a cement pavement, and would then blow my top. She was much handier at those chores than I, until arthritis called a halt to her activity. She was a girl of great humor and gusto, and God knows, patience and unselfishness, else how could she have put up with me for so many years? She was also a lifelong and adamant Democrat. And kind of violent, like a lady Father Day. In Hitler times she would read about him in the Herald Trib until she couldn't stand it any longer. Then she would fling the newspaper from her with a cry, "That old Hitler! Why don't somebody SHOOT him!" Well, Hitler himself finally obliged her. Tom Dewey was another un-favorite of hers, mainly because he had the temerity to oppose her hero, FDR, and when she read about some crack he took at FDR, away the newspaper would go across the room and "That old Dewey! Why don't somebody SHOOT him!" Her voodoo didn't work with Tom.

I regret you never met Kate because I feel you and she would have got along fine. Her favorites among my friends were Crouse, Ross, Ford and Gus and Jean Lobrano.[13] They all stopped off here from time to time. Thurber* was in Saratoga a

* James Thurber. See note 65, page 265.

couple of times but never came to the house, which I regret because I *know* he and Kate would have hit it off. From what he
wrote about his mother, I'm sure Kate and she had a few points
in common. I'm sure I have told you about Kate's first meeting
with Ross, so I will tell it again. He came by one August noontime early in the New Yorker era and met Kate. I left them on
the front porch while I went in to make the drinks. I no sooner
got to the kitchen than I heard that clarion voice of Ross—"Now,
Kate, goddam it, make Frank do some PIECES." Five minutes
after he met her he was not only on first name terms but also on
goddam terms. She loved him. She thought Crouse and Ross and
Gus and Ford were Good Influences on me. Others came by,
Johnny Cheever[14] once or twice, and one morning in August
(that's when most of my friends came here) Norman Anthony[15]
dropped in after a night at the roulette wheels with Broun.[16]
He was flat broke and had a hangover that, to use Dotty's[17]
phrase, was a museum piece. I fixed him up with fare back to
NY but Kate provided more immediate relief—a huge breakfast
of ham and eggs and a gallon or so of coffee, which restored
Anthony to membership in the human race. He never forgot it,
or her. Kate also deserves a tablet of some kind as being the
only person I ever heard of who bawled out Aleck Woollcott and
made him like it. One night in January Aleck came by, he was
stopping overnight in Saratoga, en route from Bomoseen[18] to
NY or vice versa, and we were going out to dinner. Aleck was
impervious to cold, being well insulated by all that fat, and he
skipped in wearing neither hat nor overcoat. It was too much for
Kate and aroused all the Ministering Angel in her. She lit into
him severely and asked him what he was thinking of to come out
on a January night like that, he'd catch his death of cold, etc. I
stood by waiting for Aleck to blow up and tell her to mind her
own business. To my surprise, he didn't. He stood there meekly
and took it, like a schoolboy being rated by his teacher for flunk-
ing arithmetic, and said something like, "Yes, Miss Sullivan, I
guess you're right." The "Miss Sullivan" was rare. As you know,
everybody called her Kate. It came natural.

Since I suspect that you constantly besmirch my character and deny my saintliness to Jacqueline[19] I wish you would tell her that on Holy Thursday I was honored by being asked to be one of the twelve "apostles" who go upon the altar for the ceremony of the washing of the feet. I acquitted myself all right but I admit I had stagefright and feelings of guilt, every kind of neurotic misgiving from a fear of there being a hole in my sock when I took off my shoe (though I knew I had checked carefully and unearthed the only pair of sox I own without holes) to an apprehension that I might faint away or scream, or that somebody might hurry up the aisle and cry, "Get that impostor off that altar, he's no apostle." The monsignor, 76 years old, went from one to the other of all twelve of us on his knees, giving the right foot a token wash, and it was pretty unsettling for a sinner like myself to see that good old man do that. But I guess it taught me something about humility, and high time.

Yours,

F

Saratoga, October 9, 1964

Dear B.,

I thank you for your kind birthday greeting. I got a handsome present on my 72nd birthday. I gave it to myself—a set of bedsprings, or whatever they are called. I had been sleeping on the old bedsprings for thirty-five years, since about the time I moved in on Ford at 51st Street and had to buy a bed for my own use. Thirty-five years puts a strain on a bedsprings, even if the occupant lives the saintly, celibate life I have led. A chap like you would have to go through life buying bedsprings constantly, I suppose. At any rate, my bed—if you are really interested in all this intimate detail—felt very odd under me for the past several years and though I suspected the source of the trouble I never really realized it until a couple of days before my birthday when I had to get down on hands and knees to retrieve a book that had slid beneath the bed—and saw that the bedsprings was or were touching the floor. Small wonder I had thought I was sleeping in a ship's hammock. So I gave myself the birthday present of a bedsprings. I bought them from my high school classmate, Ed Starbuck, and told him he was to regard the springs as a birthday present, since I was to be 72 the following day. But Ed said he had become 72 a month previously, as I might have suspected, and that he could not recall I had sent him a bedsprings or any other present, and that therefore the springs would be charged to my account, as usual. BUT when Ed's workmen arrived next morning they set the springs on the porch as I held the door open for them, and then they sang Happy Birthday. Good voices, too. An intimate Saratoga touch that may give you an inkling of why I am content to spend my rapidly declining days here.

Thornton Wilder just left here after a week's visit. I invited him to dinner every night and he accepted every night but when I reached for the check he yelled, "This is on 'Hello, Dolly!' "[20] and seized the tab. I succeeded in grabbing the check on only one occasion and I am being a Monday morning quarterback trying to figure how I failed to outfumble him that once. What a delightful man. And what vitality. He's just finished a novel after a year and a half in Arizona. Worked every day he was here. Made me sick.

Yours,

F

Saratoga, December 8, 1966

Dear Mr. Bryan,

I would have written you earlier only I have been so completely crushed at not being invited to Truman Capote's party that I just haven't had the heart to do anything. And I had the perfect mask all ready, too. My own face. Nobody would have guessed and I would have got first prize. Second prize, I understand, was sleeping with the host.

Bryan, have you ever had a cat in your cellar? No, I don't mean a tiger in your tank at all. For four days, until yesterday, a cat was trapped in the cellar of this house and at the end of that period I was taking half a dozen tranquilizers a day in an effort, perhaps vain, to keep my sanity. How can you, when you are awakened at 3 a.m. by blood curdling yowls that would make the baying of the Hound of Charlie Baskerville[21] sound like a dove cooing? I could not locate the damn thing and I had visions of it caught some place in the house foundations and dying there and perfuming the house for months. I finally got the cops yesterday and one of them spotted the poor feline within a minute after entering the cellar. Perched on the masonry in a secluded corner. As soon as I saw it I recognized it as belonging to a neighbor, and then I called off the cops, feeling that the frightened mammal could be more easily coaxed out by its proper owner. Who of course was out of town for the day. He got home eventually, came over, and talked honeyed words to the thing, and in no time it jumped down into his arms. I went up to Siros and jumped into a flock of highballs in sheer relief.

Ford's all finished with the book,[22] as far as I know. I did the preface. He has sent the ms to Marc Connelly to read. I told him Marc would rewrite the whole thing.

Your very true friend,

F Sullivan

Christmas card from Plum Wodehouse. He's quite alarmed, he says, because he's about to become a great-grandfather. What can he expect, at 85—

Saratoga, April 22 or so they tell me, 1967

Dear Mr. Bryan,

Arthur Daley, NY Times sports columnist, had an essay recently reminiscing about Casey Stengel, God's gift to sports reporters and the English language, and he included one quote which I hereby forward to you because you are probably in Portugal or Irkutsk and missed it. It was Casey sounding off to the reporters on his 70th birthday and among other things he said: "You know, most people my age are dead and you can look it up." I think that ranks with Dave Clark's, "Don't miss it if you can" and his other classic "I may be wrong but I'm not far from it." Or with any of the sayings of Ford's Hollywood friend, Bunny McLeod.

I have just finished reading a hilarious English mystery "Lonelyheart 4122" by a Colin Watson whom I never heard of. There is a rowdy and bawdy heroine who should be played by Margaret Rutherford if they ever make a movie of it, and they should. And it had the funniest ending, just one last page, I ever read. Humor all very quiet and understated. The English do that much better than we; we have to throw custard pies to make our point. Don't miss it if you can.

It is cold and raining. I am just staying in bed ignoring the cosmos. Ford muttered through these parts, including my bedroom, recently. I was laid up with bronchitis. He was laid up with his hunting dog, on his way to Virginia to—you guessed it—hunt. His book is now scheduled for September publication. I hope I will stop shivering by then.

Give my love to La Belle Jacqueline. And yourself.

Very truly yours,

Myself

Saratoga, Feb. 8, 1969

Dear III,

Don't get me started on Dickens or we'll be here all night. While you were re-reading David Copperfield I have been spending January re-reading Pickwick Papers and Nicholas Nickleby. Re-read Nickleby, please, even if you only re-read the chapters on the Vincent Crummles theatrical troupe. So wonderful, in particular two descriptions of broadsword play by Crummles' sons and another of a ballet starring the Infant Phenomenon (Crummles' daughter if you recall). The ballet description is pure Benchley, and I feel sure both Bench and Dickens will be pleased at that remark. . . . Nobody ever stops to ponder that although Wilkins Micawber has become a symbol of futility and mismanagement, he is the one who puts everything to rights in Copperfield; he's the only one who has the prudence and courage to do it. If his plan to expose Uriah had misfired, he really would have been destroyed. Nobody but poor old Wilkins had the guts to go after Heep although it does seem that Copperfield might have had resource enough to find a way to get old man Wickfield out of Heep's clutches, and get Aunt Betsey's 8000 pounds back. Traddles said it after Heep's exposure when he remarked that Micawber could handle everybody's affairs successfully except his own, or something to that effect. I knew a man, an old friend, here in Saratoga who was Mr. Micawber to the life, poor soul. And Mrs. Micawber is about the most lovable girl in Dickens' galaxy. She's a sweetheart. Did you happen to see the film Hollywood made of Copperfield many years ago? Edna May Oliver was Aunt Betsey Trotwood and W. C. Fields was Mr. Micawber and I never could understand why Aleck Woollcott insisted they were both examples of miscasting—even though Fields did mug a good deal. I read that when the film was being made Fields wanted to interpolate his juggling act but I find that hard to believe, because Fields was an intelligent man and he was a reader of Dickens and would not be likely to commit a blasphemy like that. Although an actor's ego knows no bounds. Some noted hams have re-written Shakespeare to fatten their parts. There was an even better picture made of Great Expectations. It was made in England and I can't remember the cast except that I'm sure that wonderful actress Martita Hunt was Miss Havisham. (I still cherish the memory of Martita Hunt playing the Madwoman of Chaillot in NY some years ago; they have just turned that fine play or fantasy into a musical, God forbid.)

I will now leave you and listen to the Saturday afternoon radio opera. Rosenkavalier today, and my favorite one.

Wilkins Micawber

BENNETT CERF[23]

Saratoga, September 22, 1959

Dear B,

Three score and seven years ago today Mrs. Dennis Sullivan brought forth on this continent a new infant, dedicated to the proposition that all work and no play makes Frank a dull boy. We are met today to determine if that infant or any infant so dedicated can long survive. Well, I've survived for 67 years but do not anticipate being around as long as my grandparents. None of the four of them ever had a shot of penicillin in their lives but they all lived into their nineties.

I have read Moss's book[24] with delight and I'll bet you and he have read the reviews with delight. Those I've seen have been raves. I have the dusty soul of a proofreader so when you publish second and third and fourth editions change his statement on Page 10, if it is practical, that Little Emily died, in "David Copperfield." Nobody would notice this but an old Dickens fan, which I am. Little Emily didn't die, at least not in the book. She emigrated to Australia with Mr. Peggoty and did penance for having hit the hay with Steerforth. Moss may have been thinking of Dora Copperfield, who did die in the book, or perhaps of Little Nell, who died in The Old Curiosity Shop, causing Oscar Wilde, some years later, to remark "The man must be indeed hard of heart who can read the death of Little Nell without laughing." As a matter of fact Little Emily, Little Nell and Dora were little prigs, and they should have been shot in the first chapter. As Ross wrote once at the end of some comments on a proof of mine, "I am just writing this to be interesting."

Love,

Frank

"Act One" is the best book I've read on the theatre, and the most honest and candid.

Saratoga, October 6, 1967

[*Sullivan had a race named after him at the Saratoga Race Track.*]

Dear Mary[25] & Pop Cerf,

I have pasted your dear birthday telegram in my memory book. I am on the 27th volume of my memory books now and must hasten to complete the current one because my memory isn't as good as it used to be. You haven't heard from me because I really have had no time to write my more plebian friends like publishers and publishers aides. I have been hellin' around in sporting circles presenting trophies to assorted Whitneys and since I don't believe for a moment that you will believe that, I enclose visual evidence of me at the Saratoga racetrack last August on the occasion of the running of the Frank Sullivan stakes, presenting the trophy to Mrs. C. V. Whitney, flanked by her husband C. V. and with their trainer Ivor Balding on the left, and little Jockey Angel Cordero in there alongside You Know Who. I was glad to present the trophy to Mrs. Whitney as she had just been robbed of $870,000 in jewelry and I wanted to do what I could to console her.

This was part of an observance of my 75th birthday, which finally to my relief took place in September. I would also have you know that in June I got made an honorary doctor of humane letters by Skidmore College and would be obliged if you would wire instructions on how to be humane to letters. I have been abusing them all my life and cannot stop now, as you cannot teach a new dog old tricks. And just before my birthday they gave me a public shindig at the Saratoga library. I'm glad neither of you were there because they served only coffee and doughnuts. But Gene Markey, a Saratoga resident now in summer, saved the day by showing up with a bottle of J&B Scotch neatly wrapped. *There's* a chap who knows how to console an old man for being 75. After all this tumult I scarcely had strength enough left to raise a glass of champagne to my lips on the occasion of my actual birthday, which I had with the aforesaid Gene and his lovely wife, Lucille. However, things worked out all right. Gene held me while Lucille poured quart after quart of vintage wine down my gullet and by the time three quarts of Mumms Extra Dry had entered my gullet I was a new man, full of fun and games, and ready for a frolic.

This gives you a rough idea of what my life has been and now the leaves are falling so I think I will fall too, on the bed, and take it easy until the robins sing again.

Peace,

Old Sullivan

RUSSEL CROUSE
AND ALISON SMITH

Saratoga, New Year's Day, 1936

Dear Crouse & Smith, Inc., Women's Apparel, Drugs, Ales,
Wines, Liquors & Cigars:

Thought I would drop you a line to tell you that the labor
pains have started. I am getting ready to move from here to there.
I am coming down in about ten days. The holidays being over,
it is time I stirred my stumps, took the bull by the horns,
bearded the lion in his den, braved the elements, ran amuck,
bade farewell, played the game, pocketed my pride, faced the
music, knuckled down, pulled up stakes, took a firm grip on myself, shook a leg, girt my loins, put my best foot forward, kept a
stiff upper lip, got down to brass tacks, put my shoulder to the
wheel and lit out for the Big City.

I just wrote Dr. Schilder[26] requesting him to brush up on my
libido and be prepared to take a mid-year quiz covering the
period between my first discovery that my preference for girls
wearing overshoes was an indication of latent dendrophilism to
the period when I learned that my elevator phobia was due to the
fact that my father once told me what I wasn't worth a pinch of.

And I have found out what you two are, incidentally. You are
both confirmed aelurophiles, in contrast to Peg Feldman[27] who
is aelurophobic to a degree approaching the morbid. Do not ask
me where I discovered that word, as I have no intention of telling you. I have found a mine of words like that, a kind of secret
Comstock Lode, and I am going to keep them for myself, trotting
them out to confound one-syllable boys and girls like you at
strategic moments when you may give signs of failing to be prop-

erly impressed with my erudition. So aelurophobe to you, and also agoraphobia. I carefully avoided getting tangled with the New Year's Eve celebrations here, that is to say, the more formal celebrations. I don't mean to give you the impression that I didn't go out and cut capers until rosy-fingered dawn was creeping up over the Saratoga Battlefield, which I feel today as if I had been in—the Battle. I went downtown intending to have one drink at the Worden with my friends, at midnight, for sentiment's sake, and Auld Lang Syne, and should auld acquaintance be forgot and John Anderson my Jo John and all that sort of thing. So I had twenty drinks.

Got home around fiveish. Rode home with a friend who was so, shall we say, tired that he almost had to be lifted into the car. But I wasn't so tired that I didn't let out a yell of panic when, as we were zipping along the icy roads at a nice pace, I looked over at him and saw he had both hands off the wheel. I don't know why I got in the car in the first place, even though skished. At any rate, as a result of that ride I am convinced I could weather any nervous strain. One highlight of the trip—X, for such is his name, recognized a late homegoing celebrater walking; a fellow he didn't like, so he tried to run him down. The lad ducked just in time and I think an old elm tree on the sidewalk ducked just in time, too. I got out of the automobile unharmed physically but bearing fully a score of psychic scars. I was also suddenly cold sober.

I trust we shall have a happy 1936. I intend to, and I intend you two shall, or I'll break your damn necks.

Yours determinedly,

F.J. Sullivan

St. Louis, May 6, 1936

Dear Crouse,

Glad to hear from you and from the old town. I wasn't surprised to hear they have finally decided to build a subway. New
York is getting so crowded it was bound to happen, but I venture to predict this means the end of the horse. I feel rather
badly on that account, as a friend of mine, Mr. Blank, makes his
living by raising horses and doping them so that they will win
races.

Say, don't say anything about it yet, but I think there's a
comer among the newspapermen here and I venture to predict
(again) that N.Y. will hear from him ere long. He's a young
Austrian named Pulitzer and he has founded a paper named
the Post-Dispatch. Quite a paper.

They are thinking of having a World's Fair here soon and I
had an idea for a song, which I may submit to David R. Francis,
who is chairman of the committee. Something about "Meet me
in St. Louie, Louie, Meet me at the Fair." I venture to predict
(again) it would be a go but I need a tune.

There are 600 psychiatrists here and I have found out a great
deal, including what is really the matter with you. However, I
plan to let it make no difference whatever in my attitude toward
you, although naturally, from now on, I'll have to be a little chary
about being seen with you. A man in my position, the friend
and confidant of 600 psychiatrists, has to mind his Ps and Qs.

Barring a few spasms of wild desire to get the hell back to
New York the trip has been a great success. I am delighted I
came. I'm with the Doc and three of his colleagues from Bellevue, all of them swell, and terribly nice to me.

There are 3,000 bars here and one of the Bellevue party and
I have visited 2764 of them in an attempt to find the Barbarossa
beer you recommended so highly, but no one has ever heard of

it. You probably dreamed you drank it during one of those attacks of delirium tremens which, I am given to understand by oldtimers here, studded your career as a journalist in these parts. The best beer is Griesedick; nobody drinks anything else here as far as I can see.

I'll be back Saddy, Gabe.

Yours,

Sullivan

Saratoga, April 6, 1950

Dear R.,

Your note made my year. It came unexpectedly, which makes it all the nicer. Certainly, if two people like Annie and you think well of me I cannot think that my span in this vale of tears has been in vain. I say the same things right back at you both, and thank you for the comfort and bolstering I get from having you as friends. I have been lucky all my life in my friendships, but in none so lucky as in yours; and I try to remind myself of this at moments when inclined to self pity. I really haven't deserved such good friends as I have been blessed with. Crouse, it is approaching thirty years since we were first acquent, and never a cross word or blow struck. This is due to your merit. I have had no other close friend for as long a time as I've had you. I haven't known Annie thirty years but I wish I had, and anyhow she is a kind of concentrated girl that you like ten years worth for every calendar year, so I really have known and loved her for fifty years. You are two great people.

That dinner we had Sat night was the perfect windup to a pleasant two months in New York; I had a lot of fun just being with you, and not the least feature of the evening was the sight of Nature Boy my godson skipping around in his birthday suit. Really, I begin to think I pick godsons pretty well; Tim is a great guy, and I was delighted that he accepted me with such gay camaraderie. I'll get Lindsay Ann later; my plan to captivate her was foiled by the medical profession but I'll captivate her next year when she has a more adult appreciation of the good, the true and the beautiful, especially the last.

Spring is here, though there is still a snowbank three feet deep on the north side of this and other houses. They had a terrific snowfall here, which is one reason I suppose why they rarely have a water shortage. I'm scarcely able to walk for stiffness, due to unaccustomed labors in the garden, uncovering leaves from the tulips, which are sprouting like mad things.

That letter of yours, on account of its tonic effect on me, convinces me that friends ought to remind each other every so often that they do like each other. Remind me to remind you that I love youse both.

F.S.

Saratoga, February 14, 1964

Dear C.,

Well, I grow weary of picking up the morning paper and getting smacked with news about an old friend. The other day it was Chotzy,[28] and I spent the day thinking of all the fun we had at his and Pauline's[29] house. I never would have met Maestro Toscanini but for the Chotzys. They used to invite me up when they were having him to dinner. And one night I got placed next but one to him at the table, with Florence Vidor,[30] then married to Jascha, between us. I had an awful feeling that he might cast that formidable eye at me and ask me something about music, and that of course I wouldn't be able to answer, not knowing nothing about music. But I needn't have worried. Florence is a mighty pretty gal and a mighty nice one too, and the Maestro was so busy all during dinner talking to her, and giving an occasional look down her low cut gown, that he didn't even know I existed.

I loved Chotzy and Pauline and Mama Heifetz. I was the only Irisher I guess used to go to that Russian household and one day Pauline and Mama H. decided I would have to have a Russian name, so they tried to translate my name into Russian. It was a tough job but they finally decided that Fyodor Sullivanovich would be close enough, so for a while I was known as Fyodor Sullivanovich, and felt like a character out of Dostoievsky.

Hoping you are the same,

I remain,

Fyodor

WILL CUPPY[31]

New York World. May 17, 27

Dear Mr. Cuppy,

My delay in answering your letter has not been due to lack of courtesy, for if I do say it, my bringing-up was of the best. Even now I curtsey whenever I am presented to my elders or to anyone who matters. Once in a while I lose my temper over this damned typewriter, but at those times such oaths and expletives as I emit are done in a nicely-modulated, aristocratic falsetto.

The truth is, I was piqued at your remarks about the atom. I don't like that strain in you, Cuppy. Anyone who kids the atom, kids me, and as Mother said, when she fixed my necktie and sent me out into the world, "Boy, if you ever see a cuppy kidding an atom or hitting one below the belt, gird your loins and rush to its defense."

Well, you should see my loins. You never saw loins girded so, and, Cuppy, I don't want you to make any more cracks about the atom.

The "d" on this typewriter seldom hits, unless I gather all my force and wallop it. It is on vacation and so am I, only its vacation is permanent and I go back to work June 9, to do Broun's column and then Adams'.

I am so tired of dragging myself down to a newspaper office every day to be funny on schedule, every hour on the hour, that I am thinking seriously of taking a course in bricklaying and earning an honest living. If I may bore you with my mental state, I do think the modern "daily feature" idea is the most stultifying, killing factor the brisk mind of the American editor has invented. The last two years, since I was torn from a very comfortable, happy and cloistered sinecure as a reporter, have made a neurotic out of me, and I envy you your being away from that sort of thing. One simply hasn't got something to give every day—especially not 1600 words or thereabouts, which is what those wide measure columns on the World demand.

Sometime when you are in town, perhaps we can get together over a beaker of Scotch, if you scotch. I have scotched too much this past winter and am now temporarily on the wagon, after having got home one morning at eleven o'clock after being out all night. I thought that was too insane, and of no constructive value to me or any children I may have. I think that young men, when they go out like that, and drink too much, often become inflamed by the baser passions and, casting caution aside, cohabit only too often with women of easy virtue, with the result that, alas, their great-grandchildren are often born with palsy. Is palsy something you garnish planked shad with? I must look that up.

In the meantime, Heaven send you her choicest blessings.

Yours sincerely,

Frank Sullivan

COREY FORD[32]

Saratoga, April 12 [no year]

Dear Ford,

Your note was unnecessary because I read the piece on Ireland yesterday and was about to send you this to tell you I thought it was magnificent. You stirred the old Celt in my blood and made me wonder if I oughtn't to pack up and get back there and spend my declining years where my ancestors lived. It sticks out all over that piece that you really fell in love with Ireland. This was not your first trip there, was it? Only a sassenach like you could write that way about Ireland. I think sassenach is what I mean but Protestant will do, if sassenach doesn't fit. One of the paradoxes about Ireland is that most of the great Irish patriots who have led in the fight against English rule have not been Catholic—Tone, Lord Edward Fitzgerald, Robert Emmet, Parnell, and others—and you.

Did you know the classic about Alison and the Irish taxicab driver? He wasn't in Ireland, he was in New York, and she and I got in his cab one night, and when he spoke, we heard as rich a brogue as you'd hear the length of Ireland. Alison was in love with Ireland and so she fell in love with the driver, and asked him what part of Ireland he came from. He said, "Kilkenny, ma'am." Alison just meaning to make gay conversation said, "Oh, that's where the cats did all the fighting." He turned around, gave her a stern look, and said, "An' why shouldn't they stick up for their rights, ma'am?" That squelched Miss Smith for a spell.

When they came back from Ireland, the Crouses spoke of a thing you also mention—the unearthly greenness of the place. I'd like to see it but I suppose I never will. My father and mother were just such friendly souls as you encountered. Schilder and

I, in the course of our delving, could never unearth anything detrimental to either of them that we could blame for the collection of neuroses I had accumulated. My father came from Listowel, County Kerry, and my mother from Limerick, two spots you didn't visit on this trip.

Do you recall that about a year ago the newspapers carried quite a bit about something that had happened in Ireland? Some important engineering project was involved and when the engineers told the laborers to excavate a small hill that was in the way, the men walked off the job to a man, and the bosses couldn't get any others to take their places, either. The reason: that hill was well known as a rendezvous of the little people and no Irishman in his right mind would dare disturb them. I believe they had to dig around the hill. There was a good deal of humorous patronizing of the superstitious Irishmen by us smart uptodate fellows but I wish there were enough of that kind of superstition in New York to keep the greedy bastards who are ruining—who have ruined—Manhattan, from throwing up those ugly waffle-iron skyscrapers.

All right, MacGiollarnath. Slainte!

FS

Saratoga, Nov 2 [no year]

Dear Ford,

My godson Tim Crouse thinks he may go to Amherst and Crouse is considering asking for a letter of recommendation for Tim from our old World colleague, Lord Jeffery Amherst, currently of London. When the Crouses were in London two summers ago Jeff gave them a whirl including lunch at the House of Lords. It was nice to have the two Crouse kids see the House of Lords, as it seems to be growing extinct. I'd be proud to see my godson ushered into Amherst with a letter from Lord Jeffery Amherst himself. It would be as though I had gone to Cornell with a letter from Ezra Cornell, or you had gone to Columbia with a letter from Nicholas Murray Butler. Come to think of it, you did *leave* Columbia with a letter from Dr. Butler, didn't you, requesting you to do so.

I feel quite cheerful. I don't know why. It must indicate an enfeebled mind. My cousin who is a G E executive got me a G E portable television, first I've had in six years. Threw the old one out and swore I'd never get another. But this has a wonderful gadget—a small box with two buttons. I can sit in a chair with the TV across the room, press one button, and shift to any channel by remote control. But better still, by pressing the other button, I can shut off the sound and I spend most of my time shutting off commercials. It's wonderful to be able to choke those goddam asses of commercial announcers, male and female. Great outlet for suppressed sadism.

I recall that one day here last spring Rich Barber[33] asked me why I didn't learn my own telephone number. I wondered why, but to please Dr. Barber I did learn it, and one night when I was downtown I called the house here—and I answered. It took three doctors and Chas Addams[34] to bring me to. Tell Rich to mind his own business hereafter.

Yours sincerely,

F.S.

Saratoga, August, 1931

(During the summer, and in the absence of Ford and Sullivan, their joint New York apartment was entered by persons unknown, who, it seems, had themselves quite a time, especially after locating the liquor.)

Dear Ford,

As I often said to you in our Sunday afternoon forums, sex is one of the most powerful influences in the life of man and this occurrence at the apartment certainly proves my theory, you will admit. I am a little disturbed to learn that my chaste couch has been used as a seat of carnal nonsense by elevator operators and their molls. I don't want to contribute, even indirectly, to the breeding of more elevator operators. There are enough now. In fact, I, as you may know if you have read my speeches before the Congressional committee on the Proposed Abolition of Elevators and Elevator Operators, have long since been in favor of de-sexing all elevator operators and scrapping all elevators. I certainly wouldn't want to think that my bed had been used as a crucible wherein to conceive more of these pixies. Did the bed fall apart? I have led such a monastic life myself of late that I am sure if any cavortings or counterpane capers took place on it, it would have collapsed from surprise, or joy. I suppose now when I go back and try to get a quiet night's sleep in the bed, I will seem so dull that it will walk out from under me in the middle of the night and fly over to some more lively apartment.

Did they swipe my winter overcoat? I hope so. If they did I will have to go to Florida or Hollywood and it would be good for me to do so.

Whom do you suspect? Keep me posted. I have mulled over all the possible suspects, such as (eighteen names deleted) and I have come to the conclusion that none of them is guilty but that the culprit is none other than X, that objectionable friend of yours. The time he came up to see you he was probably getting the lay of the land. We won't develop that theme any further.

I am vague about one point in your account of the outrage. How did they get at the booze? Did they break the lock of the booze closet, or did you go away leaving Scotch lying about? If you did, I'll have a commission appointed to look into your psyche. One thing more—I think we ought to lay a trap for the miscreants in case they come back. Remove the slats from the bed. I'll be back late in September and in the meantime I wish you would arrange with the X. Realty Company to have chastity belts placed on all their doormen and elevator operators.

As ever,

Vernon P. Sullivan

New York, Tuesday, March 7, 1933

Dear Ford,

I have always wanted to see history in the making and by God I got my wish. You're really missing something by not being here in New York these past few days. It's pretty exciting and I can only compare it with those war days just after we got into it. Fortunately for the sanity there comes a moment when you just automatically give up worrying. I learned about the bank holiday Sat. on getting up but didn't quite get its significance somehow. Mrs. Moffitt[35] and I listened to the radio when Roosevelt was taking the oath. I had my breakfast on the table in my room. Then Alison came over and we started for Coney Island, your old stamping ground, and so little did I realize that cash might be at a premium that instead of economizing and taking the subway I got Julius the taxi driver and he took us to Coney. Then later on Crouse came down with the late afternoon papers and in the W-Telly I saw a picture of a crowd gathered in front of the ———— Bank where I have every damned cent in the world that—

(interim caused by an interruption by Ross; I'm writing this chez New Yorker)

—I have labored to store up all these years, and believe me it took the wind out of my sails. We came back from Coney and made a point of taking a look at Times Square to see what was happening and it was more crowded than ever. Apparently everybody had been possessed by the "Oh what the hell, eat drink and be merry" spirit. Monday I woke up with about 3 dollars in cash and it was very funny, and salutary, to go over to Broadway and say, as I did myself, "Guess I'll drop in at Bleeck's for a drink." and then realize that you had only $3 in cash and no assurance that you would get any more. So I had a cup of tea instead and then walked up to Crouse's, and he was rolling in wealth, being the possessor of $20, of which he gave me $5.

Monday night, as I say, I had dinner at Crouse's, and poor Alison got nervous indigestion from the strain. Later on, Marise came down, pretty depressed, and she thinks she'll pack up and move to Honolulu. Then Crouse came back from the Guild[36] and we went over to Jim's to see how things were going there, and there were seven or eight people there, including Mike Romanoff,[37] who was simply uproarious with mirth at the plight of everybody else. It was really funny. We had a drink apiece —not seven or eight drinks apiece as is our wont—and went home very soberly—after *signing* the *tab*.

I woke up today feeling perfectly swell; I slept like a top on account of being exhausted. Fred Freese, the manager of the Bank of Manhattan branch, called me and said, "If you're short of cash I can cash your check for anything up to $50." Well, Baby, you could have knocked me up with a feather! I popped right over there and it was only with the greatest difficulty that I refrained from embracing Freese heartily.

So on the strength of that and also following the general policy of what the hell, I popped over to De Pinna's and bought me a swell new hat and a half dozen Irish linen handkerchiefs. I also took the occasion to pay the newsman on First Avenue the $3.80 for last month's papers and when I dealt out four one dollar bills to him, you ought to have seen his face. Delighted.

Then I came over here to the NYorker and to complete the picture there was the usual killjoy, some guy who says we've seen the last of money for a long time and that this is only the beginning of a terrific period. Maybe it's true, maybe he's right, but we might as well take it. Ross says there are undoubtedly hundreds and hundreds of banks and business corporations in the country that are on their last legs, and that their collapse may have to be faced. I wish it could have been avoided, but as long as it couldn't be, let's get through it as best we can. Roosevelt has suddenly become to me a great symbol of reassurance and when he took the oath last Saturday, these old cheeks were streaked with something that was not water from the faucet in the bathroom. God, I hope he does live up to our expectations! I hope he doesn't disillusion us. I don't think we could stand another disillusionment.

Crouse, Marise, Smith and I are having dinner chez 433 tonight and going to Max Anderson's play later.[38] I'm opening a bottle of our old Burgundy. What the hell! Let the corks pop. Let the pops cork.

So long,

Sul

Saratoga, June 29, 1937

Dear Ford,

Arrived safely, in the rain. The country is lovely, particularly Saratoga, and the house looks superb, all painted white, with the grass tinted green and fragrant foreclosia clambering all over the mortgage. Kate has had a new kitchen sink installed but her false teeth are beginning to chip. She has been telling me the detailed story of the events of the four months I have been away and has got as far as the second week. She is a modern Sche—Sheh—I can't spell it, Sheherezade in a bungalow apron, and I have threatened to behead her unless she tells me one fascinating story per night for the next thousand nights. She, on her part, has threatened to behead me just on general principles anyhow, but mainly because I flick cigarette ashes on her rugs, but she is not going to do it until she has finished this thousand night engagement, because she has grown so absorbed in telling me these tales of life in our neighborhood during my absence, that I have become essential to her Art. It is very involved; you wouldn't understand. Go away. I am safe anyhow for a thousand nights and I can get everything done that I want to do, and see everything I want to see, by the time a thousand nights are up. I will be ready for the block, but I warn you, I will be a tough old bird by then, very stringy and not much fat on me.

I had a going over from Al Barach.[39] He says I have the arteries of a boy of twenty, the spleen of a boy of ten, and the mind of a boy of five. Woollcott says that at a rehearsal of his play one night an actor spoke of someone having a broad beam, at which George Kaufman spoke up and said, "Mr. X, I want you to know that in making that remark you have insulted Mr. Woollcott grossly—and therefore you shall have a gold medal."

Hastily,

F.S.

NUNNALLY JOHNSON[40]

Saratoga, Jan 7, 1955

Friend Nunnally,

You must make an effort to conquer this pesky vanity, which I can see is eating at your very vitals. I can see it so plain because I sit here in this cloistered retreat and have a perspective that you fellows whirling around in the marts of trade cannot possibly get. I ought to have got maelstrom in that sentence somewhere; will you re-parse it and insert maelstrom where it would seem to belong. I should think that if there was one person a person would be free-handed and generous about, it would be a person's little woman, and not consumed with jealousy when she gets mentioned by poets in one of their odes.[41] I believe I mentioned you several years ago in one of my odes and I thought that would satisfy your craving for the center of the stage, but I guess some persons are never satisfied and will ride roughshod over even their near and dear ones to gain their selfish ends. If I were to mention your name twice in as many years the editors of the New Yorker would say right away, "Well, Sullivan has mentioned Johnson again. This makes twice, and unwilling as we are to concede this, it indicates that his Muse is flagging. Alas, we have no other alternative. We must get another poet to do that Ode." Also, your name doesn't rhyme with anything but Funnily. I suspected this was so but to make sure, I had some of the best poets in the country go over the situation carefully and check. All of them, including Robert Frost and Carl Sandburg, verified my impression that the only word you rhyme with is Funnily. Dorris, on the other hand, rhymes with Boris, chorus, wee doch an dorris, Morris (Ryskind,[42] for instance), Norris (the late Senator George W.), and others too numerous to mention.

I should think that instead of complaining when I put the little woman's name in the poem, you would have said, "Pal, it was jolly white of you to mention Dorris's name. I was hoping all along that you would put her name in it, in fact, I would have preferred it if you had put in her name instead of mine that other year, because there is so little sunshine in her drab life. Slaving over a hot stove all day long while as for I—what can fame or fortune or mention in your poem mean to me, who have had wealth, glory, success, kudos, more kudos and even skouras, heaped at my feet? Thank you a thousand times on behalf of my helpmeet."

But I prefer to think that the letter I received does not represent the real you, the real Johnson or Johnston. I do not think you are basically a cad. I think you just succumbed to a rash impulse and wrote hasty words you would now give a King's (Dennis King's[43]) ransom to recall. As far as I am concerned it is just as if you never wrote those words. You are still up there on a pedestal, with Brackett,[44] and I must see the marble people about getting a bigger pedestal because I noted when he was here that Brackett is falling into flesh, and I doubt that pedestal will be

big enough for you both much longer. I don't want either of you
falling off on your cans.

REPENT !!!

A Friend

Saratoga, Thanksgiving Day, 1958

Dear Nunnally,

I hasten to reply to yours of last July. I would have answered
your letter before you even wrote it, except that I have had a
strenuous and very wearing year and am just about all in. Last
January I did a piece for the New Yorker which took me three
days of unremitting toil to do and then a few weeks ago I had
to buckle down and do that Christmas jingle I have been doing
annually for the New Yorker since the year Martin Luther
nailed those 99 theses on the cathedral door at Wittenberg. Ah,
those were the days. That Martin was sure a card when he got a
few drinks under his belt. The only man in our profession,
second oldest profession in the world, who has done more work
than I did this year is O'Hara, whose 897 page novel[45] I have
just finished reading, and am suing Bennett Cerf for printing it
in type so small. And I am writing O'Hara a pretty stern letter.
I thought that he was a fairly industrious fellow but what is one
to think of a fellow who writes 897 pages and then is too lazy
to make it 900! Anthony Trollope would have written 900 pages
and then he would have said What the hell, Live Dangerously,
and would have written three more pages just for the hell of it.
By the way, this new book of John's is his best, although I don't
think it will ever be made required reading in the various
monasteries and convents of the land. In fact even I could have
done without a few of the screwings that dot his pages liberally,
but then my attitude toward that phase of life is a lot more ob-
jective, alas, than it used to be.

Mr. Cagney[46] was here a couple of times during the summer, drawn to Saratoga by his interest in trotters. I had a letter from Jim a few weeks ago, from Dublin, where he is making a picture, and he wrote that at that moment they were shooting on the docks, down near the brewery where Guinness's stout is made. He said the aroma was delightful. Why wasn't I born with a face and personality that would draw the populace to the movie theaters instead of, as is the case, being just plain handsome, but not photogenic? You fellows live the life of James Whitcomb Riley. You personally rub elbows constantly with Cary Grant and Loretta Young, and Brackett and Dame Edith Sitwell exchange small talk over the nuts and wine.

I thought I was too old to be astonished any more but the Beard[47] did it. The night before the Pope was elected, I was having dinner at the Colonial when he came in from his teee Martoonis at the Gideon Putnam bar and started discussing the Papal election in an erudite manner. He was speculating on what name the new Pope, when elected, would take and he went on something like this: "I don't think it will be another Pius. You know they haven't had a Pope John in, let me see, about six hundred years. Maybe the new Pope will be a Pope John." And lo! See what happened. It turns out that the Beard is very well read on the history of the Papacy and could discuss the subject learnedly with Bishop Sheen. I think we may eventually get the Beard. He said to me one time, "I envy you" and I said Whatever for. Well, he said, I woke up this morning at 4 o'clock in an awful state of despair and apprehension, you know those 4 a.m. moods, and I thought of you sleeping peacefully over on Lincoln Avenue because you have a faith to comfort you, and never have those 4 a.m. doubts. I toyed with the temptation to let him go on thinking that I pass my nights in a state of serenity but my conscience got the better of me and I had to tell him that I too, faith or no faith, have those bad moments occasionally at 4 a.m., but I say a Hail Mary, take a Miltown, and in ten minutes or so, get back to sleep. I recommended that if he couldn't bring himself to say the Hail Mary, he ought at least to take a Miltown when the black dog got into bed with him at 4 a.m.

Well, let me know how tricks are, at your convenience.

Frank

Saratoga, January 30, 1959

Dear Nunnally,

Young Walker's[48] Variety piece (for which thanks) sounds as though he had found the secret of happiness like that fellow Candide who cultivated his garden. I say Young Walker because after all he is only a whippersnapper alongside of me, as indeed you are too. I went to the New York Herald to work in January 1919, still in uniform, thought I'd better grab the offer of a job and get a suit of civvies later. That was the *old* Herald, commonly referred to as the James Gordon Bennett Herald. And that year 1919 was the last year of its existence, before the fell hand of the repulsive Munsey choked it off. Now I don't remember just when Young Walker came to work on the Herald, or even whether he came to work there before another young cub called Cornelius Vanderbilt. I know I was there before either of them and always took precedence over them at court functions and lining up at the window to get the weekly pay. I think we three were the last three reporters to be hired on that nice old newspaper and that being so I think some kind of banquet ought to be tendered us. Or perhaps a nice piece of group statuary featuring Young Walker and Neely Vanderbilt and me. We three could be writhing in the coils of a huge serpent or anaconda, labelled Munsey, and I have just the spot in Central Park picked out where the statuary could be placed—just this side of the statue of Balto, the dog that rushed the serum to Nome of blessed memory, and a little to the north of the Men's Rest Room.

Young Walker has an imposing list of friends but I confess

I didn't think he went back far enough to know De Wolf Hopper.[49] Wasn't De Wolf Hopper dead by the time Walker and I got to NY? Or am I thinking of Lincoln? Anyhow, I don't believe that Walker knew Lord Jeffery Amherst, a Soldier of the King, but I did, and to this day we exchange Christmas cards. Did you ever run into Lord Jeff in your salad days in NY? He came to work on the World in the mid-Twenties and was known as Jeffery Holmesdale. Most of the staff pitied him as a belted earl who would never make the grade as a reporter on a fast-moving sheet like the World, but he did. The way he stuck it in the face of seemingly insurmountable obstacles gave me an insight into British bulldog pertinacity and I saw how come the British Empire had won through. Just such fellows as Jeff and, before him, his great-great-great-etc-granddaddy who took Quebec or something and had that song written about him. They put him on ship news at first and then word got around that Mrs. Cornelius Vanderbilt and other dowagers kept calling him at the World to know if the Viscount Holmesdale would come to dinner. That's what he was at the time, a viscount, and he would have none of Mrs. V. He spent all his spare time investigating new speakeasies and he hadn't been in NY five months before he knew more good speaks than we Yankees had been able to discover in five years. In fact, it was Jeff who introduced me to one of the two best speakeasies I knew—Dan Moriarty's on East 58th Street (the other, Bleecks, of course). Then Aleck Woollcott grabbed Jeff for the drama department, which was an easier job than ship news. Soon after he started being a drama reporter he startled Alison Smith one day. He was doing a feature story about economic conditions among actors, and he said to Alison, "I say, Alison, what would you say was the average weekly screw of the Ameddican actor?" Alison, though convent bred, had been around, and tho she didn't know what the English meant by "screw," she damn well knew what it meant in American, so she jumped three inches and hit four wrong keys on her typewriter. Well that was straightened out to everybody's satisfaction, and it may have been the reason Jeff decided to learn American. He did this, as Abel Green[50] can testify, by subscribing to Variety and reading it with the diligence of an archaeologist poring over old stones dug up in Asia Minor. Then Jeff's father died and Jeff became the fifth Earl Amherst and had to go home. We gave him a sendoff and said goodbye but he said it wasn't goodbye—"Ay'll be back," he said, and by God he did come back, and worked two or three more years on the World, the only peer of the realm on the reportorial staff of a New York newspaper. Let Young Walker tie that. Then Jeff finally got a job in British aviation and I guess that's what he still does. And last time I saw Abel Green, he said Jeff still subscribed to Variety. He lives in Cadogan Square and I think it would be a lark if we all trooped over there some day and polished up the pearls on his coronet, just before the House of Lords opens. I have lived a rich life, Nun. I also knew One Eye Connolly. (And I know Marc Connelly, who I hear is doing a wonderful job in the new Crouse-Lindsay hit, "Tall Story").

Yours ever,

Frank

MR. AND MRS. JOHN KIERAN

Saratoga, September 26, [no year]

Friends, Romans and John Kierans:

Thank you for your birthday greeting. There was quite a celebration here that day. A cannon salute at 8 a.m., Mass at St. Peter's later, followed by a street parade and in the evening a display of fireworks. Candor compels me to add that all this was not in observance of my 70th. The local Italians were celebrating the feast of one of their favorite saints. However, I told everybody it was for me.

Now that I am seventy, what do I do? Wire instructions.

Yours,

Frank

GODDARD LIEBERSON[51]

August 6, 1969

Dear Goddard,

How nice to get that letter from you, and thoughtful on your part. The fact that I see you and Brigitta only once every twenty years or so brings home to me what a cock-eyed life I lead. Hardly ever seeing the people I would like to see, the people who are *my* people. Well, I suppose one doesn't have to see friends every day to feel close to them. Anyhow I so often have tangible evidence that I am in your thoughts—those records that have come so often these past years. I hope I have always been on the ball to thank you for them. I can't be sure because now in my seventh decade as a member of the so-called human race I find I have amnesia every other Tuesday, and forget things. I keep in touch with Anna Crouse regularly and some time ago she mentioned that she and Brigitta had been at Cambridge to see some kind of dance recital that the Pride of Radcliffe, Lindsay Ann Crouse, had a part in. As you may know, Timmy Crouse (my godson) is back from his Peace Corps stretch in Morocco, to the unbounded delight of his mother. He threatens to come and see me later this month. I hope I know how to behave in the presence of the youthful generation. I don't see much of youth, unless you count Jeannie, a six-year-old living down the street, who cross-examines me every time she spots me going past her house to the store.

She said: "Why haven't you got a wife, Frank?" (they all Frank me around here, and I consider it a great compliment). I said, "Well, I never could seem to find one, Jeannie." And she said, handsomely, "Well, you can have my grandmother." Later I told that to her grandmother. I do not think she was any more amused than Queen Victoria was on another occasion.

Well, I am all right, I guess, relatively. I creak considerably, on the verge of seventy-seven, but I can still walk about, something some of my old friends can't do. And too many of them are turning in their dinner pails and leaving for the Other Side. Two weeks ago Corey Ford (perhaps you knew him) had a stroke at his house in Hanover, N.H., and did not recover. I had known Corey nearly a half century. It knocks me a bit to see old friends like that leave . . . Obviously, you and Brigitta and the sons are in fine fettle. The boys grown up, like Tim Crouse. There ought to be a law against them growing up so fast. My love to all four of you and as my Irish mother used to say, "May your shadow never grow less!"

Ever,

Frank

I read with delight Groucho's letter addressing you as "Dear God." I told him I wished I had thought of that.

HOWARD LINDSAY

Saratoga, December 7, 1965

Dear Howard,

It didn't raise my particular spirits a bit to hear from Buck that you are hospitalized again. Damn it all, you have had more than your share of hospitals and pneumonia and such these past

years. Ancient Buck (six months less ancient than I am) seemed
in good voice when we talked Sunday. He looked rather wan and
undernourished those two days Annie and he spent here in
August but they both had a ball at the racetrack, as he undoubtedly told you, and won consistently, in contrast to me, who
lost consistently. I dropped three months social security in my
operations at the parimutuel windows and almost, but not quite,
wish the racetrack were thirty miles distant instead of three
blocks. Well, what the hell—easy come, easy go.

And all signs indicate my mind is going; I assembled a bunch
of clothing for something called the Bishops Clothing Drive—
wearable clothes for needy persons in Baluchistan—last week,
turned up a wearable winter coat that might as well be passed
on, and found after the clothing had been turned in at the
church, that I had given them by mistake my best winter overcoat. $175 bucks only a couple of years ago at Walsh's swank
haberdashery in Albany. Either I now wear the worn overcoat I
meant to give to the poor or I ask the Bishop to put on a drive
to get a new winter overcoat for Sullivan. In any case I ought to
get a good mark and some stamps to improve my standing Up
There. I have been trying these past few years to atone for a
misspent life by going about doing good and have had hopes
that I had accumulated enough green stamps to shorten my stay
in Purgatory considerably. On the other hand when I do good too
much people are apt to snarl at me. You can't win. Maybe you
and I had a better time when we were in the 303rd Regiment,
76th Division, just about this time 48 years ago. At least we were
healthier.

I recently wrote what I hope was a rousing letter of praise
recommending your goddaughter Lindsay Ann to the Admissions
Committee of Cornell University. You probably know that she
went to Cornell with Anna for an interview and fell in love with
the dump, as indeed I did myself some centuries ago. Well, I have
a feeling that letters from alumni don't count for too much, but
they are chumps at Cornell if they don't grab the daughter of

Crouse, the goddaughter of Lindsay and the granddaughter of John Erskine[52] for their Arts College. And she can write, too. I have seen some things she has written.

I spent the four hours we were blacked out here as bearably as anyone could. My next door neighbor is something in Civil Defense and he was called out to patrol the town and asked me if I'd like to go along. We were to be on the lookout for pranksters, looters, rapers and the like, and it was eerie to drive around the darkened town but with a brilliant full moon making it almost daylike. We cruised for two hours, saw no rapings, and since we kind of hated to go back to police headquarters and report no action, we got out of the car and raped a few ladies, just for the hell of it.

I do hope this finds you feeling better. All my love to ditto and your bride.

Affectionately yrs.,

Frank

LEONARD LYONS[53]

January 12, 1937

Dear Leonard,

Get Sam Chotzinoff to tell you the story about Toscanini and the slang, or, if you prefer, here it is: The old man is entranced by American slang and American ways, was very homesick for New York after he left last spring, wore American clothes, wouldn't eat anything but American food and had collected an assortment of what he considered slang. One day at Salzburg he got into an argument with a German scenic designer over a set for "Die Meistersinger"; didn't like the set a-tall, and blew up about it. Chotzy, or someone, heard him. He called the poor little

German everything he could think of—"Assassin!" "Canaille," pig, dog, etc., and finally with a last effort hissed at him, "Sez you!"

Yours,

FSullivan

Constant Reader.

ALISTAIR MACBAIN[54]

Saratoga, 27 October, 1948

Well, this is the new, pensive Bill,[55] pondering on the problems which will face him when he goes out for crew at Cornell, or consoles his old man by entering Columbia for a postgraduate course. He is a boy in this one. He was a baby in the Cornell sweater picture. March will be time enough to send me the picture of him having his first shave.

The new Bill is greatly admired by Kate and her cronies. You are lucky you don't live on this street, or your child would be thoroughly spoiled. That is Kate's mission in life. She makes passes at every kid on the block and went downtown today to get five dollars in nickels, in preparation for the Halloween rites.

I have had a real sadness. There was a young lady pup in this neighborhood named Pokey. She was a mutt and the most charming dog I ever met. She could laugh and she was more intelligent than most humans. She belonged a block away but she had adopted this neighborhood, having the bone concession in several houses hereabouts. She also doted on me, and God knows I on her. Every morning she accompanied me to the corner to get the papers, and also helped quite a lot in the garden, by sitting on the places where I wanted to plant bulbs, and laughing at me. When you told her not to do anything, she had a way of gesticulating at you with her paw, as if to say, "Oh dont be such an old crank" and that gesture used to render me helpless, and got her her own way in anything she cared to do. Yes, a car got her.

Judging from the build on Bill I should say both crew *and* football, don't you think?

Happy Election Day.

Your sincere friend, and the adored godfather of your child,

F. John Sullivan

New York, November 19, 1951

Dear A.,

It hurts me more than it does you to tell you this but I just today came on some very depressing news about you. You are only a Sept. I don't mean September, I mean Sept. I would be less than candid if I did not tell you that this is bound to make a difference in our relations. Had I known you were only a sept I doubt if, in my position as a scion of one of the oldest families in Ireland, I could have afforded to take on the responsibility of being godfather for William, who only belongs to a sept. You are probably wondering by now so I will explain that I went into that Scottish shop of Forty-fourth Street today, thinking to pick out some choice gift smacking of heather or glamis or scones to give to my godson this Christmas. There were some tartans there for tots (Tartans for Tots, that's very good) and I said "I will take one of these if you can give it to me in the MacBain plaid." He said, "Who?" This fellow, I might say, was all togged out in a kilt and a sporran and a pibroch, and a tam, but I think he was a phony, or a spy named Halloran or McGinty, put in there to sabotage Scotland and undo the work of Robert Bruce. I said, "MacBain" and he again said "Who?" so then another man came up with a book and he opened it and found the tartan of the Clan MacBean. No, says I, I want MacBain and MacBain is not Mac-Bean, not the same thing at all. "Yes it is," said the both of them,

"The MacBains are a sept of the Clan MacBean." Well, I could not gainsay him offhand, and I thought to hit him with something for the affront to the good name of my godson. Are you a sept? If so, why didn't you confess it frankly to me long ago, and I would have forgiven all. I'll bet if your father, infirm as he is, heard that this ersatz Harry Lauder that waited on me called the MacBains a sept he would be down there in twenty minutes brandishing his claymore, to work havoc. The Sullivans are, of course, not a sept, but the whole cheese, practically, in Ireland, as you know. I suggest that to save face it might be well to change Bill's name to Sullivan, or we might compromise on MacSullivan. His mother's side could not possibly be of help. Who wants to be a Smith? They are a dime a dozen.

In the meantime the problem of Bill's Christmas present is in abeyance and in conclusion I can only add, Where the hell were you at the pipe night for Frank Adams' 70th Birthday last night, one of the nicest parties at The Players in many a year.

Love,

The O'Sullivan

GROUCHO MARX

(Groucho had sent Sullivan an inscribed copy of The Groucho Letters.*)*

Saratoga, March 29, 1967

Dear Groucho,

On behalf of my friend Groucho Marx I am bringing suit against you for one million damages for writing in that inscription that Groucho should write less and I should write more. It may interest you to know that at the February meeting of the Saratoga County Dairymen's League a resolution was passed viva voce recommending that you should write more (and the reviews of the Letters will bear this out) and that I should have started writing less years before I did. But since I have written nothing in ten years how can I oblige by writing less than nothing? I'm doing the best I can to please . . . What I am trying to say is, a thousand thanks and bless you for the Letters, and for the grand inscription, and for that "Love" at its close. I can do with all the affection I can wangle from my friends these years but it seems to be getting harder all the time to get any. People keep saying "Go away" when I ask them to be kind to me.

The book got here toward the close of a two week imprisonment in this dump, alone, with la grippy. La grippy was enough of a bore but I may add that although I yield to no one in admiration for the sterling qualities of that saint in human form, F. J. Sullivan, two weeks alone in his company comes under the head of cruel and unusual punishment. I had run out of reading matter and was about to flip my lid when the Letters came. The la grippy abated immediately, I told F. J. Sullivan to get the hell away from me, that I vastly preferred you, and I spent the next two days laughing. Also, marvelling at your insight. That letter you wrote the president of Chrysler in 1954 about the death traps automobiles had become preceded Master Ralph Nader's exposé by a dozen years. He should give you half his royalties and half the million dollars he expects to win in his lawsuit against GM for setting dicks on him to prove he led an immoral life.

I'm pleased as hell to be carrying a spear in the cast of Letters. If I had realized you were going to use letters to you as well as from you I would have bombarded you with letters daily and might have racked up enough mileage to rank with Sheekman,[56] Ace[57] and Tom Eliot.*

Under separate cover, if any, I am not sending you a copy of the book I did not write last year or the year before, just to make you quit saying I should write more. This is called phantom

* See next letter.

giving. You won't be able to read the phantom inscription but you can take my word for it that it is signed

With love,

Frank

HERBERT MAYES[58]

April 4 [no year]

Fondest of Herbs:

That letter you wrote me in January has been read and reread. I appreciated it the more, coming from a busy man like yourself. Nobody takes the trouble to write letters like that any more. In my time I have inundated my friends with long screeds, and I guess it was because I sequestered myself up here and letters were the only way to keep in touch with the loved ones, like you and Crouse and Ferber. I just wrote Groucho, after finishing reading his Letters, and told him I was going to ask Congress to name him the Horace Walpole of today. The only man in the world who would have and did have the temerity to call T S Eliot "Tom" is Groucho, and Tom obviously loved it. And Groucho's immortal note resigning from a club: "Herewith my resignation. I don't want to belong to any club that would have me as a member." I first saw, and fell in love with, the Marx Bros in Jan 1919 (long before Woollcott and the other big shots discovered them). With the gold of a shavetail's bars still glowing around my shoulders, I fell out of my seat laughing, and still remember one line, where Zeppo came in and said, "Dad, the garbage man is here" and Groucho said "Tell him we don't want any." And to my delight in one of the letters to a dame who had asked him to name his favorite Marxist lines, Groucho put that one down.

I get stray bulletins of you and Ferb and other friends from that great woman, Annie Crouse. She has been wonderful. I take it you know my godson, Tim Crouse, is a co-author of the book for the current Hasty Pudding musical and it is a great smash hit at Harvard. I wish Crouse were here to savor that triumph. Caution—you mustn't answer this, I have no intention of imposing a burden of correspondence on a busy man. The postman just left a letter from Cerf; I glanced thru it and I think it is abusive but will know for sure when I read it. Love to Grace and you.

Frank Solomon

ROBERT E. SHERWOOD[59]

[This was written ten days after the death of FDR.]

Saratoga 4.22.45

Dear Bob,

I did not have access to a radio during those three days but I have just read in the Memorial Book just issued by Pocket Books your tribute to him and I want to tell you that I love you for it. I envy you; you knew him intimately. I have to be content and will be content with the great solace of knowing that I was in that company, and a good-sized one it is to be sure, of those who knew from the first that he was a great man, and appreciated him. That is something I will be proud of all my life. I would hate to be now in the position of those who have been sniping at him, or at least passive and dumb about him, and now cannot do anything about it. Or those who are now saying, and I have met them already: "Well, I never voted for him but he was a great man." What an indictment of them that remark is. My neighbor John Rydberg, born in Sweden, and another friend, Johnny Cassidy, supt of public works up here and I—the three of us agree that our appreciation of FDR is something we can cherish the rest of our days. I registered my faith in him by voting for him seven times and I feel damned proud of that record. If I brag about it too much in the future, or get to seem smug, let them as don't like it do what they know they can do. In the meantime I still feel as though I had lost my father all over again and I have some insight into how you who knew him really, must feel.

Remind me to tell your wife some time that I admire her extravagantly.

Yours,

Frank

MARK SULLIVAN[60]

Saratoga, August 7, 1939

My dear Mark Sullivan,

After a number of years the situation is getting out of hand and I must request you to Take Steps. The situation in question is as follows: An old gentleman who came here to Saratoga to take the cure, settled for his stay in a cottage near my house, and one night recently, during my absence, he paid a visit to my sister, and in terms of the most extravagant superlatives he extolled my merits as a writer and begged the privilege of an audience so that he might bask in the sunshine of my presence and drink in whatever words I might choose to let fall upon him. I was greatly set up when I came home and my sister told me about this visit, for nobody had said a kind word to me for months and my morale needed a tonic. You can imagine with what haste I prepared to return the gentleman's call, so that I might derive renewed vigor from his adulation. I popped right over to his house—only to find that he thought I was Mark Sullivan. He had never heard of Frank. I crept home, a beaten man, hiding my sorrow beneath a smile. As I believe I told you once in Washington when I had the pleasure of meeting you at lunch one day with Arthur Krock,* this happens often to me. During one of the major political conventions in 1936 I was bawled out severely by a lady who said I ought to be on the ground, interpreting events for good Republicans. In vain I protested to her that I was a staunch Democrat and, if you will pardon, a Roosevelt Democrat to boot. My lot is a hard one. People either take me for you, or for Ed Sullivan, a gossip columnist on the New York News. This is all very bad for my ego, which shows signs since this last debacle similar to the symptons noticeable in the cornfields around here after the third week of the late drought. I need the rain of a little reassurance. You couldn't possibly write, could you, and tell me that someone had mistaken *you* for *me*? What the hell!

Yours in the bonds of our clan,

Frank Sullivan
(of the New Deal Branch)

HERBERT BAYARD SWOPE, JR.[61]

Saratoga, January 20, 1968

Dear Ottie,

When I read about your mother it made me feel like the last guest at the party, who lingers on after the others have gone and can't think of a way to say Good Night. I could write a volume about my own pleasant memories of Maggie and Swope and that wonderful, gay house at Great Neck. For days afterward the memories kept crowding in, all of them fond. It must have

---

* Arthur Krock, New York Times Washington columnist and author.

been around 1925 that your father first invited me out for a
weekend and it was the first of a succession of weekends,
and there was never a dull moment. At first I knew none of the
guests except those I knew from the World office. Broun, FPA.,
Stallings,[62] etc., but I soon got into my stride and formed friendships there that have lasted—Al Barach, Edna Ferber, Gerald
Brooks,[63] so many others. Maggie knew I was—God help the
word—shy at first and she could not have been nicer or more tact-
ful in making me feel at home. Peggy Leech was another friend
I made there and I maintain that Peggy and I met in a bathtub.
It was one of those things that happened in that house. One
Sunday morning I rose, went to a bathroom across the hall and
found a bath all drawn and ready. I marveled at what an efficient household Mrs. Swope ran, to anticipate her guests' wants
so. I got into the bath and bathed, got out, and on leaving ran
into the future Mrs. Pulitzer, who informed me she had drawn
that bath for herself, not for me. But she was amused, not ir-
ritated. (I was always running into Peggy in bathrooms, somehow. She and Ralph stopped off here one August afternoon on
their way to the track, and that time she got herself locked in
my bathroom and I thought for a while I'd have to call the fire
department to get her out. But the lock yielded just in time.)

I recall a characteristically kind thing your mother did one
night for Broun. The poor fellow was having a nervous break-
down and it seems he often got panicky when among people.
That night, in a room full of people having supper, Broun suddenly rose and stumbled out of the room in a kind of daze. No
one sensed he was ill except your mother, who followed him out,
walked him up and down and calmed him until the seizure
passed and he was able to come back.

I was in on a hilarious episode at Great Neck one New Year's
Eve. Ruth Hale[64] wanted to get your father to perform some
ancient tribal rite with her, at midnight. They were to hold hands
and jump off the bottom step of the porch, into the New Year.
Then Swope was to kiss Ruth. He swore he'd be damned if he'd
kiss Ruth or anybody. It was like a scene from Life With Father.

I'm sorry I can't remember who won but I'd bet on your father. Correct me if I'm wrong, but I think I was also in on your matriculation at prep school. Your father took you to a school in Connecticut and you telephoned your mother shortly that you disliked it there. So your mother went up and fetched you back home. HBS swore discipline must be maintained and he took you back to Connecticut and next day your mother brought you back to Great Neck. I think there was a compromise finally and you landed in a school in Riverdale. As I say, correct me if I'm wrong. All the Operation Ottie was carried out amid volumes of advice from twenty or thirty friends of the family.

It never occurred to me to wonder how that remarkable household happened to run so smoothly in the face of so many opportunities for chaos—luncheon at 4 p.m., dinner around ten, etc. It never struck me that Maggie, with competent assistance from the Admirable Crichton, May, was responsible. I have an old man's memory. I recall quite well what happened fifty years ago but I can't remember where I put my eyeglasses fifteen minutes ago. I remember such details as your mother's aversion to ashtrays full of butts. She kept an eagle eye out for them and swooped down the moment she spied one, and got rid of the butts. She didn't want anybody near her who had a cold, and I don't blame her there. She was a girl of uncommon fortitude. She had to be to be married to and keep up with Swope, and to preside over that establishment and cope with us guests.

Well, I said I could write a book about the Swopes and I seem to have done it, almost. This is not a letter of condolence. At seventy-five, I don't write them any more, and I doubt if you would welcome any conventional, doleful letter. Consider this a love letter to the memory of two wonderful people whom I'll always cherish. I can't bring myself to believe that I won't see them again, somewhere, somehow.

Yours, with affection,

Frank S.

I was reading recently in Woollcott's Letters and came on an item that said, "I had lunch today with Ottie Swope, the only Swope who is speaking to me." It took me back.

JAMES THURBER[65]

Saratoga, September 26, 1955

Dear Jim,

You are probably familiar with Satchel Paige's Rules of Life but I cannot take a chance on your not having seen them. A friend handed me a copy and I do not know where she got them, but here they are, for the guidance of Helen and yourself:

1. Avoid fried meats, which angry the blood.
2. If your stomach disputes you, lie down and pacify it with cool thoughts.
3. Keep the juices flowing by jangling around gently as you move.
4. Go very light on the vices, such as carrying on in society. The social ramble aint restful.
5. Avoid running at all times.
6. Don't look back. Something may be gaining on you.

Yours,

Frank

Saratoga, June 3, 1959
[*The party was given by his publisher, Little, Brown, for the publication
of Thurber's* The Years With Ross, *which he dedicated to Sullivan.*]

Dear Jim,

I am a country boy and it takes me a week to get over a few
days in New York. I am now back in shape after last week's visit
and its highlight, the party at the Algonquin. It was a grand
party and I wouldn't have missed it for anything. The only flaw,
from my point of view, was that I didn't get enough of you and
Helen. I got in a hug for you when I arrived and gave Helen a
kiss but I effaced myself then because there were too many calls
on you both and it would have been selfish to demand more of
your time under the circumstances. In the course of the party I
got myself a quite pleasant little brannigan and later on I took
Ik Shuman[66]—or did he take me—to the Players for dinner, and
we had a few more there, in your honor.

If the party was grand the reviews I have seen are even
grander. I clipped the two daily reviews from the Herald-Trib
and the Times and also the two from the Sunday book sections
of those papers, and air-mailed them to Nunnally Johnson, because I know he will want to see them. Also that heart-warming
editorial from the Herald Trib about you and Ross. It's nice to
get good reviews on the book but when you rate an editorial as
well, you're in.

When you called me at Christmas time and recited the dedica-
tion I don't think I was able to come anywhere near an adequate
thanks. One reason, you took me by surprise, and another reason, which you may have suspected, was that I was so close to
busting into tears that I could only mumble something foolish.
Well, I never had a book dedicated to me before but if by some
occult arrangement I could have picked the book I wanted ded-

icated to me, this would have been the one. I would have turned a deaf ear to Proust, Shaw, Maugham, Hemingway and all such when they begged me to let them dedicate books to me, and I'd have said to them, "No, I'm sorry, but Jim Thurber is going to write a book along about 1958 which he will dedicate to me, and I prefer to wait for that, thank you."

One small nice thing I would like to mention. You got my sister Kate in, in a quote from a letter Ross wrote me. She loved Ross and she would be so pleased to be mentioned in Thurber's book about him. She cannot thank you audibly but I can, in her behalf, and hereby do.

I will leave you now to rest on those laurels, with my best love to Helen and yourself.

Sullivan

The 1st Dedicatee of His Time.

Morris R. Werner[67]

Saratoga, September 9, 1968

Dear Mr. Werner,

I regret I didn't contact you when you were here. "Contact" is a new verb I just thought up and have sold to Batten Barton Durton and Osgood for use in their blurbs. I am processing another new verb which I am thinking of calling "finalize." Would you let me have your best thought on this idea?

I am not very dependable these days, as I grow increasingly fragile. Another birthday is far too close for comfort and as my age is far from being a secret I will tell you that goddamit, it will be my 76th. And if you don't think I feel completely alienated and out of things these days, you're just not 76. I try to dig the modern scene but fail.

I get up to the racetrack about twice a week, which is more than I expected to do, and I have a new perversion—I like to sit in the grandstand. This from a darling of the clubhouse set like myself will no doubt astound you. But I like hoi polloi in that there grandstand because they enjoy themselves and holler and scream when the nags come down the stretch, and root their horses home, and curse and swear and mutter to themselves when they lose. They are no doubt also a bonanza to any stray mutuel clerks who may—perish the very thought—be inclined to pull fast ones on the customers, because a lot of the birds in the grandstand are only occasional customers and really don't know how to bet, or how to watch their change and see that it's correct. Why even I, a gambler of long experience about whose methods text books may well be written in future times, have been short-changed. You get excited and don't give a damn.

I did get to the Hopeful in the distinguished company of my doctor, Albert Yunich and his wife, and the State Tax Commissioner, Joe Murphy and his wife. The commissioner is a splendid fellow. I did not mention your failure to file a return in 1931; I thought you wouldn't care to have it brought up. Somehow or other, probably because of the Commissioner, our party wound up sitting in George D. Widener's[68] box, and I am really sorry you couldn't have seen me there. You would have been down on the lawn among the proletariat but I would have nodded to you. Let it never be said that Sullivan forgets a friend just because the latter hasn't quite made the Diamond Horseshoe.

And remember in the coming days when the leaves will be falling and there will be a tang of autumn in the air, that it's all done with mirrors.

Courage, mon ami!

Frank

THORNTON WILDER[69]

May 30 [no year]

[*The gambit was a device for motorists so that they could escape from being arrested while speeding.*]

Dear Thornton,

Your letter came and I read with delight that you had fooled the state troopers so neatly with the Just Married gambit. Then, last Wednesday, I took off for New York myself and yesterday noontime as I walked along Park Avenue by the Waldorf there was a great clatter of motor bikes and screaming of sirens, and a tumult roaring up Park. Of course my first thought was that the troopers had caught up with you. "They've got Thornton!" I cried. "They're moving in for the kill. They've got him out-numbered about a thousand to one but they'll know they've been in a battle before this day is over. Wilder will never be taken alive and many a state trooper's wife will be a widow this night." (I said all that to myself) Then, instead of you, it turned out to be only the King of the Belgians arriving for some old lunch-eon. Rarely have I encountered such a dismal anti-climax.

I went to New York to go to the shindig Little Brown gave for Jim Thurber and his book on Ross, at the Algonquin. You never saw such a crush. Tout le mond (all the world) was there and the place was jammed. You couldn't move, there was such a crush. I loved it. I guess what a sedentary fellow's spirit needs every so often is a good crush. I saw old New Yorker friends I hadn't seen in years. I also made a highly gratifying discovery. Jim, the dear old fellow, had dedicated the book to me and I found myself getting compliments on all sides. Thus I shared in the kudos without having done any of the work. This is a wonderful labor saving device and I wish Thurber had thought of doing it earlier, and oftener. It would have saved me much labor in past years. I don't suppose anything else will ever be dedicated to me now, though I might possibly rate a bird bath or two of a memorial nature in the public plaza here after I pass on. Or I may leave my residue as a fund, the income to be used to put on a sumptuous dinner at Ashgrove twice a year for Wilder and Woolley, with the choicest wines and viands, and preceded and followed by drinks at the Colonial.

I came home last night tired but happy and am so glad to see the mass of green which is Saratoga at the moment. Why is green so restful? I don't think I'd have been so glad to get back if the trees here were blue, and I don't think I'd have come back at all if my lawn and the other region greenery were scarlet. There must be a reason for this. Life is so mysterious, don't take it serious.

Next year I may try to crash the meeting of the Academy.[70] They sound so lively. Your account of the cabal this year to keep you from Marilyn, and last year I recalled O'Hara writing me about a lady poet he sat next to. When an award was given Mrs. Parker, the lady poet hissed catty remarks in O'Hara's ears and, rising to the defense of Dotty, John and she almost came to blows.

Happy summertime, and come back soon.

Your devoted

Frank

My homage to your sister.

ALEXANDER WOOLLCOTT

Saratoga, Sept. 1934

Dear Alec,

I have taken an apartment at 2 Beekman Place and the Albert B. Ashforth Company demanded social references as they are very particular so I gave you as a sponsor. Your duties as sponsor will not be onerous; all you have to do is hold me in your arms while Albert B. Ashforth pours a little water on my head and mumbles the few words that make me an Ashforth tenant. Then you also have to attend to my religious instruction, and, of course, pay the rent.

Love,

F. Sullivan.

Saratoga, July 17, 1939.

[*There was a party for authors for FDR.*]

Dear Alec,

Sorry you can't make it Sunday on acct of Hyde Park. Matter of fact, I was invited to Hyde Park for this weekend, too, but I told the President I had a luncheon engagement Sunday with you, so couldn't come. Now if I had only known you had accepted an invitation from Hyde Park to spend the weekend with the second assistant gatekeeper and his family, we could have gone down there together. Are you going to remain at Krum Elbow to spend the following weekend with Father Divine, or will you be spending it with Lord Tweedsmuir?[71] Really, you meet more interesting people than anyone I know except Danton Walker.[72] If you are not lunching on the following Sunday with anyone entitled to more than six pearls in his coronet, why don't you stop off here and slum it with plain old me? We're jes plain folks, pardner, but nobody kaint say they ever went away from Buzz Sullivan's door hungry. I'll get you a companion befitting your station that day if I have to go over to the Saratoga Battlefield and dig up Gen. Burgoyne. I cannot come to the Island at the moment as I have just been inundated with a flood of orders for magazine articles of a comical turn and I plan to spend the next few weeks thinking them up, pausing every once in a while to chuckle. I suppose you will roar up and down the Ethan Allen country now that I am coy and desire to be wooed, but I can't help it; I also desire to eat. Business before pleasure. Pitch a little woo with Beatrice Kaufman for me, and give my regards to Lloyd Lewis,[73] my veneration for whom is second only to that I entertain for the Holy Ghost; in fact I would think more highly of the Latter had He written "Sherman." Take care of yourself, old man, mind the protocol next Sunday, wear three ostrich plumes in your hair, and curtsey.

Yours,

Frank.

TO THE NEW YORKERS

Roger Angell[1]

Saratoga, Sept. 22, 1959

Dear Roger,

Thank you. Hearing so pleasantly from you made it a family quorum, since both Katharine[2] and Andy[3] had taken the trouble to send me communications too. Those are the thoughtful things that make life worth living and get the people who do them into excellent aisle seats in Heaven. Today I had a birthday telegram from John O'Hara. He never fails to send one and it always touches me, because John is a man who would hate to be thought sentimental. But he is, about old friends.

I would as soon have skipped this birthday, having been put in my place about birthdays two weeks ago. I was a guest at the birthday of an up-and-coming girl named Grandma Moses and as you may have read it was her 99th. She is frail physically but as active mentally as ever, and so sweet and good-natured. Perfectly at ease, knows just what to say and when, and a Life photographer popping flashbulbs at her didn't bother her in the least.

A New Yorker reader named Mr. Cunningham wrote me about a casual I did in the early Thirties and warmed me very much by telling me he had dug it up and was quoting it all around, since the recent Lady Chatterley fuss. I had remembered it myself and had been kicking myself for having a good idea twenty-five years too soon. I had read a bootleg copy of Lady Chattlerley and got to wondering about what would happen after they flew the coop to Canada or the United States and the bloom came off the lust, and they got sick and tired of each other. Very cynical idea, but a psychiatrist who read the piece told me it was excellent psychology. Anyhow, the piece described Lady C. and Mellors living in sin and Philadelphia a year later, and she is awful tired of sexual intercourse. For the time being at least, and as far as Mellors is concerned. I remember it took quite a bit of soul-searching on Ross's part before he could decide to use it, and one phrase I used in particular bothered him. I said something about Mellors' "glistening flanks." Surprisingly, Ross let it by. Ah, those were the days. The piece was called One Year Later.

I must go out now and feel 67.

Yours,

Frank S.

Saratoga, January 26, 1963

Dear Roger,

My latest thought—and I would appreciate it if you'd manage to keep a straight face when I talk about working—is a cliché piece[4] on murder mysteries. I have had it in mind for some time, off and on, and it keeps recurring. It might work. It certainly would involve a wide audience. I have been an addict for the past ten years or so but I am somewhat handicapped by being strictly a Scotland Yard boy. I don't want to sound unpatriotic but all except a few of the American mystery writers leave me cold, and so do their fictional detectives. I suppose Scotland Yard has the glamor of distance and London fogs and so on. I am convinced that the English write better mysteries than we do and that English women write better mysteries than English men— witness the peerless Agatha Christie, and Ngaio Marsh (New

Zealander but still Empah); and Margery Allingham; and the unfortunately defunct Dorothy Sayers and Josephine Tey.

No British murder can even start to be solved until everybody concerned has had tea. Every time they find a new clue or a new suspect, they have tea on the head of it. Sometimes they wake up the corpse and give him a dish of tea, or so it seems. Nobody must touch anything or move the body until Scotland Yard arrives and Dabs comes. (Dabs is the Scotland Yard nickname for the fingerprint man.) Then everybody has to tell where they were when the deceased was bumped off. When Agatha Christie has a tea break, every few pages, she really does it right, and serves scones and crumpets. As some magazine whose name escapes me puts it, There'll always be an England.

This might work out, and then again . . .

Yours,

Inspector Sullivan

GUS LOBRANO[5]

Sept. 15, 1951

Dear Gus,

I will defer to Ross on the diff. between stealing and stopping a show, as he is a stage door johnny who knows these things, and who also knows Ginger Rogers. Mary Martin stopped a show when she sang My Heart Belongs to Daddy first time and she also stole the show for the same reason. To me the difference is a nuance and only God and Abel Green know the truth.

If you had passed through here one night shortly before the races ended and had not called me, you would have missed a hilarious evening, as on that evening I was out with Joe Palmer, racing expert of the Herald Tribune, and we ran into a trio com-

posed of Eddie Arcaro and Ted Atkinson, the jockeys, and Liz
Persons, formerly Liz Whitney, in a small bistro near the track.
I learned more about horses from those four experts (Liz knows
as much as any of 'em) than I have learned in my 58 years
around here, 59 come September 22. Jockeys have changed.
Little Atkinson learned from Joe that I wrote for the New
Yorker and recognized my name then, and made much of me,
and discussed things he had enjoyed in the New Yorker by different writers through the years. He don't miss an issue, and he
is a smart cookie. I went home, depleted, at 3 a.m., but the other
three went to Arcaro's house and talked horses until six and
Arcaro got up, or rather didn't go to bed, and won three races
that afternoon.

I have multitudes of ideas but work so slowly I have no hope
of doing them all. I wish I had a collaborator like Lindsayand-
crouse. For instance, I feel sure a pleasant fantasy, or something,
could be made from either of two similar ideas that occurred to
me some time ago. Perhaps I have already mentioned this. I read
that Abercrombie & Fitch were selling a super-sonic(?) dog
whistle which, on being blown, would produce a sound inaudible
to human ears but clear to the more sensitive ears of dogs. Mercy
on us, what hath God wrought, thinks I, and then thinks I, suppose some guy should get himself one of these whistles and blew
on it and the result was that the goddamndest most unheard of
animal that ever existed in fable or Alice in Wonderland appeared, like Aladdin's genie. It would serve him right. It and
the consequences also might make the story. Similar was an idea
I got along the same lines last spring reading about the possible
use of super sonics (my science is weak and would have to be
bolstered before attempting anything) in growing things in the
garden. Well, same thing happens, except that some dreadful
flower responds. Maybe too close to John Collier,[6] and maybe
dog whistler idea is too close to Harvey.[7] I thought of that.

I also want to do an idea I've had for years; in fact, a draft of
it has been around so long it is yellowed with age, and I take it
out and look at it every so often, and that is something tentatively

called The Flitch of Gloversville. An American town stages a
Flitch of Dunmow contest, in which, as in the old Dunmow
tradition, a flitch of bacon is awarded the married couple who
have gone through a year without quarreling. Chamber of Commerce puts it on, and maybe the couple that get into the finals
go right through to the eve of winning and then have a knock-
down drag-out fight over how they want the bacon cooked. Something like that.

Well, I have fixed your day. After reading this, it will be time
to shut up shop and go home.

Yours,

Frank

HAROLD ROSS

Saratoga, 1932

Dear Hal,

I am glad you liked the Passion piece. I did it as a burlesque
on these Hollywood gals who are always airing their amours,
real and imaginary, in the newspapers. You will not be sued by
any of the movie actors mentioned in the piece because I understand only three of them can read.

You say I have been writing good pieces. I wish to say that
any small success I may have had lately in that direction has
been due to right thinking and clean living. Honest, I don't take
four drinks a week up here, and I haven't been out to a social
function since Fleischmann⁸ was here and treated me to a dinner
at the Brook. Many have commented on the resulting improve-
ment in my looks, the old Sullivan pallor having been supplanted by a firm, ruddy mien, sparkling blue eyes, and sensitive red lips that curl readily in a jovial, friendly smile to show

two lines of teeth that vie with the pearl in their snowiness. In addition I am much less impotent than I was when I left Ny.

I haven't any idea on the makeup of the short story thing. Ross, I don't know about makeup, now. As for picture, why not any outlandish picture—King George, Ben Turpin, or, possibly better, one of John Gilbert, labelled as me? In fine, you work this makeup problem out for yourself, Hal. There is a certain point up to which daddy is willing to work things out for you, and then he thinks Harold ought to make some effort for himself, so that he will grow up strong, and self-reliant and with lots of nice character, so that he can cope with the world.

As ever,

Daddy

Saratoga, December 11, 1946

[The New Yorker *printed a Christmas list of books written by its contributors. However, it had a rule that no book could be included unless one third or more of its material had appeared in the magazine.*]

Dear Ross,

I have decided to adopt a dignified, hurt attitude toward my exclusion from the Christmas list of books by New Yorker contributors. I cannot afford self-pity. Self-pity is unbecoming at any age, but especially in one over fifty, and arouses distaste in the beholder more often than the sympathy it yearns for. However, when I am gone you will regret that you treated me, a charter contributor to your magazine, in this fashion. I don't feel well, either, right now. Facts and statistics, indeed. One-third. We must have standards (I quote you). Do you recall what happened to Thomas Gradgrind, a man who worshipped facts and statistics? Suppose I didn't attain that 33 1/3 per cent. The two best pieces I ever did for you or any other magazine are in that book. But I suppose you are right, in these atomic days, to go in strictly for the quantity standard. It's a percentage world, and you realize it because you are a man who has an ear to the ground. You are right to adhere to statistics. You would have been crazy to let any such sentimental consideration as for instance the fact that I am a charter contributor to the Nyorker, outweigh that 33 1/3 per cent rule.

I am dining here with Charlie Brackett tonight. He is a man who would not be apt to lose his sense of proportion over facts and statistics.

Yours, precisely to the extent of 33 1/3%.

F.S.

One-third of a Merry Christmas to you.

April 5, 1948

Ross:

It is not clear to me what your qualms are about that Russian piece, though I had forgotten about it, until you mentioned it. Did you think it was loaded *pro* Commie, or loaded *anti*. I didn't think it was either, just a catalogue of the chestnuts. I got it out, too, and re-read it, and I still don't think it's such dreadful dynamite, and neither do a couple of seasoned observers I've showed it to. Would you be willing to sell it back to me in the event I got a purchaser for it? I haven't tried, but the idea occurs that some other editor might not have your qualms. These remarks are addressed in a reasoned, amiable, benign tone, as I have to be very careful in handling you. If I so much as emit a mild cry of pain or protest, you accuse me in the presence of Mayor Bill O'Dwyer, of "sulking." Christ, I am the least temperamental of all the aggregation of manic-depressives, paranoiacs, psychoneurotics, prime donne and other fauna that go to make up your magazine, including yourself. You should be grateful to have such a calm, nicely balanced psyche on your payroll as mine is. I had my psychoneurosis many years ago when psychoanalysts were only ten dollars an hour, and I am glad I got in on the ground floor. All that is left of my earlier turbulence is a tricky colon, which itself is largely neurotic, but bothers nobody except me. Now you must tell me how *you* feel some day, Ross.

Love,

Sullivan

June 15, 1948

Dear Ross,

A sign in front of the Church of the Ascension on Fifth Avenue says "Lawn Service Sunday 8 P.M." but another sign, on the lawn, says "Keep off the Grass."

We upstaters come down here and notice such things.

F. J. Sullivan

Saratoga, September 9, 1948

Dear Harold,

I have an ending to something that I might get a beginning for. I had it for some time and then you touched on the subject in a talk recently about those goddamned cigarette machines. There is one up here in a saloon I go to occasionally. It never works. Hasn't worked in a year. They still keep it, to trap unwary customers, but now the barkeep has a stock of cigarettes behind the bar, which he hands out, personally, when the machine fails to come across, after the quarter, formerly two dimes, has been deposited. I like that triumph of the human element. It marks the complete circle and the defeat of the machine age. My ending was that some lucky son of a bitch would come along some night and hit the jackpot. Put a quarter in and by magic get a shower of everything that ever came from a machine—salted peanuts, gum, card telling your fortune and weight, all kinds of cigarettes, somebody's baggage, chocolate bars, nickles from a pay telephone, a free trip to Hwood, an order on a 5th ave tailor for a $250 suit, etc. Then it plays a record, one of those tunes stolen from Chopin or Rachmaninoff.

I dont know whether to do it as the triumph of a man long beaten by machines, or how. I once did a couple of burlesque fairy tales for you, and this might be worked out that way. The guy befriends an old crone and when the king has told him he can have the hand of the princess if he gets a pack of cigarettes out of that machine, why just as he is trying to do that, the old crone comes along, turns into a fairy, no cheap cracks, please, and presto! out pours the jackpot. I will do it, somehow.

I will be down as soon as my tulip bulbs come. I have to plant them before frost comes.

Sincerely,

Havelock Frothingham

A lot of people here during the races asked about you but I cant remember her name.

KATHARINE WHITE

[no date]

Dear Katharine,

Thank you for the kind words about the book, which, as far as I know, is not being bought by anybody in particular.

I told Ross a story but that old wool-gatherer probably will forget it and I thought it an unusual enough kid story to make it worth while. It concerns Ann Kaufman, George and Beatrice's daughter. I am told she is making a Xmas present for her father, a statue of liberty modelled in clay (she's six!) and in the course of a conversation with her mother about the project, she explained: "Of course, in *my* statue, instead of holding up a revolver, she's holding an ash tray."

My God, she's the coming American satirist.

Ever,

Frank

Saratoga, April 17, 1956

Dear Katharine,

I planned to come down this week but I got an idea Sunday that might work out and I want to see if I can do it while the iron, etc. The Herald Tribune on Sunday published a rotogravure section as a benefit for the NY Infirmary (they do it annually) and it comprised photographic ads for various foods, autos, clothes, etc., all modelled for free by Society ladies, the Duchess of Windsor, Mrs. Rhinelander Stewart, Mrs. Henry Ford II, etc. One of them is examining very knowingly a complicated adding machine, another is just back from a housewifely trip to the A & P and Mrs. Henry Ford II is right where any up-and-coming gal would be if she were Mrs. Henry Ford II —in Harry Winston's jewelery palace, picking out tiaras. It all struck me as rather comical and reminded me of a hilarious story I once dug up in the morgue of the Sun when I was writing an obit on Lillian Russell—it was a column and a half of lovely humor about Lillian borrowing a cup of sugar from Marie Dressler for some cooking she was about to do. The two ladies had taken apartments up on 57th Street and were learning to be housewives.

I'm not sure what point to stress because several angles popped up, and one of the most fascinating is the pearl necklace situation. I never realized it before that Society gals wear a uniform but I do now that I've gone into it. They are all photographed in plain black (but I'll bet costly) frocks, and they *all* wear pearl necklaces. I haven't rechecked on it but I went over the rotogravure once and every one of the fifty or sixty women pictured is dolled up in a pearl necklace except Mrs. Charles Amory, and that intrepid rebel will be the heroine of my remarks, I think. Furthermore, what is the protocol that regulates the number of strands of pearls a girl may wear? Most of them wear two or three, and Mrs. John A. Morris wears seven (the record) but Wally Windsor wore only one! Who regulates this? Does a committee of well-dressed women get together at the Colony and make the rules, as the A A U sits down and makes the rules for Wes Santee?⁹ Well, I will get to work instead of asking you questions.

Love,

Frank

Saratoga, Sept. 11, 1956

Dearest Mrs. White,

In a note to me dated August 10 you rashly placed a postscript saying, and I quote, Let me know how you are. So this is to let you know how I am, and maybe it will teach you a lesson never to ask people how they are because, you know, they almost always tell you. I never ask anybody how he is. I follow FPA's practice: I saw him encounter one of the club bores at The Players one time and Frank said, "Hello, Fred, howareyouthat'sfine" and Frank was gone before Fred had a chance to open his trap to tell him how he was. He probably told some other sucker with less agility than Frank.

Well I found, to my astonishment, that I am a good deal of a phony because as soon as I got going to the races every day and playing the horses I got so wrapped up in enjoyment of the same that I forgot all about those ills that flesh is heir to, about which I was moaning to you in late July. I ought not to confess this to you because now I will probably never again get any sympathy out of you or Andy when I feel under the weather. And there is no use, now that I have spilled the beans, in telling you that since the races have left and I am faced with the prospect of getting to work again after a two month layoff, all my symptoms have returned. But do not send flowers or jellies. I made my bed and I will lie on it.

Breathes there a man with soul so dead who wouldn't have had a good time playing the horses last month when all the hilarious things happened to him that happened to me? In the first place I had that bonus and a lot of other assorted checks from the New Yorker, and another unexpected check for doing a piece on Saratoga for Sports Illustrated, so I felt I could go up to the Saratoga track, a three block walk from where I sit at this moment, and kick the old goddess of fortune around a bit. I did, but candor compels me to state that the goddess got in a few licks herself, and is not yet to be flouted with impunity. I will mention a few highlights of my gambling which will illustrate why I spent most of August poring over form sheets.

One day I had lost six straight races and was in a fury with the goddess. That was a day when she was doing the kicking. I was sitting moodily on a bench in the paddock when I suddenly turned to an old racetrack character (he looked like one at least) sitting on the bench, and shouted, "I'M going to bet every god dam long shot in this race, do you hear?" Since the man was a total stranger to me, he looked at me after this outburst in understandable alarm and distaste, thinking probably that the freshman class in some nearby institution for the feeble-minded was having an outing at the track that day and that I was perhaps secretary of the class. But I had to shout something to somebody and he was the goat AND I went in and put four two dollar bets straight on the four longest shots in the race, and one of them won, at twenty to one, and I broke even on the day.

But the greatest triumph of my gambling career, which made everything that came after seem anticlimax was the day I bet on a horse called Turbillonte. I bet a $15 combination on him, which means $5 straight, $5 place and $5 show. It is a conservative bet, frowned on by the daring souls who believe in living dangerously by playing horses only to win. Well, Turbillonte finished fourth and there was a slight ripping sound as wounded horse players throughout the track tore up their tickets on the nag. Just as I was about to follow suit, the Objection sign went up on the tote board, meaning that a foul had been claimed. Not knowing what was in the wind I clutched my ticket in my hot little fist and waited for an agonizing ten minutes and then, lo, the judges disqualified ALL THREE OF THE FIRST HORSES AND PUT TURBILLONTE IN AS WINNER. I assure you there is no more therapeutic feeling in the world than to win a bet like that.

Most of my losses and reverses happened in the final week and I attribute them not to fatigue but to a state of mental distress into which an acquaintance plunged me, perhaps inadvertently. He nearly drove me crazy, to put it bluntly. I saw him at the track one day looking very morose and asked him the question customary among us horseplayers—"How you doing, Jack?" He said, virulently, "I've had a lousy season and you can say that with a capital B." I said "That's too bad" and walked away and I was out in the paddock before the full implication of his remark began to penetrate. "I've had a lousy season and you can say that with a capital B." I began to worry about that capital B and why I should say Jack had a lousy season with a capital B. It threw me completely off, I didn't win another bet that day, and I had to take two sodium amytals that night instead of my customary one.

Now you know how I am and all that remains to be said is that I heard on the radio that Muskie is reelected in Maine, which if it is true is wonderful news indeed.

Love,

Frank

TO SARATOGIANS
AND OTHER FRIENDS

CHARLES BRACKETT

Saratoga, January 6, 1958

Dear Charlie,

Congratulations on the Christopher Award. I was entering eleven o'clock Mass yesterday and met Elizabeth Gorman[1] departing from the ten o'clock one, and she was all steamed up, a week later, about your award and was taking some vicarious credit, as one of your mentors in your formative years—and I know you'd want her to take that vicarious credit. I must say it was no news to me, as I had already awarded you the Christopher thing, and I have awarded you a baker's dozen other prizes, none of which I have yet put a name to, and none of which carry any cash honorarium. All but one of them are of an affectionate nature, designed to shower esteem, regard, appreciation and fondess on you for having been Charlie all these years. The one derogatory medal I may give you will be inscribed something along these lines: "To Charlie Brackett, the rat, for not coming back to Saratoga often enough to chew the fat with sedentary old pals of his like old Sullivan." That is only a rough sketch of the inscription. I will work out the details later. The inscription will be in Latin, of course.

I have not seen Mr. Foye, your pastor at the Presbyterian Church here, since your Christopher Award but he is a Christian charitable man and I do not think he will excommunicate you for having taken this pourboire from the Vatican.

All your friends here thrive and do as well as advancing age and a troubled world permit. Dr. Woolley is just back from an endorsing session before the mikes in New York, endorsing some kind of wine which has never passed his lips, and he got nine grand for doing it. Before that he was in Detroit for a week doing something for the tycoons out there and that netted him five grand, so his current worry is not whether he will have enough to pay for his nightly Martinis at the Gideon Putnam, but how he is going to keep his income tax at a minimum.

Award Muff[2] my love, will you, and award yourself a lot of it, too.

As ever,

Frank

JOHN J. CASSIDY[3]

Saratoga, March 23, 1962

Dear Son,

Professor Kac and Professor Srb came from one and the same issue of the Cornell Alumni News. I doubt if any other Ivy League institution has two faculty members named Kac and Srb, both pronounced Cholmondeley. My preference though is for Mr. Cloud Wampler, chairman of the board. He wamples clouds, I suppose—but I bet *you* couldn't wample a cloud. Nunnally Johnson, past worthy exalted inside guard of the Nomenclature Club, once unearthed an Austrian actress in Hollywood named—if memory serves and it does—Gisella Werbezerg Piffl. That was her name. I would have suspected Johnson added that Piffl just to be playful except that of course he submitted a clipping with her name right there, Piffl and all. Then I remembered that Piffl is a name fairly common in Austria. I once covered an event in New York at St. Patrick's Cathedral when about fifteen Cardinals assembled there, on their way to a Eucharistic Congress in Chicago. It was the most Cardinals ever to gather at one time in St. Pat's and the nave was rife with scarlet. And I recalled the name of the Austrian Cardinal present—Cardinal Piffl.

I suppose I told you long ago about two of the first or charter exhibits of the club—both New York lawyers, and both in the telephone book at that time, and I am sorry to report, both since passed to their reward. One was named Hyacinthe Ringrose and the other Friend Hoar.

Yours,

Cloud

Saratoga, Jan 3/68

Dear John,

I had a couple of charming letters from David and Liz[4] thanking me for the endowment I slipped them at the Yuletide. They both state that they are banking the money, presumably with the intention of going through college on the accumulated interest when the time comes. If they were to take my advice they would spend it immediately and as foolishly as possible. I like to get letters from kids. They are simple and direct and come right to the point. David ended his note with a sentence that seemed to me to be the model of courtesy. "Thank you for reading my letter." Well, thank you David for writing it. I had a letter from Ogden Nash and he included quotes from two letters he had recently from kids. One wrote "My Mom and my teacher say you are dead but I am writing to you anyway." The other: "My teacher has told me to write a term paper on your works. Please send me your works right away." See what I mean by simple and direct?

Now that the Christmas frenzy is over (and it nearly did me in this year) I have had time to dip into the Lure of the Limerick, and many thanks for it. I wondered about the name of the compiler—Baring-Gould. There was a parson in England years ago named Baring-Gould, known to fame as the author of Onward Christian Soldiers. If the current Baring-Gould of the Limericks is a scion of the old dominie then all I can say is that the Baring-Goulds have come a long way since Onward Christian Soldiers. The latter-day B-G has got 'em all in. And he has taken advantage of public domain to use some titillating illustrations by Aubrey Beardsley, proving that the limeys of the gay Nineties knew what a phallus was just as well as Freud did. Beardsley draws them with loving care; I seem to have read that he was partial to his own sex. Further that he became a Catholic when stricken by TB and destroyed all his fancy drawings before his death. Well, he didn't quite get them all; Baring-Gould has dug up a few. It is an entertaining book. I am learning some of the more plain-spoken ones by heart and would be the life of the party around here, if there were any parties.

Yours,

FS

DONALD M. GOODFELLOW[5]

(Goodfellow asked Sullivan to send a letter to be read at a banquet for Henry K. Kirkpatrick, a retiring colleague who had been Sullivan's classmate at Cornell in 1914.)

Saratoga, May, 1959

I have known Kirk man and boy these sixty-six years. Kirk was the man, I was the boy, and the sixty-six years are mine.

Kirk himself must be about a hundred now but the last time I saw him he was awfully well preserved. When I was a little boy in kindergarten Kirk used to take me by the hand and lead me to school, across the dangerous street crossings. The traffic was awful in Saratoga in those days. Fully every half hour a horse and buggy would drive along, menacing life and limb. When the older boys picked on me, Kirk would fight my battles, which he usually lost, but I will always be grateful to him for protecting me.

I haven't got the exact dates at hand because my memory is not what it was before I started drawing Social Security but I finally caught up with Kirk in some way and became the same age as himself. I imagine this was because Kirk stayed in high school fifteen or twenty years. The faculty loved him and were loath to part with him. With me it was different. Each June a teacher heaved a sigh of relief and sent me skimming along to the next grade, and first thing I knew there I was, same age as Kirk. Now it is my turn to take him by the hand and lead him to high school, across the dangerous horse and buggy traffic.

Kirk and I went to Cornell and he held my hand all through those four years, too. He also helped me up those Ithaca hills to the campus on many a midnight after we had been downtown helping celebrate a Cornell football victory. Or did I help him up? These details become so misty as the years go by.

As a result of our incredible carelessness in not having been born the sons of John D. Rockefeller or some other millionaire, Kirk and I had to work our way through Cornell. We worked in the Cascadilla Hall, a student dining commons. They put me to washing dishes and I washed several millions of them before getting my degree of pearl diver summa cum laude. Kirk had something to do with cooking and after we graduated he went to India. He said it was to teach English to a young Indian named Nehru but there was a rumor around that he chose India because it seemed a safe, far-off refuge from a posse of young Cornell grads who had experienced his cooking at Cascadilla Hall and were out looking for him, armed with a long rope.

Kirk was always a kind-hearted boy and full of fun and pranks. I remember how the police in Saratoga laughed the time he broke into the local bank and took ten thousand dollars. "That Kirk!" the cops chuckled. "He'll sure be the death of us yet." Then there was the time in 1914 that he shot the Archduke in Serajevo and started a war. We who knew Kirk knew that he bore the Archduke no ill will, and that he had just shot him on impulse. His years at Carnegie Tech have had a calming influence on Kirk and I really do not believe he would shoot an Archduke now, except in self-defense.

Kirk will deny all these facts I have stated but please pay no attention to anything he says on this momentous occasion. He is only the guest of honor and he has no rights or privileges. Just bury him under laurels and love and tell him to keep quiet. I can't wait to see Kirk in the long white beard of the emeritus professor. All I can say is that Carnegie Tech's loss will, I do hope, be the gain of those of us who love Kirk and will now have a chance to see more of him and Agnes in the years that lie ahead—years that I hope will be full of contentment and serenity and pleasure for them both.

Frank Sullivan

TRUDY HEMSTEAD[6]

Saratoga, May 10, 1966

My dear Trudy,

I did not, as you state in your quaint Altmanese, "rat out" on the Hemstead Easter orgy. I laid off of it a-purpose because I suspected you were going to eat dinner at some ungodly hour like two in the afternoon. As it turned out I was right, or so near right that I claim a near-miss. Furthermore, as Exhibit A in my evidence I adduce the fact (learned from my spies who are everywhere) that you personally fell asleep immediately after that dinner and woke up stupefied by food just in time to catch the night train to Altmans. I have given up eating anyhow. It is a pagan custom, and expensive. I admit I shoot out to Old Lady Heslin's every time she invites me to have sausage and pancakes en famille, if that is the phrase, and I charge into those delicacies full speed. The old gal makes a wicked pancake. I call her Aunt Jemima and am going to ask her to make her pancakes in blackface in the future. I can easily out-pancake-eat my aged classmate, Famed Urologist Heslin.

Do not feel guilty about not travelling with Cornell men. They are not the breed of which their ancestors (me) were made. Haven't got the verve. Which Ginsberg does your Lincoln School date teach? The son of the so-called poet with the heavy growth of hair and beard who looks like an identical twin of Krao, the Bearded Lady in the Ringling Circus forty years ago, who was— no kidding—a friend of mine.

I was also a friend of Martha the Armless Wonder and have a photo of her somewhere, autographed with her toes. When I was on the New York Sun several light years ago I haunted the circus press room when it came to Madison Square Garden and could never get enough circus. I got to know nearly all of the clowns, a good many of the elephants (very dear people those elephants) and most of the freaks including Zip the Original What-Is-It who was just a plain friendly old colored man with a head shaped like a cone. And for God for country for Yale and for the dear old Sun, I disrobed one night, was dyed a chocolate color like Othello from head to foot and went on in the sideshow as Amok the Igorote Head Hunter (who was a friendly Filipino lad trying to make enough money to go to law school back in Manila; I hope he is the Chief Justice there now). I was a wow, too, as Amok until some drunken newspaper friends came in and threw ice cubes at my bare skin, which not only caused me to shiver unduly but wherever they hit my epidermis they washed the dye off and left a white spot and there were cries of "Fake" from the customers. I was hastily retired. How did I get on this circus kick? Well, if you don't believe I actually went on in that freak show I have a scrapbook right here to prove it.

My godson's sister, Miss Crouse, went up to Cornell last fall to case the joint, fell in love with it, and had me writing letters by the barrel to get her in. Well, I wrote *one*. Then when Cornell accepted her she exercised a Woman's Privilege and opted for Radcliffe. I suspect she did it because her brother Tim will be a junior at Harvard next fall and is a member of the Crimson staff and all those things and can get her a lot of dates. She is a very dateable lass. But I have warned her that all Radcliffe girls are expected to picket something for two hours every day—Get Out Of Vietnam, Justice for Alabama Whites, Equal Rights for Wearers of Tight Pants, More Pay For Homosexuals or Tear Down President Pusey. I confidently expect to hear some day next fall that she is in the hoosegow for bopping a Cambridge cop with her placard. I am glad you are an old woman and not apt to picket anything.

Peace!

Father Time

DOCTOR AND MRS. JOHN HESLIN

Saratoga, Feb. 18, 1956

Honored Pals,

It is a fine snowy day here and everybody feels fine, especially kids reaping a golden harvest by shovelling sidewalks. It just cost me $1.30 to get mine shovelled. the asking price was 1.00 but big-hearted plutocrat that i am, I gave them a bonus of thirty cents. *You* are probably panting with the heat, bothered by flies and mosquitoes, and overcome by the peculiar smell of the West

Indies which they tell me is not unlike that of the village dump here. But I told you not to go.

i had a magnificent time at the Guvs that night, and it was magnificent because it was so plain and friendly and just like walking into *your* house for an evening of fun and frolic. wonderful people, those two, in my opinion. i went down and came back the same evening, on the midnight (that is I came back on the midnight). the eats were of the best, wild rice and something, and rare vintages calculated to stir the pulse of even an old poop like me were circulated freely by well-trained and agreeable butlers. and I dont know why but i shared the place of honor with the FRENCH AMBASSADOR TO THE UNITED NATIONS, if you please; he at Marie's right (there would be war with France if he hadn't been placed at her right) and i on her left, and a small wire-haired dachshund sitting on the floor between Marie and me. there were two young couples there, the men are in some posts on the Guv's staff, a mr and mrs Bingham and a mr and mrs Kaiser, all *tres agreable;* and there were some old pals of mine, George Backer and Dick and Dorothy Rodgers. No nonsense about dressing up at all and no formality at all. the wire haired dachshund gave me an occasional look as if to say Here's a guy that maybe cannot be trusted with the gubernatorial silverware, but on the whole he seemed well disposed toward me, and I really did not come away with any loot except a couple of match covers with "executive mansion" on them, which I brought away in order to impress virulent Republicans up here and make them envious, and sorry they never became Democrats. This goes for you, too. after dinner, dick rodgers sat down at the piano and played things from his scores for an hour, to the delight of one and all. I was the only one remembered an early Rodgers opus, done with Larry Hart in their early days, called Peggy Ann, and it seemed to please Dick that somebody remembered that old one, as well as South Pacific, etc. and believe it or not the French ambassador did imitations, which were hilariously funny. Nobody asked me to do anything as nobody thought I had any parlor tricks except the one where I sit on my hind legs and bark when offered a scotch and soda, but I fooled them. I volunteered to do my act. I had to suggest that they all keep quiet while I played the overture to william Tell on my cheeks with sound effects, because they thought I was not able to do anything like that, but the commotion and furor that resulted when I did play the overture—on my cheeks—was certainly rewarding, and even the Governor seemed a changed man for several minutes, and as for the Governor's Lady, she nearly fell off the chair laughing. Haven't I ever done that trick for you? Well, if I haven't, I will do it for you as soon as you get back, and will continue doing it for you all summer long, until you have to hire a sentinel to keep guard at lake lonely and warn you of my approach, so that you can all run for the cyclone cellar.

I came back on the midnight and what do you know—those two grand people called me the next day TO MAKE SURE I GOT HOME ALL RIGHT. Now I ask you—the Governor of the State and Lady worrying about whether *I* got home all right! If that sort of thing keeps up there is not going to be any standing me.

I wish I had as an endowment what those paintings Marie Harriman has hung in the mansion, are worth. You've seen them. They belong to her and Averell and I'll bet they are worth a million. There are also several fine old paintings lent to the Mansion by the Metropolitan Museum of Art. I couldn't get away with any as the dachshund had his eye on me.

Oh to be in April now that the Heslins are in Jamaica. Come back soon.

Your loving pastor,

Frank

New York, May 3, '59

My dears,

I thought you might be interested to know that altho I have been here only 2 days I am practically the Toast of the Town. The first thing I did was to start crossing Fifth Avenue at 42nd Street against the light Sat. and nearly got pinched as a jay walker. Gracious sakes, I've been dodging taxis against the lights here for 40 years and I didn't know the law had got so stuffy about that. A cop halted me in midstream while a hundred NYorkers laughed heartily and the cop called me "Mac" and asked if I could not read that there sign. Well, there *was* a sign that said "Don't Walk" but I didn't have my glasses on, and couldn't have seen it if I did, as I only wear reading glasses. So I told him I didn't know about the new rules as I was from out of town, so he said, "Well, you know now. Go ahead, Mac." (The sign now said "WALK.")

Let this be a lesson to you.

I wished he had pinched me. I might of got a piece for the NYorker out of it and I would have split it 50–50 with the cop.

Love,

F.

This afternoon I went to see young Holbrook[7] do his one man show on Mark Twain and it is the most wonderful thing I have seen in the theatre in years. But I love old Mark and maybe that's why I loved it. The boy is marvelous. I wish you would see it. Didn't I bring this letter to a close some yards north of here?

Compliments of a Foe

CLARENCE KNAPP[8]

(*Knapp was aide to the New York secretary of state when this letter was written and one of his duties was to edit the annual* Legislative Manual.)

Saratoga, August 22, 1933

Hon. Clarence Knapp,
State Capitol,
Albany.

My dear Mr. Knapp,

May I express my sincere gratitude to you for sending me the lovely copy of your new book, the Legislative Manual of 1933? It is delightful, and quite surpasses anything you have given us in the past, except possibly "Lady Chatterley's Lover." Of course I have long been a fan of yours and when I heard you were dropping light fiction to try your hand at this more ambitious form I was not among the few who felt and predicted that you were getting in too deep waters; I was among the few who predicted that you would achieve a *succés fou.* And I am delighted to tell you that although the Manual arrived only ten minutes ago, I have read it from cover to cover (skipping in between) and find that it fully justifies every statement made by those who have hailed you as the leader of the new surrealist movement in American literature. It is a new Knapp we find in this tome, a Knapp who (except in the chapter on Sex) occupies himself with the higher, sublimer things of Life. For brevity and wit I think your list of the State's Governors is unsurpassed since Twain's Jumping Frog of Calaveras County and in the Declaration of Independence you have written a document that has dignity and force, and is a ringing challenge that will find many an echo in these colonies, for, as you very aptly point out, "all men are created equal," and it is high time somebody said that to George III. Your "Constitution of the United States" equals anything I have read of Wodehouse, or Sarah Orne Jewett, and in your magnificent table of contents I for one believe you have successfully challenged the supremacy of Gertrude Stein. There is so much depravity in literature today that it is a relief to find in your Manual a book I can send to a friend convalescing in the hospital, or let my little sister of fifty-two read, safely. I do hope you will give us many more of these charming tomes, Mr. Knapp, and in conclusion allow me to hail you as the William Dean Howells of 1933. I may call you "William Dean Howells," may I not? You can call me "Rex Beach" or "Sweetheart."

Yours sincerely,

F Sullivan

P.S. A friend of mine, a bookseller, wonders if, as an advertising stunt, you would stand in his show window, naked, some day at high noon, signing copies of the Manual.

DOCTOR ALVAN BARACH

Saratoga, Dec 7 [no year]

Dear Al,

Congratulations on the award from the Inhalation Therapists. I learned about it when my old high school classmate, Dr. John Heslin, sent me the clip from the AMA Journal. John has heard me speak of you often. He recently got an honor himself; he was elected president of the American Urological Society. I may sue John for slander. I was in Albany Hospital for ten days to get rid of a painful attack of our old friend, diverticulitis. One night

John came into my room and said, "I just had a look at your chart and I think there's one mistake on it." I was all ears at this and said What. John said, "They've got you down for a negative Wasserman test; that can't be true." All I could think of to say was, Is that so. But I felt complimented that the Albany Hospital thought it worth while to take a Wasserman of my celibate blood. You will recall Dotty Parker's poem: "I'd rather flunk my Wasserman test / Than read a poem by Edgar Guest."

I hope to get down after Christmas and see some old friends and some shows, in the order named; and Frederica and you are high on the list, if you are in town.

Ever yours,

Frank

MARISE CAMPBELL

THE DELAWARE & HUDSON COMPANY

Ticket Office, Saratoga Springs, N.Y.
October 25, 1932

Dear Madam,

We feel sure that you, as a big holder of railroad stock, will be interested in the coup which the Delaware & Hudson Company has just accomplished, in the face of the keenest competition from other railroads.

WE HAVE SECURED MR. FRANK SULLIVAN AS A PASSENGER ON OUR CRACK TRAIN, THE LAURENTIAN, TOMORROW, WEDNESDAY, OCTOBER 26! ! !

We feel justly proud that the noted numismatist has chosen to take his annual autumn hegira to the metropolis via the Delaware & Hudson. It is a tribute to the Service which has been a watchword of our system since the memorable day when Commodore Vanderbilt said "The customer is ALWAYS right." It is especially a tribute in view of the fact that Mr. Sullivan chose OUR road in spite of MANY FLATTERING OFFERS TO TRAVEL TO NEW YORK VIA OTHER ROADS.

It is our understanding that the Chicago, Milwaukee and St. Paul company wanted Mr. Sullivan to make the trip via Montreal, Manitoba, Fond du Lac, Chicago, and Weehawken. It is no secret in railroad circles that for some months the Southern Pacific has been attempting to jockey a deal whereby the Beloved Vagabond would make the trip from Saratoga by way of Sacramento, Santa Fe, New Orleans and Chattanooga. The Atchison, Topeka & Santa Fe road was only estopped from shanghaiing the noted pyromaniac by a sharp reprimand from the Interstate Commerce Commission that such practices would not be tolerated.

Mr. Sullivan also had an attractive offer from a dog sled company in Saskatchewan. Nor was the competition confined to overland routes. We understand the Italian American Line solicited the permission of the Great Lover to transport him to New York via Saratoga Lake, Fish Creek, the Hudson River, Lake Champlain, the St. Lawrence, Newfoundland Bay, the Cape Cod ship canal and the Atlantic Ocean on their new cracked ship, the Rex.

In the face of these offers the famous dendrologist chose our road to travel on and although we are naturally elated we can readily understand his choice, for the Delaware & Hudson is and has been THE RAILROAD OF THE PEOPLE, BY THE PEOPLE AND FOR THE PEOPLE—and the Laurentian is its *crack* train—all Pullman, club car, private bedrooms, maid service, all steel modern equipment, elevators, no extra fare, delightful comfortable ride along the Hudson and through the charming Adirondack region. Montreal is just a good night's sleep away from Manhattan on this superbly appointed non-stop train. Leaves Montreal daily at 10 a.m. Arrives New York 8 p.m.

Sincerely yours,

F. Sullivan
GENERAL PASSENGER AGENT

January 27, 1934

Dear M,

I suppose by the time you get this, Sistie Dahl[9] will be President, I will belong to the Ages and you will be a gentle old lady with white hair, sitting in your armchair. I am hereby notifying you that I am being true to my vow, and that New Yorkers are being sent you regularly, strictly according to the address instructions you left. So if you fail to get them, blame the postal services of one or the other of the ninety-three countries you are bounding over.

The diversion of the week has been reading about the doings on Welfare Island. The new commissioner of prisons raided it suddenly last week and found two hundred pansies all dressed in girl's clothes, mascaraed and rouged. They all had adopted names like "Lillian Gish" "Marilyn Miller" etc., and when the cops came into their wing of the prison, they all said, "Whoops, look at the lovely cops" and made a rush at them, and the cops, blushing furiously, ran like the very devil. It's funnier, when you read the details in the tabloids.

Dotty Parker is installed in her new apartment, 444 East 52, and called me up the first morning after arriving to ask me what you did with garbage. She had called Mr. Benchley, who was not very helpful. He told her to put it in the bed and cover it up with a sheet. I brought her a hausegeschenk that afternoon, a little box filled with orange rinds, tea leaves and lamb chop bones. She hates the place. Somebody asked her how far east she lived on 52nd Street and she said "Far enough east to plant TEA!"

I will write you a longer budget later but Mr. Hearst is crying for copy at my door, and I must feed him. Have a good time, and mind what I say, the New Yorkers are being sent you, so don't think Sullivan is not a man of his word.

Here is a timely hint for you, as a globe trotter—when you

enter a Japanese house, you remove your shoes. When you enter a house in Corsica, you remove your corsicets.

Love,

Frank

saratoga ny august 23 1943

[Mrs. Campbell had gone overseas with the Red Cross.]

dearest marituch,

i heard an awfully good trade last for the red cross while in new york. seems there was an old lady decided she would knit something for the boys, and she picked out the boys in alaska as her pets, and decided that the most practical thing she could knit for a boy in alaska was a pair of good warm drawers. so she did knit it, but alas she didnt purl at the right place, if purl is the word, with the result that she left no orifice at the front, where, if you know your anatomy, an orifice ought to be in a male garment designed for below the belt. she took it to the red cross, the lady inspector examined it and was quite enthusiastic over the quality of the knitting until she observed the fatal flaw, and at that she blushed prettily, hemmed and hawed a bit and told the old lady that in closing up the front she had so seriously wronged the architecture of the garment that a man could not wear it for long without serious embarrassment. the old lady was depressed for a second but then found a solution and brightened up. "well, couldn't you give it to a bachelor," she suggested.

i hope your bosses in the red cross do not read your mail before you do. i would not like to feel that i had been the occasion of your being paraded before the regiment and stripped of your insignia and drummed off the field, because of a slightly obscene story i had sent you.

in telling you the following personal experience i do not want to discourage you from being kind to soldiers. but one hot night here a month ago an extremely travel-stained and tired soldier came to me on broadway and asked me if there was a YMCA in town where he could shower and shave; he had travelled two days and had a two-hour wait for a train into the adirondacks. there was no YMCA, there is no USO here and so i took the lad into the worden with the intention of hiring him a room for an hour for his toilette. well, the worden gave him the room and wouldnt take any dough, but anyhow, after he had gone upstairs, i put some dinner money in an envelope and left it with the clerk, with no name attached, as he looked hungry. that was all for the time being; i did not see him when he came down and was handed the money, but mrs. jewett the clerk must have peached my name, because t'other day i got a letter from him, thanking me very much for having given him that money and wondering, since i had been so generous, would i do something else. would i take a train, go up to a place in the adirondacks where an aunt of his lived, and fix things up so that a bank would not foreclose on the mortgage on her farm. he signed the letter "Yours in Christ." well, i got dinner money for a buddy once in a while, but i aint got enough to pay off aunts' mortgages.

keep well, and write if you can spare a moment.

yours always,

Frank (Sullivan)

Saratoga, December 22, 1947

Dear Marise,

Your Christmas card received and contents noted. Thank you. I *will* have a Merry Christmas, or know the reason why, and you will oblige me by having one hell of a Merry one, too. I trimmed a tree for this house yesterday and it is a brilliant and shimmering apparition of delight, resplendent in three dozen new ornaments from Czechoslovakia which I bought in New

York last month. I bought the ornaments, that is. Czechoslovakia I cannot afford.

Kate has wrapped up eighty-two Christmas gifts for regional children and now as she was about to place them under the Tree, cannot remember which goes to which, and is judging which is which and whose is whose by general feel, appearance and weight. I predict that the intensely virile Mike Burke, age eight and scornful of the female sex, will get a perfumed scarf intended for Miss Louise Schrade, aged eleven; while Miss Carol Porter, a redhead of ten, will get a football or a baby rattle, the latter intended for Mr. Joe King, age four months.

Crouse is delightful in his new metamorphosis and as happy as, I suppose, it is given to us here below to be. I needn't tell you how felicitously life has turned out for him. My godson, Tim Crouse, is so like Crouse in looks that when Kate first saw the baby's picture, she announced, in a stern, almost belligerent tone, "Russel can never deny THAT child!" Can't you picture Crouse being stopped just as he is about to rush into the streets and cry "I deny that child!" You may know that he will have a chance next spring not to deny another Crouse, who Anna and he hope will be a little Miss Crouse. They are in their new home, which is lovely.

Of your other old friends I have seen only Professor Connelly, whom I told about his cousin. I had just read in the Trib that the muezzin who calls the Moslem faithful to prayer in a mosque in Port Elizabeth, South Africa, is an Irishman name of Connelly. I was sure he must be a cousin of Marc.

Mr. Michael King, age four, has arrived, for the seventh time today, on a double mission. He wishes to see the Christmas tree illuminated, and also would not spurn a homemade sugar cookie, if pressed sufficiently. I have to go down and crawl under the Tree and turn on the lights. Kate cannot bend any more, and matter of fact, I don't bend so easy myself as I used to when I scored those triumphs of acrobatic charades at your house on 66th Street, the year of the Beecher-Tilton scandal. For instance, if you were to drop the lower fifteen pounds of a million dollar stomacher at a night club today, I couldn't possibly get under the table to pick it up. Love and a Merry Christmas to you. The Merry Christmas is for this year; the Love is permanent, and use it, as there is plenty more for you where it came from.

As I said before, Love

Frank

Saratoga, May 8, 1955

Dear Marise,

It occurred to me that a simple direction might save you inquiring about my hovel next Friday. I assume you will be coming up Route 9 from Albany way. As you get to the outskirts of Saratoga you'll spot the Spa and some white bathhouses on your left. A little farther on, off to your right, you will see a cemetery, placed there to remind the entering visitor that Saratoga is a health resort. On both sides of you, you will see a congeries of filling stations, diners, ice cream booths and other eyesores placed there to remind the visitor that Saratoga is right up to the minute and modern, and not to be outdone by any city in the country in the ugliness of its approaches. Now slow down, because the traffic light you hit after you pass the filling stations is at the intersection of Broadway and Lincoln Avenue, and all you have to do is turn to your right at that light, and bowl up Lincoln Avenue until you come to 135.

This will save you going on into town and making inquiries of the local police, who have a dossier on me. I have not lived in vain: last winter one Saturday Madeline and Bob Sherwood and George Backer were spending a weekend with Marie and Averell Harriman at the Executive Mansion and somebody had the idea to invite me down for dinner. They had some trouble finding me by telephone, because my telephone is in Kate's name, and the only other Frank Sullivan in town is a farmer who raises pigs, and wishes I lived someplace else, as he is constantly being routed out at 3 a.m. by convivial visitors with a yen to talk to me. On the other hand, I wish Frank would move out of town as we patronize the same doctor and on several occasions I have narrowly escaped being treated for his ailment, which, I hear, is much more serious than anything I have. Anyhow, whoever the telephone operator at the Executive Mansion appealed to up here in trying to locate me, it was someone who knew my habits. George Backer was informed that I could be reached at the Colonial Tavern or the Worden Bar and Grill, choice of one. As a matter of fact I was home.

It will be grand to see you again and I think we'll dine at the Worden Bar and Grill.

Ever,

Frank

MARGARET FELDMAN

New York, Sunday, March 22, 1942

Dear Peg,

I came down here a week ago and have felt mentally low ever since. War, I guess, and general hysteria. I had with me for two days a young fellow, an ensign, on leave, who has been in Iceland for 6 months, and who about a month ago set out on an expedition from his ship, in a launching with a dozen men— and two came back, himself and a seaman. The ensign is a kid from Schenectady, a big good-natured lad with the build of an ox, the heart of a lion and the temper of an angel. After I saw him to the door of The Players as he was leaving to go back to his ship—they were due to leave for sea—I had a lump in my throat and smoke in my eyes. I felt humble and unnecessary alongside of him, and he is only one of a great many. I hope these kids will have a better world to live in as a result of what they are sacrificing, than my generation was able to construct. There are a great many of them around this club, coming and going constantly.

I am going to stay down here until April 27, then go to Saratoga and register for the senile dementia draft on that day, and then I guess I'll stay in Saratoga.

Yours,

FS

ANNE FORD[10]

Saratoga, March 2, 1954

Dear Miss Mifflin,

Aware that you are perishing to know what I have been up to, I will not keep you in suspense. The answer is Nothing. I sat out the winter here in comfort and peace, reading, working, movie-going and polishing up just the right number of Scotches at downtown taverns to keep my metabolism in good spirits, although I may fling caution to the winds come St. Patrick's Day when I plan to attend the annual dinner, with wine and black tie, of the Friendly Sons of St. Patrick, of whom I am one of the friendliest.

One day I went to confession at the Redemptorist church here (St. Clement's) and afterward while waiting for a pal who was to give me a lift home, I got into conversation with a fine broth of a boy from Boston. He asked my name, I came clean with it, and he said he had read my stuff. Then he said very confidentially, "Tell me, Frank, did you ever get that marriage of yours straightened out?" I did a double take and recovering my composure said I was a bachelor. He said, "Oh, come off it, now. You can talk to me. I know you married outside the Church, and who knows, if it hasn't been fixed up, I might be able to help with advice." I assured him I had never married and was a pronounced bachelor and that I wouldn't be telling him fibs ten minutes after going to confession. I always wait until two days afterward before I start telling fibs again. We parted the best of friends, although I got the impression that he was still unconvinced and thought I was just being contrary in not admitting things. The story has made life brighter for the friends I have told it to and I thought it might amuse you in moderation, without causing you to turn handsprings up and down Boston Commons past the statue of Ralph Waldo Longfellow. Incidentally, the consensus is that the Father got me mixed up with *Ed* Sullivan who, somebody said, had some such difficulties. That is my penance in life. I am always being taken for either Ed Sullivan, or Mark, who is dead. For all I know a lot of people may think I am Maxine.[11]

Yours,

Liberace.

PS—Kate gets downstairs in the morning before I do, sees the papers and when I come down, gives me a brief sketch of the chief news. This morning when I showed up, she said, "Well, they nearly had an accident in Washington." How many Congressmen do you have to shoot before it qualifies as a real accident?

ANN HONEYCUTT[12]

Saratoga, March 29 [no year]

Dear Ann:

Welcome home, sister, always provided that you didn't take
one look at NY, get one sniff of the weather, and turn right
around and fly back to equatorial regions. They say it is Easter
and also Spring but they're not going to trap me into taking off
my chest protector and my heavy underpants. In fact, I'm not
going out until I get word that it is 80.

I am glad to hear you have decided to become a freelance
sister. I always suspected there was a kernel of virtue underneath
that raffish, devil-may-care Sadie Thompson crust of yours. I may
be able to help you in this matter. During August in the past
seasons two sisters always sat at the clubhouse gate as the crowds
thronged into the track and welcomed any coins bighearted
gamblers chose to bestow. I imagine they had a pretty good thing
of it, too, because my researches prove that ninety-two per cent of
two-dollar bettors, including myself, are Catholic, and of that 92
per cent probably 84 per cent took those black-garbed figures as
Catholic nuns, and thought that a little donation might bring a
blessing on the form and bring home a nice daily double. It took
some years before the cops and Pinkertons got wise to the fact
that the ladies were not nuns of any denomination but just hard-
headed business girls who thought that nun's garb would be a
good prop to help bring in the shekels, and they were right. They
got the bum's rush couple years ago, but I was thinking that if
you were to become a bona fide freelance nun I might wield some
slight influence I have, and get you the franchise to sit at the
clubhouse gate every August afternoon from 12 m to 2:30 P m,
with your tambourine and appealing smile. I would expect only

ten per cent of the take, and if anybody questioned you about this you could say the ten per cent went to a deserving orphan, and you would not be perjuring yourself, for I am a deserving orphan if there ever was one. Oh, and you would have to black up. Those other sisters that got the bum's rush were rather chocolate colored and we would not want to break with tradition, would we?

I hope you had a good time at Key Largo.

Things are looking up for this battered old burg because the legislature passed the measure that will make sure Belmont is rebuilt and also Saratoga. This track has scarcely had more than a coat of paint since old William C. Whitney built it in 1901. And neither have I. Instead of frittering away the public's time and money the legislature might well have also appropriated money to rebuild me. I could be restored and would be a very interesting landmark for tourists to visit. All I need is a new body. My soul is like Little Eva's.

Your loving friend,

F J Sullivan

Saratoga, December 23, 1959

Dear Anna,

Confidentially, I don't mind wishing you a Merry Christmas but don't tell the hucksters I did. In me you see a disgruntled curmudgeon beside whom Scrooge would appear as one of the Cheeryble Brothers. I have been reduced to this state by the devastation wrought on a grand old feast day by the television, the radio, and Madison Avenue, and by the newspapers, too. I go downstairs these mornings to make my coffee and turn on the radio—or I did; I've declared a moratorium until December 26—and I get the lovely old Christmas carols and THEN a glib, bored announcer gets in his commercial barking at me to run right out and buy a lot of stuff and then he wishes everybody a Merry Christmas in a bored, phony voice. I say to you, Anna J. Honeycutt, that Cromwell and the Puritans, in the days when they made it a penal offense in England to celebrate Christmas, never wrought the havoc on the old festival that the cheapness and tawdriness of today's commercialization has done.

Many thanks for your invitation to come to New York in 1960. I accept gladly and will be pleased to be your guest from about February until next November. With August off, of course, to come up here. You will find me an easy guest to please. Breakfast in bed, and I like to be awakened to the sound of pleasant music, and suggest you have the Budapest String Quartet or E. Power Biggs come every morning to play soft music. If you have no organ for E. Power Biggs to play, why I believe one could be installed for a reasonable figure, such as $30,000. I will need a bedroom, sitting room and bath for myself, and a bedroom and bath for my manservant. He likes to be wakened by soft music too. In the cooking line, don't fuss, for Heaven's sake—just some ortolans, or lark's wings, and of course caviar and Montrachet with each meal, and I like a pony or two of Napoleon brandy with my coffee. I will let you know other little things as they occur but above all, don't go to any bother about little old me. I refer of course to your old pal, signature below, as follows:

F. Sullivan

Saratoga, June 13, 1967

[*Dorothy Parker had just died in New York.*]

Dear Miss H'cutt,

I could write you so much about Dotty that I don't dare get started. Jim Cagney telephoned today from Milbrook in a mild state of shock about her death. He said he just wanted to make sure I was here, as a link with former and happier days. Well, it threw me into pensive shock too. Her departure is as much the end of an era for me (and you) as the departure of the bulk of the NY papers. She was a *strong* person, Honey. And you said it, what you wrote: she was at war with herself all her life. Maybe most of us are and some negotiate cease fires occasionally, which seldom last. All the digs she took at people, friend and foe alike, were really digs at herself. And I don't need to tell you that her wallops were almost inevitable for anyone who at any time gave her a helping hand. I never gave her a helping hand, having nothing to offer her in that line, so as far as I know she never lambasted me. On the contrary I am going to remember her not for the wisecracks but for what she did at the outset of our friendship (because I did count myself as her friend). In 1925 FPA married Esther Root and they took off for Europe on a 2 month honeymoon. Swope pushed me into the job of doing the Conning Tower while FPA was away. It nearly wrecked me. You know what a pair of shoes *that* was to fill. I had a hell of a time filling that column. Dotty heard about it at Swope's or Tony Soma's or somewhere, or with her intuition sensed it from reading my flounderings, and by God one day two poems arrived from her! I still remember the note she sent with them: "If you can't use these, give them to some poor family." *That's* what she did for me, some forty years ago.

I'm surprised she made it to 73, remembering her suicide attempts back in the Twenties. I recall one time when she took sleeping pills while staying at the Algonquin (it was unrequited love), and the maid found her, and Dr. Al Barach sped her to Harkness Pavilion and pumped her out. Benchley was away and when she could have visitors, Al told me she wanted to see me, so I clipped up to Harkness. There she was, the insides of her arms black and blue from the saline injections they had pumped into her, but putting up a brave front. Well, I mustn't go into these things or I'll be keeping you up.

If there is any meaning to anything, she is now having the

good time she seldom had while here, and I hope she is having it with Mr. Benchley (her name for him always).

Anon, anon

Dr. Sullivan

JOAN IAMS[13]

Saratoga, Nov., 1962

Dear Joan,

It is not easy for me to start the mornings these days even when the news is good but this morning when I made my coffee and settled down to it, and then the front page of the Herald Tribune hit me, it pretty well shattered me. Stanley was one of the first friends I made in New York. I went to the Herald in January of 1919 and he came on from Texas later that year. In that last year of its existence the Herald took on only three new men as reporters, and the third was Cornelius Vanderbilt Jr. When Vanderbilt covered his first assignment, the other papers sent reporters along to cover Vanderbilt covering his first assignment. Along with others, S. Walker got much amusement from the career of our swanky colleague.

I was in on his courtship of dear Tot and blew a part of my weekly salary of $35 to give them a bridal dinner for three at the Brevoort. Later, I recall, we three wound up at one of the earlier night clubs somewhere in the Forties, where Gilda Gray was doing the shimmy. That part of the evening was on the house as Stanley and I both knew the press agent and he picked up the check. I hope you will not think of this as sentimental outpouring, though in fact I suppose it is. I have felt all day I wanted to talk to someone about Stanley, and I hope you won't mind being elected. After all, who else?

No editor I ever knew had such complete loyalty from his staff. I will always count it as one of the finest compliments I ever had, that when the World was sold in 1931 Stanley, abetted by Geoffrey Parsons,[14] tried to get me on the Herald Tribune. Stanley told me later the efforts of himself and Geoffrey were balked by one of the HT brass named Holcomb, who recalled that I had hoaxed the town during the 1924 Democratic convention by inventing an old lady, a long time Democrat aged 102 (or thereabouts) named Aunt Sarah Gallop, who had saved her butter and egg money to come to the convention to root for Al Smith. I had her a native of an Adirondack town called Holcomb Landing, there being no such town. But maybe that Holcomb Landing was what stuck in Holcomb's crop. Anyhow I never got to work with Stanley again. He and I agreed I was no great shakes as a reporter, but I could invent things and Stanley thought he could use me or he wouldn't have tried to add me to his staff.

Yours faithfully,

Frank Sullivan

JACK[15] AND JOAN IAMS

(Jack Iams' given name was Samuel.)

Saratoga, March 30, 1966

Dear Joan and Jack,

And how did "Samuel" get into this act? There it was, on your announcement, and since that looked like an official announcement I accepted it that way and used it that way. You ought not to confuse an old man with these subterfuges—going 3,000 miles away and then getting married and then in addition marrying a Jack who is a Samuel. I have a hard time remembering names nowadays, which I presume is the beginning of senility, and I can't even remember the names of old friends. I'm getting like Alison Smith (Lord rest her soul) when she first married Russel Crouse away back in the early 1920s when all the world was young. Alison was young too at the time but very bad at remembering names and after all she didn't know Crouse too well—they'd only been married a month. One night they both went to an opening that Alison was covering for her boss, Aleck Woollcott, and between acts they met Gil and Ada Gabriel[16] who were friends of Alison but had never met Crouse. So introductions were in order, and Alison said, "Gil and Ada, I want you to meet my husband, Mr. . . Mr. . ." Crouse pulled out a wallet, extracted his card, presented it to Smith and said, "Crouse is the name." . . . Now I am started on Alison. One time she and Crouse were in a cab and the driver of a car ahead was misbehaving badly and Smith blew her top. "I'm going to report that fellow if it's the last thing I do," she indignationed. Crouse asked her how she planned to report the driver if she didn't take down his license. "I can remember it," said Alison. "I see it. It's 023712. 237 was the number of my room in boarding school and 12—well, the twelve commandments!" A lot of joy went out of life when Alison went. Up at Corey Ford's woodsy place in New Hampshire one time, Corey took her for a Sunday walk about his acreage and they came upon a pretty little lake with evergreens crowding its boundaries. Alison was delighted. "Oh, Corey," she cried. "Look. The lake comes right up to the shore."

I am patiently waiting for some warm weather to come along and warm my chilled bone structure.

Peace!

Frank

Muriel King[17]

Saratoga, January 5, 1940

Dear Miss King,

Our records inform us that you attended the premiere of "Life With Father" a year ago last November with our Mr. Sullivan. Did you enjoy yourself? Did you have a good time? Did Mr. Sullivan satisfy you? If so, would you care to attend the premiere of "Arsenic and Old Lace" with him on the evening of Monday, January 13? Mr. Sullivan is available for that evening and will be glad to consider an application from you for his services then. We advise you however to fill out the attached blank without delay and return it to this office as Mr. Sullivan is one of our most popular men on call and there will be undoubtedly a great demand for his services. Please answer the following questions and return blank to this office immediately if you wish to attend above-mentioned premiere with Mr. Sullivan.

Age..........
Sex..........
Are you a Citizen of the U.S.?........
Have you had any of the following diseases, choice of three: Mumps, measles, psoriasis, rubeola, glanders, aelurophobia, Riggs disease, Raggs disease, Roggs disease, Ruggs disease, dyspnea, allergy, fits, acne, Hostetter's hip, housemaid's knee, housemaid's behind, syncope or elephantiasis? ....
Can you whistle?.......
What have I got in my hand?........
An early reply will be appreciated.

Saratoga Gigolo Service, Inc.

Per....F.S.......

Saratoga, February 8, 1958

Dear little Muriel,

Thank you very much for the invitation to come and crush crumpets with you on February 12, but I cannot make it, as it is too short notice. Don't you know that it now takes me twenty-four hours to make up my mind to go to the Worden bar, a distance of only one mile? And you want me to make up my mind to travel 185 miles to New York on only four days notice. Silly girl, what mad caprices do enter that tousled head of yours!

I will be down later, possibly in 1976 or, in case of rain in 1980, and the moment I get there I want to see you and resume our discussion where we left off after you finished your turkey sandwich in the Colonial Restaurant, Saratoga Springs, that night two or three years ago. I think we were discussing the quantum theory. You were against it.

You cannot say I have neglected you. When I was in NY last May I telephoned you, but a midinette answered and said you were out. Or she may have been a cocotte.

As for Mrs. Lovett, words fail me. Well, hold on, they don't quite fail me, not where she is concerned. At this party you are throwing I would like you to nominate her for President. I will send you a speech that you can read to the assembled delegates. Every day that goes by convinces me more and more that what is wrong with this country is that Adele Brown Lovett is not President. So what are we waiting for? Get the lead out, King!

Ask Mrs. Lovett also if she will be my Valentine. The post is purely nominal, quite a sinecure, entails no responsibility and, I regret to say, carries no honorarium.

The doctor shot a lot of Vitamin B into my gluteus maxima the other day, if gluteus maxima is what I mean, and I am so full of pep as a result that I think I could take you on at any time and throw you two out of three falls, and without any help from Crouse, either.

Love,

Lionel Strongfort

ED O'MALLEY[18]

Saratoga, April 12, 1967

Dear Ed,

Delighted to hear from you.

As for mysteries I really seem to be well supplied, especially in paperbacks, from the two or three newstands and stores here, and the public library, and every so often the indefatigable Bennett Cerf showers me with some Random House mysteries. John Farrar[19] comes across nobly, too.

I'm not reading any mystery at the moment because I just bought Thornton Wilder's new novel[20] and am deep in it, and of course it is perfectly fine. That fellow couldn't write a second rate book if he tried. He breezes into this town periodically in his wanderings and we paint the town red. (A pale shade of pink is about all I can manage nowadays.) It is such a pleasure to read a book by Thornton; he believes men and women have some innate decency and dignity through every tribulation, and reading him is like a cool drink on a hot day, he's utterly free of all the atrocities you are up against in the trash that passes today for novels, filled with drunkenness, perversion, drugs, incest and despair.

Your mention of Sid Perelman's "Dawn Ginsberg's Revenge" made me laugh, as I have often laughed at that wonderfully funny title. I think it is about the funniest book title I ever heard. Sid is the only humorist left on the ramparts. More power to him.

The rest of us have fallen by the wayside. Humor has got to be "sick" these days.

Thank you, Ed, for all your kind offers and one day I am going to take advantage of them. You have been most generous and I appreciate it. I'm glad to see you function as of yore. You really come under the head of an Institution. We must have a ceremony dedicating you some day, with the president of the Authors Guild crowning you with bay leaves.

As ever,

Frank S.

George Oppenheimer

(I had written Sullivan, congratulating him on his newly published book, The Moose in the Hoose *and, in the hope of extorting money out of him, accused him of stealing the idea from me.)*

Saratoga, Nov. 23, 1959

Dear George,

No use trying to claim I stole the Moose idea from you, because I have long since spent the advance royalty I extracted from Cerf by threats of exposure, blackmail and, finally, actual torture. So you won't get anything if you sue. Except *me*. And what good would I be to you? Don't answer.

I've been meaning to write to you, however, for some time to thank you for that title "In One Ear" you thought up for a book of mine in 1930. I really ought to have written you along about 1940 about it, but I have been so busy getting in the hay—I mean *mowing* the hay—and feeding the chickens and plowing the old meadow for winter wheat. Also I have been quite busy growing old and there were times when I didn't think I'd make it—but I did. I know I did because nowadays when I don't shave for 3 or 4 days my face begins to look as white as Papa Hemingway's.

When do you and I collaborate on a sequel, "Out the Other"?

The clincher that makes me know I'm old is that my fellow townsmen are giving me a DINNER on Dec. first, for God's sake. A *public* dinner. Roast beef. No speeches, or so they have promised me. Now you see what you lost by not being born in Saratoga. I don't see N.Y. giving you any dinner. I haven't even heard they gave you a block party on East 64th Street. Move up here, George. It is not too late. If all else fails, I will give you a dinner.

Yours ever

Frank

JAMES ROACH[21]

Saratoga, January 26, 1967

Dear Jas.,

That copy of the News Workshop moved me greatly and plunged me into a bout of nostalgia. Nostalgia is one of the pleasures I can still revel in. I can't take more than two drinks and the mention of sex makes me laugh heartily, in retrospect. Not only did the photo of the World city room jolt me, but the photos on a following page of the old Pulitzer building and the old Italian palazzo that housed the original Herald really broke me down. The two gentlemen statues which stood either side of the clock on the facade of the Herald were called, by the Herald staff, Stuff and Guff. They still stand in Herald Square and when I went to New York oftener and I was anywhere near Herald Square as an hour approached I would make it a point to go over and listen to Stuff and Guff bang out the hour, just for auld lang syne.

One thing bothers me. I can't identify anybody in that photo of the World city room except the man in the foreground, and his face is turned away. But I'm sure he is Jim Collins, the late Jim Collins (as so many of those boys are) who was a broth of a boy, a chap who did his full share in holding up the bar at the Roymont Club, the official World speakeasy on William Street, and who was night editor or something like that.

That photo of Park Row and the World and Tribune and City Hall in the foreground made me think of the night in October of 1922 when I trudged across City Hall Park from the Evening Sun at 280 Broadway for an interview with Swope at the World. Some slightly bitter guy at the Sun had tipped me off to what Swope would do. "He'll put on a show to impress you. You won't be in his office five minutes before he'll have Miss Millar get Governor Smith on the phone." Well, it was even better than that. I wasn't in Swope's office five minutes before Al Smith called *him*. I was one of those who loved Swope. He was always kind to me. I think he decided I was half-witted and needed constant occupational therapy. He had me down to the lively house at Great Neck innumerable times and it was a great experience. Those nine years on the World were the pleasantest of my life, though I didn't realize it until the day before yesterday.

I am moved by an impulse. I was going to have the enclosed police card buried with me, or glazed into my monument or something sensational like that but I am giving it to you, as a memento of a life not wholly ill-spent. It's my last World police card. The note at the bottom "Expires Feb. 28, 1931" is ironical. The World did expire almost to that day. The word "Reporter" is also slightly ironical as applied to me. I was a lousy reporter but meant well. The motto at the World was, Never let Sullivan within a mile of a fact. That suited me fine. I drew down what was then a princely salary for covering the Atlantic City beauty parades and the shad-boning contests held annually at Hartford,

Conn. It was fine until they gave me a goddam column, which spoiled everything.

That "News Workshop" is a real pro job. Those boys are what used to be described as On The Ball, though I suppose there's a new name for it nowadays. I am going to save the issue you sent me and look at it whenever I feel I need to shed a tear or two. Many thanks.

Conserve your health. Love to the folks. You might pin this police card somewhere where it could serve as a warning to youngsters planning to enter newspaper work. In my brief span I have killed the Herald, the Evening Sun, the World and PM. Only the Saratogian seems to have had the hardihood to survive having me as a staff member.

Ever yours,

Richard Harding Sullivan

Saratoga, January 20, 1968

Dear James,

I wrote Mr. Fleming of Alcoa a note thanking him kindly for inviting me to his cocktail party before the Baseball Writers dinner but explaining that I can't make it.

Anyhow my day in baseball is over and I think old players like me should yield the stage to youngsters like Yaz.[22] I got pretty tired autographing baseballs. However I hereby commission you to autograph a ball—a baseball, natch—on my behalf for any Times youngsters like Arthur Daley or Robt Lipsyte who yearn for an autograph from the Grover Cleveland Alexander of Lincoln Avenue . . . I could qualify to come to the dinner: I covered a World Serious for Herbert Swope's World in 1925, Senators vs Pirates, substituting for H. Broun, who got sick and couldn't make it. Goddam it, I was always substituting for Broun and when I wasn't substituting for him I was doing it for FPA.

And it was a pleasure. I'll never forget the thrill of having some admirer come up to me day after I had turned in a column for Broun or FPA and saying, "Jeeze, that was a lousy column" or "When are they going to put you back on night rewrite where you belong?" (I'm wrong; I covered 3 World Series, 2 in NY.)

You might be interested to know that I spent a portion of last night in a police car. First time that has happened but there must always be a first time. At 2 a.m., just when I had finished an Agatha Christie and was about to settle down for a long winter nap, a hundred pound chunk of ice, dislodged by the thaw, crashed off the eaves of this house with a roar and took the power line with it. I went downstairs with a flashlight to case the joint and discovered my power line on the ground and leading off to its pole across the street, at a distance of about four feet above ground. This seemed a potential danger to motorists and civic hero that I am, I put on a flock of clothes, took a flashlight and went out to do guard duty warning cars away from the wire. First, of course, telephoning the power company and the police department. It was just as confortable outdoors as it was getting to be in my heatless home. It's a great thing to live in a hamlet where everybody knows you. I realized that last night. The police car came along and somebody inside hailed me, "Hello Frank." It was my friend, Sgt. Lew Benton. He bade me step into the police car to keep warm, and that's how I got into a police car, my debut in that field. Then the power company vehicle rolled up and I got another "Hello Frank" from the boss, Frank Jones, another friend of mine. Made me feel everything was going to be all right: I was in the hands of friends. Those efficient lads from the power company repaired the power line temporarily, got my heat back, and today they came and finished the job, and strung the power line in a new position where falling ice can't hit it. I counted my blessings: it might have happened a week ago when it was twenty-five or thirty below zero.

Blessings on you and yours.

Your true friend,

F Solomon

MRS. MERRITT KIRK RUDDOCK[23]

Saratoga, December 27, 1966

Dear Maggie,

Christmas was very fine this year and I am really so sold on it that I am going to write the Times and suggest that we have it again next year. Among the pleasant features of my Christmas was your fruit cake. It solved a problem that has long bothered my conscience and that is, how to be a patriotic Irishman and drink or take Irish whiskey. Years ago, under the tutelage of that great man Dan Moriarty (about whom Lucius Beebe wrote a couple of years ago in American Heritage), I tried to learn to drink Irish whiskey but it was no go. It did not play fair; it made me drunk. I returned to Scotch and Dan, who was born in Ireland in the next village to the one where my father was born, put me down as a rather feeble scion of a doughty race. Now I know how to take it—in fruit cake. In fruit cake supply by Miz Ruddock. I thank you a thousand times. I was not able to get away with it all, I will confess, but I shared it with a couple of congenial souls who thank you also.

Christmas Eve, being tired and with the usual Christmas low spirits that come to old men with too many memories, I planned to go to bed and read a bloodthirsty mystery, but some old friends routed me out and insisted that I spark their Christmas Eve celebration. They are a remarkable clan and they wanted me there because years ago I was adopted into the tribe as an honorary member. It was the loveliest Christmas I've had in years and I'm delighted I went instead of staying home and acting Scrooge. I was the only outsider there. There were about twenty of the family, ranging from four to a matriarch approaching eighty (or maybe already there). They know how to keep Christmas if anybody ever did. Nothing stylized or cliché about their Christmas, and there isn't ever any bickering, such as usually is bound to crop up in family gatherings that large. They are all fond of each other and proud of each other and they are all definitely and delightfully nuts. One 15-year-old boy who plays the snare drums in a high school combo (his god is Gene Krupa) just kept walking through the rooms all evening long, when he wasn't eating, holding a smoking glass of dry ice. It fascinated him. His mother and everybody else would say as he passed, "Toby, put that stuff away before you burn yourself" and then the matter would be forgotten and Toby would keep right on walking in and out with his smoking potion. Another boy, about as handsome as Gregory Peck must have been at twenty, came along and his great-aunt, the matriarch, introduced him to me and said, "John never keeps a job more than a month." Something in her manner struck me as odd and then it dawned on me that she was *proud* that John didn't choose to go to work more than a month. He was supposed to go to work as a reporter on his uncle's newspaper but instead he went to some place like Guatemala with a pal to hunt iguanas. I'm sure George Kaufman wrote this family. It was all like "You Can't Take It With You." Maybe dear old Russel Crouse and Howard Lindsay wrote them too, in "Life With Father." Come time to sail into the buffet, laid out on what is known as a Groaning Board, everybody formed a procession. The youngest, the four-year-old, led it, by tradition, and bringing up the rear were the two seniors, Grandmamma and me. And did they sing Adestes Fideles or Hark the Herald Tribune? Not this crowd. We marched in procession around the Groaning Board singing I Want a Girl Just Like The Girl That Married Dear Old Dad. Don't ask me why. I had a magnificent time.

Yours ever,

Frank

PETER TURGEON[24]

(Written to Turgeon when he served as Pipemaster at a Pipe Night at The Players to pay tribute to the memory of James Thurber.)

Saratoga [no date]

Dear Mr. Pipemaster:—

Bernard Shaw's love letters to Stella Campbell are all rather public so why can't a pipsqueak like me write a public love letter to Helen Thurber, for whom I have cherished a requited passion these many years. My favorite Certain Club honors itself doubly tonight, in extolling the memory of Jim Thurber and in adding his Helen to the roster of great ladies who have been our honored guests—Cornelia Skinner, Dorothy Stickney, Lynn Fontanne, and that French actress who got stuck in the elevator, what was her name? Bernard? Sadie Bernard? No, no—*Bernhardt*, Sarah Bernhardt.

I cannot recall exactly where I first met Thurber but it was forty years ago, and it was either at the New Yorker office or at Tony Soma's speakeasy, then on 49th Street. The two places were indistinguishable in those days. In any case it marked the beginning of a friendship that lasted until Jim's death. A friendship that was a red letter event in my life. No one could know Thurber and be quite the same afterward. Life took on a rosier hue. Never a dull moment. Who dares say he has lived in vain who has been blessed with the friendship of Jim Thurber, Bob Benchley and Harold Ross, to name three of the Great Gracious Souls I have known.

Though Helen may not recall it, I remember precisely when and where she and I first met. Not long after their marriage she and Jim came to Saratoga one August day to see the races and other sights. I gave them the Sullivan De Luxe tour of the hot spots. The town was wide open and we dined at Arrowhead Inn to the music of Paul Whiteman with an obligato of clicking roulette wheels and the gentle whirr of faro cards being dealt, probably to my World boss, Herbert Bayard Swope. We called at many joints that night and the festivities ended at 4 a.m. in the kitchen of the home of George Bull, president of the Saratoga Racing Association, with George cooking scrambled eggs and sausage. Since that occasion I have had many joyful get-togethers with Helen and Jim, at Bleecks, or the Algonquin, or their home. Helen was Jim's eyes. She was his right arm. She was his amanuensis, his shield, his wife, and his best girl. And though it was a job that took a lot of doing, it was a job that many women envied her and would have undertaken gladly. But none of them could have made the success of it that Helen did.

Dear Helen, my love to you! I raise my glass to you and Jim!

Frank Sullivan

Dr. Albert Yunich[25]

Saratoga, Tuesday . . . [no date]

Dear Al,

The Chopped-Round-Steak Kid reporting. I have followed your instructions and eaten so much hamburger that I have a rather chopped look myself. But tomorrow night I am having dinner at my cousin Mike Sweeney's home with a Franciscan priest from Siena, and if I'm any expert on Ash Wednesday the piece de resistance will be fish, not steak.

I am getting pretty tired of being smacked in the face mornings by news of the passing of old friends, but there seems little I can do about it, nor can any of us. A while ago it was Joe

Liebling of the New Yorker, a great journalist, and today news of the death of Sam Chotzinoff, one of the most lovable guys I ever knew. He was music critic on the World when I worked there. I've been thinking about him all day, and about the many hilarious times I've had at his home. Chotzy (as everybody called him) married Pauline Heifetz, Jascha's sister and they lived in a big brownstone off Central Park West, with Mama and Papa Heifetz. They were kind enough to invite me to their home often and that household was an eye-opener to a non-musician like me. It was nothing short of an education. Two grand pianos, not one, in the living room, and their parties were awash with assorted Jaschas, Saschas and Mischas, and Zimbalists and Alma Glucks. Chotzy some years previously had been accompanist for both Gluck and Efrem Zimbalist on their concert tours. There was also the guest of honor, Maestro Toscanini, and I was always grateful to Chotzy and Pauline for giving me those opportunities to get a closeup of the Maestro. For a long time Toscanini wouldn't go to any private home except the Chotzinoffs; he was very fond of them all, and they treated him informally and made him feel at home. It was Chotzy whom David Sarnoff[26] sent to Italy before War 2 to persuade Toscanini to come to NY and conduct the NBC Symphony (which he did). That adventure, as Chotzy told it, would make an Ian Fleming thriller. Toscanini hated the Fascists and Mussolini but Muss never dared molest the Maestro. But he had Chotzy followed by spies on that trip and all his mail opened . . . Good God, you won't have time to cure any patients if I go on any longer. All the best to Mary and you.

Frank

THE POEMS

In 1932 Sullivan wrote a Christmas poem for *The New Yorker* in which he hymned Yuletide greetings to people in public life whom he admired, to friends whom he cherished, and even to an occasional foe. Thirty-eight years later the custom still persists and Sullivan continues to greet all and sundry in his annual *New Yorker* ode.

To prove that he is not just a carol singer I have included the finest epic about trees since Joyce Kilmer's.

—EDITOR'S NOTE

GREETINGS, FRIENDS!

Believe it or not, friends, as you please,
But the world has seen worse times than these,
So what can you lose if you take a chance
And join again in our holiday dance?
Come, follow your aged Fezziwig
As he capers in a rheumatic jig
To celebrate the Christmas season
With doubtful rhyme, and not much reason.
In spite of all, we'll caterwaul
To compliment George W. Ball;
We'll shoot the jocund Christmas blarney
To gladden the spirits of Art Carney;
Dispense some well-meant holiday corn
For Archibald Cox and Marilyn Horne;
And stage a proper New Year bash
For Ross Hunter, Arthur Ashe,
John W. Gardner, Lee J. Cobb,
And Miss Lucinda Desha Robb!
Thanks be, the raucous campaign's done,
But now comes Congress 91,
So there's not much hope that coming days
Will give us a respite from clichés.
Ring out Lyndon! Ring in Dick!
Prexy-elect, we hope you click.
Wisdom to all your deliberations;
Bonne chance to the Paris conversations.
Well done, Muskie! Well fought, Hube!
Accept the cheers of this upstate rube,
Whose honeyed words at Christmastide
Go out to Eric Sevareid,
To Kenya's runners and Kenyatta,

And to Yasunari Kawabata.
We'll gladly waggle these ancient tonsils
To shout hurrah for the Dudley Bonsals,
For Colin Watson, Jacqueline Bryan,
Millen Brand, and Mitchell Ryan,
We'll ululate for America's youth,
So charming and, at times, uncouth.
We'll shower frankincense and myrrh
On Gene McCarthy and Raymond Burr;
We'll rain down lotus leaves and manna
On painter Robert Indiana.
Hark! Peals of bells for Walt Kelly,
Claude Chabrol, and Melvin Belli—
And bid the ringers they make sure
To add a welkin for Roger Moore.
Come, roast the bird and stuff it with oyster
To sate Vermont Connecticut Royster;
Fill the pudding with raisin and plum
For Judy Garland (née Frances Gumm),
And send a bushel or two of Bayer
To John, our patient, harassed Mayor.
May joy and peace be Joanna Woodward's,
And may we add a few more good words
To voice esteem for Arlene Dahl,
Nellie Nichols, and Judith DePaul?
We'll kick up our heels with Clark Clifford,
Janis Joplin, and Charlie Sifford;
We'll gyrate in a deft fandango
With Ishbel Ross, and then we'll tango
With Enid Nemy, Irene Dailey,
Marta Fitzgerald, and Pearl Bailey;
We'll cut in on the Tigers' Denny McLain
When he starts to waltz with Barbara Bain
(Denny, now you're free to dance
With the winsome Mrs. Cyrus Vance),
And then we'll startle Seymour Krim

With carols sung by Tiny Tim.
Descant now, Simon & Garfunkel,
To honor Theodora Van Runkle,
And when you're finished will you come and
Do your thing for Roscoe Drummond?
Yule is the time when we ought to be partial
To sterling chaps like E. G. Marshall;
It's also a time when we should not
Speak aught but love to George C. Scott,
Jacob Javits, Cary Grant,
Zoe Caldwell, Mary Quant,
Leonid Hambro, Daniel Bell,
The Grateful Dead, and Jiri Menzel.
Hail from the undersigned acclaimer
To the Packers' rugged Jerry Kramer!
Ave, Bill Freehan, All-Star catcher!
God rest you, Gary's Mayor Hatcher!
A cup of kindness for Donald Frame;
For the gallant Czechs, more of the same;
And beakers of well-spiced Christmas brews
For Wystan Auden and Senator Hughes.
Let's carol hymns in dulcet tones
To add to the glee of James Earl Jones,
Ben Shahn, Ed Bartnett,
And David and his partner Chet.
May we impose on you, John Doar,
To select at some expensive store
Some frills for Jacqueline du Pré,
Julia Child, and Elaine May?
Now, ladies, step to the mistletoe
With Canada's Prime, Pierre Trudeau!
We beam good will in particular
To Commodore Geoffrey Thrippleton Marr;
We beam it too at William Wyler,
Judy Carne, and Veronica Tyler,
And we'll assume that Wilfrid Sheed

Feels similar warmth for Kay Creed,
Boom Boom Geoffrion, Shirley Bassey,
John Wood, and Haile Selassie.
Huzza for the marriage of Williams and Vassar!
Peace to Israel, peace to Nasser!

Now at the close of our doggerel
We wish you all a fond Noël:
Friends, may the Star become a sign
Of hope and sense in '69.
From war and frights at last let's pass
To peace, says your old Wenceslas.

FRIENDLY ADVICE TO A RECALCITRANT MERCER
(*The New Yorker*, June 2, 1945)

(When Mrs. Iphigene Ochs Sulzberger, president of the Park Association of New York City, Inc., wrote Philip Le Boutillier, president of Best & Co., hoping that he would help make Fifth Avenue more beautiful by planting trees in front of the new Best store at Fifth and Fifty-first Street, Mr. Le B. answered rather brusquely that he would do no such thing. He hates trees on Fifth Avenue, thinks the ones around St. Patrick's and Radio City mar the charm of the buildings. He doesn't think the regional pigeons are any bargain, either. If trees are planted before the new Best store, it will be over Mr. Le B.'s dead body.)

In accents sharp, if not acerb,
Phil scorns to beautify his curb.
No Birnam Wood, says Best's proud Thane,
Shall ever come to his Dunsinane.
He casts a hostile, jaundiced eye
Upon St. Patrick's trees nearby
And views with ill-concealed disdain
The pigeons nesting in that fane.
Nor do the trees in Radio City
Excite his pleasure. Not a bit. He
Feels some nicely laid cement, or
Bricks, would better adorn the Center.
No leaf shall rustle, or sparrow nest,
Or dog disport, in front of Best.
No maple there, or oak, or elm,
While P. Le. B. is at the helm.
I think that I shall never see
A man so angry at a tree.

Ah, what a shame it is that trade
Should steel Phil's heart 'gainst kindly shade!
Could Betty Smith buy pretty things
If trees had never grown in Kings?

Why, forward-looking business leaders
All speak well of elms and cedars;
Every man these days foresees
A city thickly sown with trees.
It's coming, Philip, it's a trend:
Old Fifth tree-lined from end to end;
From Schwarz's toy shop to the Arch
Long rows of maple, ginko, larch,
Chestnut, ash, and all the rest—
Except, alas, in front of Best!

I see that block forlorn and bare,
Sizzling in the summer air,
A drear and arid desert scene
Amid the cool, surrounding green;
Customers falling, from heat or thirst,
At Fifty-second or Fifty-first.

Be warned, Phil, be less adamant!
Before it is too late, recant!
Get back to Nature, man, be free!
Disport yourself, go climb a tree;
Drink in the vernal chlorophyll
Or listen to a robin's trill.
Dismiss all matters mercantile,
Become a happy dendrophile,
Forget you ever worked on Fift',
And go on a hike with Otis Swift!

You'll stride back to your native mart
With laughing eye and singing heart,
Better equipped to sell fine duds
For having frolicked with the buds.
You'll find yourself rejuvenated,
Loving those trees that you once hated.

You'll write again to Mrs. S.,
This time your note a hearty Yes,
Swearing that on the Avenue
No man shall cherish elms as you;
No man more eager to sponsor a tree
Than Best & Company's Phil Le B.—
Why, you may be the first employer
To shoot the works and plant a sequoia!

THE CLICHÉ EXPERT

In September of 1934 Sullivan wrote a letter to his friend and editor Harold Ross, who nine years before had started *The New Yorker*. In it he wrote, "Here is something for your consideration. Over a period of some months I have been jotting down clichés, ones I found myself using or ones I read or heard. A structure is always imposing. A retreat is always beat—if it is hasty. A kettle of fish is always pretty. An existence, if precarious, is always eked out. Succession is rapid. Justice is ample. Ranks are serried. You, dear, are always faultlessly attired or do I mean Broun? I put these clichés down with the idea of doing something with them some day and they might possibly be worked into a piece done cross examination style. Thus: The Cliché Expert—How are you always attired? Ans.—Faultlessly. It is a purely synthetic piece but it might do for the back of the book. The idea is of course not new."

Despite Sullivan's disclaimers, Ross responded enthusiastically and the findings of the Cliché Expert, whom Sullivan christened Arbuthnot, continued for many years up front in *The New Yorker*.

—EDITOR'S NOTE

THE CLICHÉ EXPERT TESTIFIES AS A
LITERARY CRITIC

(*Sullivan at Bay*. J. H. Dent, London, 1929)

Q. Mr. Arbuthnot, you are an expert in the use of the cliché as applied to literary criticism?

A. I am told that I am, Mr. Sullivan.

Q. We shall soon find out. What is this object, marked Exhibit A?

A. That is a book.

Q. Good. What kind of book is it?

A. It is a minor classic.

Q. And what kind of document is it?

A. It is a valuable human document.

Q. Very good, Mr. Arbuthnot. Please continue.

A. It is a book in which the results of painstaking—or scholarly—research are embodied, and it should appeal to a wide public. This reviewer could not put it down.

Q. Why not?

A. Because of its penetrating insight. It is a sincere and moving study of family life against the background of a small cathedral town. It is also a vivid and faithful portrayal.

Q. How written?

A. Written with sympathy, pathos, and kindly humor. It throws a clear light on a little understood subject and is well worth reading.

Q. How is it illustrated?

A. Profusely. It is original in conception, devoid of sentimentality, highly informative, consistently witty, and rich in color. You should place it on your library list.

Q. Why?

A. Because it strikes a new note in fiction. Mystery and suspense crowd its pages. The author has blended fact and fiction and the result is an authentic drama of social revolution, a definite contribution to proletarian literature.

Q. Told with a wealth of what?

A. Told with a wealth of detail.

Q. And how portrayed?

A. Realistically portrayed, in staccato prose. For sheer brilliance of style there has been nothing like it since *Moby Dick.* Rarely does a narrative move at such a fast pace.

Q. What is it a shrewd comment on?

A. The contemporary scene. It marks a red-letter day in current literature. It is capital entertainment.

Q. What pervades it?

A. A faint tinge of irony.

Q. And how is it translated?

A. Ably. It is a penetrating study in abnormal psychology, and unlike most scientific works it is written in language understandable to the layman. It belongs in the front rank of modern picaresque literature. Ideology.

Q. I beg your pardon?

A. I said ideology. Also catharsis.

Q. What about them?

A. Well, they have to come in somewhere.

Q. I see. Now, to return to the minor classic, Mr. Arbuthnot. Would you call it a subtle and arresting piece of work?

A. Certainly I would. Why do you suppose I'm an expert in the use of the cliché? I'd also call it an honest attempt to depict, a remarkable first novel, a veritable triumph, a genuine contribution, a thrilling saga of life in frontier days, and the most impressive study of degeneration since Zola. It bids fair to go down as one of the great biographies of all time, including *Moby Dick.* In short, it has unusual merit.

Q. How does it augur?

A. It augurs well for the future of the author.

Q. And how does it bid?

A. It bids fair to become a best-seller.

Q. And how does it end?

A. It ends upon a distinct note of despair. It is a work of art.

Q. I'm glad you liked it, Mr. Arbuthnot.

A. Who said I liked it?

Q. Didn't you?

A. Certainly not.

Q. Why not?

A. Because it is, one fears, mawkishly sentimental and, one regrets, faintly pretentious. Curiously enough, it does not carry conviction. Strangely enough, it lacks depth. Oddly enough, the denouement is weak. It is to be regretted that the title is rather misleading and it need hardly be pointed out that the book as a whole lacks cohesion and form. I am very much afraid, one regrets, that it falls definitely into the escapist school of fiction. And of course, like all first novels, it is autobiographical.

Q. I'm glad you told me. I won't buy it.

A. Ah, but in spite of its faults it contains much of real value. It kept me awake till three. In the opinion of the present reviewer it would be the long-awaited great American novel except for one serious defect.

Q. What is that?

A. It lacks an index.

Q. Mr. Arbuthnot, it is easy to see that you have earned your spurs in the field of literary criticism. So much for the book. Now, observe this object I hold here in my hand, marked Exhibit B. What is it?

A. That. *That* is an *author*.

Q. Whose are those italics, Mr. Arbuthnot?

A. The italics are mine.

Q. What kind of author is this?

A. A promising young author who should be watched.

Q. What does he write?

A. Powerful first novels.

Q. What kind of storyteller is he?

A. He's a born storyteller.

Q. What kind of satirist is he?

A. A satirist of the first order.

Q. Tell us more about this interesting creature.

A. Well, he cannot be lightly dismissed. He is undoubtedly to be reckoned with, one feels, as a definite force. He is in the front rank of the younger writers.

Q. Why?

A. Because his work plainly shows the influence of Joyce, Hemingway, Huxley, Proust, Gertrude Stein, Auden, Eliot, and Virginia Woolf. Here is an authentic talent from which we may expect great things.

Q. So what do you do?

A. So I hail him. And I acclaim him. He has a keen ear for the spoken word. He also has a flair. He sets out to tell. He deals with themes, or handles them. He recaptures moods. His execution is brilliant, his insight is poetic, his restraint is admirable, and he has a sense of values. There is something almost uncanny in his ability to look into men's souls. And he paints a vivid word picture and works on a vast canvas.

Q. How?

A. With consummate artistry. He writes with commendable frankness.

Q. Using what kind of style?

A. Using a limpid prose style. He has a real freshness of approach that stamps him as an artist in the true sense of the word. He culls his material and his niche in the hall of literary fame seems secure.

Q. I'm glad you like him, Mr. Arbuthnot.

A. But I don't.

Q. No? Why not?

A. Because his talent is plainly superficial and ephemeral. He has an unfortunate habit of allowing his personality to obtrude. His book is badly documented and not the least of his many irritating mannerisms is his addiction to inexcusable typographical errors. His book is full of clichés and he does not make his characters live and feel and breathe. And he writes with one eye on Hollywood.

Q. You mean to tell me that a cad like that has the audacity to call himself an author?

A. Well now, don't be too hard on him. Although he decidedly does not justify his early promise it is as yet too early to evaluate his work. Want to know about the plot?

Q. Yes, indeed. What about the plot?

A. It is well rounded and fully developed. But it is marred by structural weaknesses.

Q. What kind of structural weaknesses?

A. Inherent structural weaknesses. It is motivated, of course. And its threads are cunningly woven into a harmonious texture by the deft hand of a skilled literary craftsman.

Q. Just one thing more, Mr. Arbuthnot. How many kinds of readers are there?

A. Three—casual, general, and gentle.

Q. Mr. Arbuthnot, I think that is all. I can't thank you enough for having come here today to help us out.

A. It has been a pleasure—a vivid, fascinating, significant, vigorous, timely, gracious, breath-taking, mature, adequate, nostalgic, unforgettable, gripping, articulate, engrossing, poignant, and adult pleasure to be of service to you, Mr. Sullivan. Good day, sir.

THE CULINARY EXPERT TAKES THE STAND
(*A Pearl in Every Oyster*. Little, Brown, 1938)

Q: Mr. Arbuthnot, you are an expert in the use of the cliché as applied to matters of eating, are you not?

A: That is correct, sir.

Q: In that case perhaps you will be kind enough to act as our guide today as we attempt to shed some light upon the incursions of the trite into the realm of gastronomy.

A: You said a mouthful, Mr. Ernst.

Q: Thank you, Mr. Arbuthnot. Now then, what kind of eater are you?

A: I am a hearty eater.

Q: What is a hearty eater?

A: A hearty eater is a man who eats three meals—three *square* meals—a day.

Q: What does a hearty eater let good digestion wait upon?

A: He lets good digestion wait on appetite.

Q: How does a hearty eater eat?

A: He eats like a plowman. He eats everything set before him. It does a person good to see him eat. He gets the good out of his food.

Q: What would a hearty eater eat a body out of?

A: He would eat a body out of house and home.

Q: And which is the way to his heart?

A: The way to his heart is through his stomach.

Q: And what are bigger than a hearty eater's stomach?

A: His eyes are bigger than his stomach.

Q: He is so hungry he could eat—?

A: A horse.

Q: What does it take to keep a hearty eater in victuals?

A: It takes a good provider.

Q: And why does he eat, drink, and be merry?

A: For tomorrow he dies.

Q: What kind of repasts does he like to sit down to?

A: Sumptuous repasts. Or, Lucullan feasts.

Q: Upon what are these sumptuous repasts served?

A: Groaning boards.

Q: How does a hearty eater describe the act of sitting down to a groaning board?

A: He refers to it as tying on the feed bag.

Q: And what is it he puts on before attending a formal dinner?

A: He puts on the soup and fish, only he doesn't put it on. He dons it.

Q: To whose taste does he then dine?

A: To the king's taste, or to the queen's. In any case he feasts right royally.

Q: And what does he do with his teeth?

A: He digs his grave with his teeth.

Q: What happens to him as a result?

A: He develops a bay window.

Q: A bay window?

A: Yes. A corporation. And when his friends meet him, they say, "Hello, Ed. Say, good gosh, you better watch your calories, and practice a little girth control."

Q: Girth control?

A: Yes. You know—birth control, girth control.

Q: Oh, yes. Now, Mr. Arbuthnot, are all eaters hearty eaters?

A: No, there are the others.

Q: What others?

A: The ones who pick at their food.

Q: I see. And what kind of appetites have those eaters who pick at their food?

A: Birdlike appetites. They don't eat enough to keep a canary alive. They don't get any of the good out of their food, as the saying goes. Nothing they eat agrees with them, or stands by them—

Q: As the saying goes?

A: Yes, as the saying goes. They are always working up an appetite, and are always losing it.

Q: Poor souls. How do they feel about onions?

A: They like onions but onions don't like them. That is too bad, in a way, because you know what onions do, don't you?

Q: No. What?

A: They build you up physically but pull you down socially.

Q: That's rather good, Mr. Arbuthnot.

A: Oh, it's not mine. Some wit said it eons ago, or, rather, put it.

Q: I see. Think of any other kinds of eaters, Mr. Arbuthnot?

A: Well, there are the gourmets, who are in between the hearty eaters and the picky eaters.

Q: Describe a gourmet, please.

A: A gourmet is a mighty clever eater who knows a hot bird from a cold bottle. When a meal is to his liking, he refers to it as a Poem.

Q: What kind of viands does the gourmet dine on?

A: Rare viands.

Q: And what does he make of his stomach?

A: He makes a god of his stomach.

Q: Mr. Arbuthnot, as a cliché expert, how would you refer to bread?

A: As the staff of life. Now, Mr. Ernst, may I ask *you* a question?

Q: Certainly.

A: Do you know what a watched pot never does?

Q: No. What?

A: It never boils. Do you know that an army travels on its stomach, and that in all musical comedies where a waiter appears he must have his thumb in the soup?

Q: Really? That's very interesting. Now, Mr. Arbuthnot, just one more question and we are through. And it is probably one of the simplest questions that could be put to a cliché expert.

A: What is it?

Q: Who ate a hearty breakfast?

A: Who ate a hearty breakfast? . . . Who ate a hearty breakfast? . . . Let me see-e.

Q: That ought to be easy for an expert like you.

THE DISTRICT ATTORNEY (*jumping to his feet and interrupting sarcastically*): But isn't, apparently.

MR. ARBUTHNOT: Who ate a hearty breakfast? Too many cooks? No. They spilled the beans. No, spoiled the beans. No, the broth. They spilled the broth.

THE DISTRICT ATTORNEY (*sarcastically*): A cliché expert!

MR. ARBUTHNOT: Why, I know it as well as I know my own name. Isn't it silly? I can't seem to think.

MR. ERNST: Just concentrate.

MR. ARBUTHNOT: Isn't it aggravating? It's right on the tip of my tongue, too.

MR. ERNST: Take your time, Mr. Arbuthnot.

THE DISTRICT ATTORNEY (*sarcastically*): Oh, yes, Mr. Arbuthnot, please take your time, by all means. We've got nothing to do until the Fourth of July.

MR. ERNST: I object to the attitude of my worthy colleague.

THE DISTRICT ATTORNEY (*sarcastically*): But my worthy colleague gave us to understand that the witness was a cliché expert. And he doesn't even know who ate a hearty breakfast. Ha!

MR. ARBUTHNOT: Hearty breakfast, hearty breakfast. M-m-m. Was it Little Jack Horner, by any chance?

MR. ERNST: Oh now, Mr. Arbuthnot.

MR. ARBUTHNOT: It wasn't Diamond Jim Brady?

THE DISTRICT ATTORNEY (*sarcastically*): Perhaps the witness will next suggest that it was Mrs. Jack Spratt.

MR. ARBUTHNOT: Was it, Mr. Ernst?

MR. ERNST: Come now, Mr. Arbuthnot. Just put your mind to it. Think! Think of Sing Sing, and Joliet, and Alcatraz, and a certain novel by Anthony Hope about Zenda.

MR. ARBUTHNOT: Zenda? Zenda?

(*Mr. Ernst hums the "Prisoner's Song."*)

THE DISTRICT ATTORNEY (*sarcastically*): I object.

MR. ERNST: Your Honor, I submit that I have not said a word.

THE DISTRICT ATTORNEY (*sarcastically*): I object to my worthy colleague singing the "Prisoner's Song" off key.

MR. ARBUTHNOT: That's it! I have it! Prisoner! It was the *prisoner* that ate a hearty breakfast! Oh, thank you, Mr. District Attorney, thank you.

THE CLICHÉ EXPERT
TESTIFIES ON LOVE
(*A Pearl in Every Oyster*. Little, Brown, 1938)

Q: Mr. Arbuthnot, as an expert in the use of the cliché, are you prepared to testify here today regarding its application in topics of sex, love, matrimony, and so on?

A: I am.

Q: Very good. Now, Mr. Arbuthnot, what's love?

A: Love is blind.

Q: Good. What does love do?

A: Love makes the world go round.

Q: Whom does a young man fall in love with?

A: With the Only Girl in the World.

Q: Whom does a young woman fall in love with?

A: With the Only Boy in the World.

Q: When do they fall in love?

A: At first sight.

Q: How?

A: Madly.

Q: They are then said to be?

A: Victims of Cupid's darts.

Q: And he?

A: Whispers sweet nothings in her ear.

Q: Who loves a lover?

A: All the world loves a lover.

Q: Describe the Only Girl in the World.

A: Her eyes are like stars. Her teeth are like pearls. Her lips are ruby. Her cheek is damask, and her form divine.

Q: Haven't you forgotten something?

A: Eyes, teeth, lips, cheek, form—no, sir, I don't think so.

Q: Her hair?

A: Oh, certainly. How stupid of me. She has hair like spun gold.

Q: Very good, Mr. Arbuthnot. Now will you describe the Only Man?

A: He is a blond Viking, a he-man, and a square shooter who plays the game. There is something fine about him that rings true, and he has kept himself pure and clean so that when he meets the girl of his choice, the future mother of his children, he can look her in the eye.

Q: How?

A: Without flinching.

Q: Are all the Only Men blond Vikings?

A: Oh, no. Some of them are dark, handsome chaps who have sown their wild oats. This sort of Only Man has a way with a maid, and there is a devil in his eye. But he is not a cad; he would not play fast and loose with an Only Girl's affections. He has a heart of gold. He is a diamond in the rough. He tells the Only Girl frankly about his Past. She understands—and forgives.

Q: And marries him?

A: And marries him.

Q: Why?

A: To reform him.

Q: Does she reform him?

A: Seldom.

Q: Seldom what?

A: Seldom, if ever.

Q: Now, Mr. Arbuthnot, when the Only Man falls in love, madly, with the Only Girl, what does he do?

A: He walks on air.

Q: Yes, I know, but what does he do? I mean, what is it he pops?

A: Oh, excuse me. The question, of course.

Q: Then what do they plight?

A: Their troth.

Q: What happens after that?

A: They get married.

Q: What is marriage?

A: Marriage is a lottery.

Q: Where are marriages made?

A: Marriages are made in heaven.

Q: What does the bride do at the wedding?

A: She blushes.

Q: What does the groom do?

A: Forgets the ring.

Q: After the marriage, what?

A: The honeymoon.

Q: Then what?

A: She has a little secret.

Q: What is it?

A: She is knitting a tiny garment.

Q: What happens after that?

A: Oh, they settle down and raise a family and live happily ever afterward, unless—

Q: Unless what?

A: Unless he is a fool for a pretty face.

Q: And if he is?

A: Then they come to the parting of the ways.

Q: Mr. Arbuthnot, thank you very much.

A: But I'm not through yet, Mr. Untermyer.

Q: No?

A: Oh, no. There is another side to sex.

Q: There is? What side?

A: The seamy side. There are, you know, men who are wolves in sheep's clothing and there are, alas, lovely women who stoop to folly.

Q: My goodness! Describe these men you speak of, please.

A: They are snakes in the grass who do not place woman upon a pedestal. They are cads who kiss and tell, who trifle with a girl's affections and betray her innocent trust. They are cynics who think that a woman is only a woman, but a good cigar is a smoke. Their mottoes are "Love 'em and leave 'em" and "Catch 'em young, treat 'em rough, tell 'em nothing." These cads speak of "the light that lies in woman's eyes, and lies—and lies—and lies." In olden days they wore black, curling mustachios, which they twirled, and they invited innocent Gibson girls to midnight suppers, with champagne, at their bachelor apartments, and said, "Little girl, why do you fear me?" Nowadays they have black, patent-leather hair, and roadsters, and they drive up to the curb and say, "Girlie, can I give you a lift?" They are fiends in human form, who would rob a woman of her most priceless possession.

Q: What is that?

A: Her honor.

Q: How do they rob her?

A: By making improper advances.

Q: What does a woman do when a snake in the grass tries to rob her of her honor?

A: She defends her honor.

Q: How?

A: By repulsing his advances and scorning his embraces.

Q: How does she do that?

A: By saying, "Sir, I believe you forget yourself," or "Please take your arm away," or "I'll kindly thank you to remember I'm a lady," or "Let's not spoil it all."

Q: Suppose she doesn't say any of those things?

A: In that case, she takes the first false step.

Q: Where does the first false step take her?

A: Down the primrose path.

Q: What's the primrose path?

A: It's the easiest way.

Q: Where does it lead?

A: To a life of shame.

Q: What is a life of shame?

A: A life of shame is a fate worse than death.

Q: Now, after lovely woman has stooped to folly, what does she do to the gay Lothario who has robbed her of her most priceless possession?

A: She devotes the best years of her life to him.

Q: Then what does he do?

A: He casts her off.

Q: How?

A: Like an old shoe.

Q: Then what does she do?

A: She goes to their love nest, then everything goes black before her, her mind becomes a blank, she pulls a revolver, and gives the fiend in human form something to remember her by.

Q: That is called?

A: Avenging her honor.

Q: What is it no jury will do in such a case?

A: No jury will convict.

Q: Mr. Arbuthnot, your explanation of the correct application of the cliché in these matters has been most instructive, and I know that all of us cliché-users here will know exactly how to respond hereafter when, during a conversation, sex—when sex—when—ah—

A: I think what you want to say is "When sex rears its ugly head," isn't it?

Q: Thank you, Mr. Arbuthnot. Thank you very much.

A: Thank *you*, Mr. Untermyer.

AFTERWORD

By George Oppenheimer

This has been a labor of love—love of the material and of the man who supplied it. Among other rewards, it gave me the opportunity of renewing my friendship with Sullivan, which had, of necessity, waned, since I was working in Hollywood the greater portion of the time that he was living in New York and when I returned, he had moved to Saratoga and stubbornly refused to be routed out.

In the early Forties Alexander Woollcott had the idea of collecting Sullivan's letters and, with his man Friday, Joe Hennessey (now running a bookstore in Saratoga), he began to assemble the correspondence. Before they had gone very far, Woollcott died and the project was abandoned. The letters were returned to Sullivan, who, in turn, sent them to his Alma Mater, Cornell University, at the request of Professor George H. Healey, curator of the Department of Rare Books.

Some time later, Sullivan's close friend, Russel Crouse, spoke about renewing the project but nothing came of it. Finally, I had the idea to edit a volume that would include not only his letters but a sampling of his pieces and poems.

I first met Sullivan in the Twenties through, I believe, Beatrice Kaufman, wife of George S., an enchanting catalyst who delighted in bringing people together and in furthering their contacts and their careers. When Harold Guinzburg and I were operating the Viking Press, we published *In One Ear*, selections from which have been included here.

Unhappily a correspondence with Sullivan that lasted over several months cannot be located in the Viking files. It started when Sullivan discovered some galleys with our imprint, the Rockwell Kent drawing of a Viking ship. They were lying in a gutter, having fallen off a garbage truck to which we had consigned them, as we did all old galleys.

The book was a reprint of a Russian semi-classic, *Sanine* by Michael Petrovich Artzibashev. Sullivan picked the galleys out of the gutter and returned them to us with a stern note pointing out that this was no way in which to treat the works of Viking authors. Instead of answering, we merely sent him our form letter of rejection.

Some days later we received a supercilious note from Sullivan stating that we were fools, dolts and insensitive fellows devoid of acumen and taste. As proof he included an enthusiastic review of *Sanine* by none other than Count Leo Tolstoy. We wrote back and suggested that he keep his log-rolling friends out of this. That started a battle of words and I deeply regret that Sullivan's are lost to posterity.

Then there's the inscription that he wrote on a book which he sent to Marise Campbell: "To dear Marise," it read, "without whose sympathetic help the undersigned would not have written this book," signed Frank Sullivan, Fiesole, May 4, 1930 (he has never set foot outside of the United States). The inscribed book was a Staten Island telephone directory of 1929.

I visited Sullivan in Saratoga in January of 1969, a visit that was unfortunately curtailed by a severe bout of his diverticulitis. However, I did have one festive evening with him, when it took no time at all to discover that he was the best-known and best-loved citizen of that sporting spa.

Even the dogs knew him and he them. On our way to his neighborhood pub, Siro's, we were waylaid by a small black mongrel bitch who, at sight of Sullivan, became hysterical with joy and practically threw herself out of kilter with the wagging of her tail.

Sullivan patted her fondly, then addressed her. "Flossie," he said with a note of severity, "you know you're not supposed to be on this block. Remember what that police dog did to you last year."

Flossie cocked an eye in recollection. Then, although I have only Sullivan to back me up and he is a notoriously unreliable witness in matters of this sort, I could have sworn that Flossie said, "Thank you, darling. I forgot," and trotted off, throwing kisses at her mentor as she left.

In one of his letters that is not included in this book in order to keep it from becoming a twelve-volume set, Sullivan wrote to Joseph Bryan, III, "The autumn coloring is at its height and I am simply beautiful, all reds and gold. People come from miles just to see me."

It is well worth the trip.

I want to thank all those who went to the trouble of finding and sending me their letters from Sullivan. Their names are listed in "The Letters" section. Apologies to those whose letters were not used. There were so many that some had to be omitted.

Thanks are hereby tendered to Curator George H. Healey for his and his assistants' aid in providing me access to and the use of letters in the files of the Cornell University Department of Rare Books; Paul H. Myers of the Lincoln Center Library of the Performing Arts; to Louis A. Rachow of the John Drew Library at The Players; to the *New York Times Book Review* for printing my request for letters; to Harriet Pilpel of the legal firm of Greenbaum, Wolf and Ernst for providing me with letters written to Edna Ferber; to Milton Greenstein for releasing a cache of letters that Sullivan wrote to Harold Ross and other *New Yorker* personnel; to Marc Connelly for his foreword and for the publicity he gave us on TV; to Arthur Basset, my secretary, for his invaluable assistance in creating order out of the chaos that resulted when I filed Nunnally Johnson under X and Anna Crouse under Z; and to our publisher and editor, Ken McCormick of Doubleday, and to his able assistant, Lisa Drew, who have not only helped immeasurably but have made this project an altogether warm and pleasurable experience.

Finally my deep gratitude to Frank Sullivan for letting me edit his book and for his wholehearted cooperation and collaboration, and to the late Corey Ford for his early enthusiasm, encouragement and help.

NOTES ON THE LETTERS

TO THE LADIES

1. Patricia Collinge, actress, one of whose outstanding roles was that of Birdie in Lillian Hellman's *The Little Foxes,* and writer for *New Yorker* and other magazines.
2. Anna Erskine Crouse, widow of Russel (Buck) Crouse, who was co-author with Howard Lindsay of many plays including the record-breaking *Life With Father,* and the Pulitzer Prize winner *State of the Union.*
3. Timothy and Lindsay Ann Crouse, son and daughter of Russel and Anna Crouse.
4. John Kieran, sports columnist, naturalist and panelist on radio's "Information Please."
5. Jean Dixon Ely, comedienne of *June Moon, Once in a Lifetime,* and many other plays.
6. Geraldine Souvaine, Milton Cross and Edward Downes, producer, announcer and moderator of the Metropolitan Opera radio broadcasts.
7. Edna Ferber, distinguished American novelist, short-story writer and playwright.
8. Richard Rodgers, one of America's foremost composers, of such musicals as *Pal Joey, Oklahoma!, South Pacific, Carousel, The King and I* and *The Sound of Music.* The book of the last was written by Lindsay and Crouse.
9. Actress Dorothy Stickney, who co-starred with her husband, Howard Lindsay, as Vinnie in *Life With Father* and *Life With Mother.*
10. Madeline Hurlock Sherwood, widow of Robert E. Sherwood. See note 59, page 265.
11. Alice Guinzburg, widow of Harold K. Guinzburg, founder and head of the publishing house, the Viking Press.
12. Corey Ford. See note 32, page 264.
13. Gene Markey, film producer, screenwriter and author.
14. Max Gordon, Broadway producer of *The Band Wagon, Dodsworth, The Women, My Sister Eileen, Born Yesterday, The Solid Gold Cadillac* and many others.

15. Kate Sullivan, Sullivan's older sister, with whom he shared the Saratoga house until her death in 1957.

16. Alison Smith, assistant drama critic of the New York *World* and first wife of Russel Crouse.

17. Ruth Hammond, actress who appeared with Howard Lindsay and Dorothy Stickney in *Life With Father* and *Life With Mother,* and her late husband, Donald Macdonald, actor and musical comedy star.

18. George S. Kaufman, one of the most popular comedy writers and directors of his time, collaborated principally with Marc Connelly, Edna Ferber and Moss Hart on a long series of hits.

19. Helen Hayes, a first lady of the American stage with such plays to her credit as *What Every Woman Knows, Victoria Regina* and the recent revivals of *The Show-Off, Harvey* and scores of others, and author of *On Reflection* and other books.

20. Laurence Housman, author of *Victoria Regina* and other plays.

21. Charles MacArthur, author with Ben Hecht of *The Front Page* and other plays and books, husband of Helen Hayes.

22. Beatrice Kaufman, wife of George S. Kaufman.

23. Alexander Woollcott, drama critic, writer, editor, Town Crier of radio fame, who even took a turn at acting himself in one of the many companies of *The Man Who Came to Dinner.*

24. *The Letters of Alexander Woollcott,* edited by Beatrice Kaufman and Joseph Hennessey.

25. Adele Brown Lovett, wife of Robert A. Lovett, banker, Undersecretary of State under Roosevelt and Secretary of Air and Defense under Truman.

26. John O'Hara, well-known novelist and short story writer.

27. Margaret Leech Pulitzer, novelist and Pulitzer Prize historian (*Reveille in Washington, In the Days of McKinley*), and widow of Ralph Pulitzer.

28. Harold Ross, founder and editor of *The New Yorker.*

29. Cleveland Amory, author of *The Last Resorts, Who Killed Society?,* etc., and columnist in *TV Guide* and the *Saturday Review.*

30. Tony's, a popular speakeasy on Forty-ninth Street named for its proprietor, Tony Soma.

31. Dorothy Parker, poet, short-story writer, critic, playwright, screenwriter and wit.

32. Charles Lederer, screenwriter and friend of Sullivan, Woollcott and many of the Algonquin group.

33. Charles Winninger, comedian on stage, screen and television, the original Cap'n Andy of the musical *Show Boat.*

34. Alan Campbell, husband of the late Dorothy Parker, with whom he

wrote many screenplays, including the first version of *A Star is Born*.

35. George Backer, writer and former editor and publisher of the New York *Post*.

TO SUNDRY GENTLEMEN

1. Lord Jeffery Amherst, direct descendent of the famous general for whom Amherst College was named, and a colleague of Sullivan on the staff of the New York *World* for several years in the 1920s.

2. Clemence Dane, pen name of Winifred Ashton, British novelist, playwright and poet.

3. Paul Schrade was with Robert F. Kennedy when he was assassinated, and was hit by one of Sirhan's bullets.

4. Nathaniel Benchley, novelist and biographer of his father, the well-loved humorist, Robert Benchley.

5. Bleeck's, a bar that was practically an annex of the *Herald Tribune*.

6. The Royalton Hotel on Forty-fourth Street, where Benchley kept an apartment for many years.

7. Marise Hamilton, now Marise Campbell, an old friend of Sullivan. See page 258.

8. Joseph Bryan, III, writer and squire of Brook Hill, Richmond, Virginia.

9. The Players, a club founded by Edwin Booth in his house on Gramercy Square for actors and others connected with the arts.

10. Lucius Beebe, chronicler of café society in his *Herald Tribune* column, editor, and author.

11. Mary Boland, film and stage comedienne and star of many musicals.

12. Charles Ruggles, stage and film comedian who played in a series of films with Mary Boland.

13. Gus Lobrano, see note 5, page 266.

14. John Cheever, short-story writer, and author of several novels including *The Wapshot Chronicle* and *The Wapshot Scandal*.

15. Norman Anthony, founder of the comic magazine *Ballyhoo* in the twenties, author and editor.

16. Heywood Broun, journalist, columnist, critic, author and crusader.

17. Dorothy Parker. See note 31, page 262.

18. Woollcott founded a club on Neshobe Island, Lake Bomoseen, Vermont, where he lived and entertained for many years.

19. Mrs. Joseph Bryan.

20. *Hello, Dolly!*, highly successful musical version of Thornton Wilder's *The Matchmaker*. For Wilder, see note 69, page 265.
21. Charles Baskerville, artist.
22. *The Time of Laughter*.
23. Bennett Cerf, publisher and co-founder of Random House, editor, columnist, writer, lecturer and television panelist.
24. Moss Hart's *Act One*.
25. Mary Barber, Cerf's girl Friday at Random House.
26. Dr. Paul Schilder, Sullivan's psychoanalyst.
27. Margaret Feldman, an old friend of Sullivan.
28. Samuel Chotzinoff, accompanist to Heifetz, Zimbalist, Alma Gluck and others, music critic of the New York *World*, director of music for NBC, and author of two volumes of reminiscences.
29. Mrs. Samuel Chotzinoff, sister of Jascha Heifetz.
30. Florence Vidor, silent motion-picture star.
31. Will Cuppy, columnist, author, humorist.
32. Corey Ford, parodist under the name of John Riddell, author and one-time roommate of Sullivan.
33. Richard Barber, young Dartmouth College friend of Ford.
34. Charles Addams, whose drawings of ghouls, monsters and their like appear in *The New Yorker* and come to life on television.
35. Mrs. Moffitt, housekeeper for Sullivan and Ford.
36. The Theatre Guild, for which Crouse was at that time press-agent.
37. Michael Romanoff, royal restaurateur.
38. *Both Your Houses*, which won a Pulitzer Prize.
39. Alvan Barach, Sullivan's New York doctor.
40. Nunnally Johnson, director, producer, writer for stage and screen.
41. One of Sullivan's Christmas poems.
42. Morrie Ryskind, playwright, author, screenwriter, and collaborator with George S. Kaufman on *Of Thee I Sing* and other musicals.
43. Dennis King, well-known actor and singer.
44. Charles Brackett, novelist, motion picture producer and co-author with Billy Wilder of such films as *Ninotchka*, *The Lost Weekend* and *Sunset Boulevard*. One-time president of the Motion Picture Academy of Arts and Sciences, and a 1910 classmate of Sullivan in Saratoga High School.
45. *From the Terrace*.
46. James Cagney of film fame.
47. Monty Woolley, instructor and drama coach at Yale, stage actor whose most important role was that of Sheridan Whiteside, firmly based on the character of Alexander Woollcott, in Kaufman's and Hart's *The Man Who Came to Dinner*, and a fellow-Saratogian.

48. Stanley Walker, city editor of the *Herald Tribune,* and writer.

49. De Wolf Hopper, stage comedian.

50. Abel Green, editor and publisher of *Variety.*

51. Goddard Lieberson, president of Columbia Records, whose wife Brigitta is the film and stage actress and dancer Zorina.

52. John Erskine, educator and author of many books and novels, including *The Private Life of Helen of Troy.*

53. Leonard Lyons, columnist on the New York *Post* and many other newspapers.

54. Alistair MacBain, writer, collaborator with Corey Ford on several books and magazine articles.

55. The MacBains' son, who is Sullivan's godson.

56. Arthur Sheekman, screenwriter who did the introduction to *The Groucho Letters.*

57. Goodman Ace, who with his wife, Jane, appeared for many years on radio's "Easy Aces," is a radio and television writer and columnist in the *Saturday Review.*

58. Herbert Mayes, magazine editor, executive and writer.

59. Robert E. Sherwood, historian (*Roosevelt and Hopkins*), playwright (*Idiot's Delight, There Shall Be No Night, Reunion in Vienna*), four time Pulitzer Prize winner, and speech writer for FDR.

60. Mark Sullivan, journalist and historian, author of the *Our Times* volumes.

61. Herbert Bayard Swope, Jr., television and theatrical producer and son of the late Margaret and Herbert Swope, executive editor of the New York *World.*

62. Laurence Stallings, book critic of the *World,* writer and co-author with Maxwell Anderson of *What Price Glory?*

63. Gerald Brooks, broker and friend of many of the Algonquin group.

64. Ruth Hale, wife of Heywood Broun, an ardent feminist, member of the Lucy Stone League.

65. James Thurber, essayist, short-story writer, humorist, playwright and illustrator.

66. Ik Shuman, an editor of *The New Yorker.*

67. Morris R. Werner, journalist and author of *Barnum, Brigham Young* and other books.

68. George D. Widener, socialite, sportsman and trustee of numerous Philadelphia organizations.

69. Thornton Wilder, novelist (*The Bridge of San Luis Rey, Ides of March, The Eighth Day,* etc.) and playwright (*Our Town, The Skin of Our Teeth, The Matchmaker,* etc.).

70. The Academy of Arts and Sciences, to which Arthur Miller had brought his wife, Marilyn Monroe.
71. 1st Baron Tweedsmuir, governor general of Canada who, as John Buchan, wrote numerous romantic adventure stories.
72. Danton Walker, columnist on the *Daily News*.
73. Lloyd Lewis, critic and writer.

TO THE NEW YORKERS

1. Roger Angell, an editor of *The New Yorker*.
2. Katharine White, for many years an editor of *The New Yorker*, wife of E. B. White, and, by a previous marriage, mother of Roger Angell.
3. E. B. (Andy) White, one of the principal contributors to *The New Yorker*, humorist, essayist, co-author with James Thurber of *Is Sex Necessary?*, compiler with his wife of *A Subtreasury of American Humor* and author of two well-loved children's books, *Stuart Little* and *Charlotte's Web*.
4. See page 176.
5. Gus Lobrano, one-time managing editor of *The New Yorker*.
6. John Collier, author of novels and short stories of the macabre.
7. *Harvey*, the play about an imaginary rabbit by Mary Chase.
8. Raoul Fleischmann, publisher of *The New Yorker*.
9. Wes Santee, long-distance runner.

TO SARATOGIANS
AND OTHER FRIENDS

1. Elizabeth Gorman, who taught English in Saratoga High School.
2. Mrs. Charles Brackett.
3. John J. Cassidy, director of public relations at the Albany Medical Center.
4. Cassidy's son and daughter.
5. Donald M. Goodfellow, Department of English, Carnegie-Mellon University, Pittsburgh.
6. Trudy Hemstead, grandniece of Dr. and Mrs. John Heslin.
7. Hal Holbrook, actor, noted for his one-man show on Mark Twain.

8. Clarence Knapp, former mayor of Saratoga and one-time contributor to FPA's column under the name of "Ambrose Glutz," and to *The New Yorker*.

9. Sistie Dahl, Roosevelt's granddaughter.

10. Anne Ford, old friend of Sullivan, a retired employee of Houghton Mifflin Company.

11. Maxine Sullivan, well-known record and nightclub singer.

12. Ann Honeycutt, old friend of Sullivan.

13. Joan Iams, daughter of Stanley Walker (see note 48, page 265), and wife of Jack Iams, the writer.

14. Geoffrey Parsons, editorial chief of the *Herald Tribune*.

15. Jack Iams, see note 13 above.

16. Gilbert Gabriel, for many years a drama critic on the New York *Sun;* Ada, his widow, is an artist.

17. Muriel King, couturière and painter.

18. Ed O'Malley, former co-owner with his brother of O'Malley's Book Store in New York.

19. John Farrar, writer, editor and co-founder of the publishing house of Farrar, Straus & Giroux.

20. *The Eighth Day*.

21. James Roach, sports editor of the New York *Times*.

22. Carl Yastrzemski of the Boston Red Sox, Most Valuable Player in the American League in 1967.

23. Mrs. Merritt Kirk Ruddock, old friend.

24. Peter Turgeon, actor.

25. Dr. Albert Yunich, specialist in gastrointestinal ailments in Albany, New York.

26. David Sarnoff, chairman of the board of RCA.